COLIN GREEN

how to run a
FOOTBALL
CLUB

THE INSIDER'S STEP-BY-STEP GUIDE

Published in 2004 by A & C Black Publishers Ltd
37 Soho Square, London W1D 3QZ
www.acblack.com

ISBN 0 7136 6992 6

A CIP record for this book is available from the British Library.

Note: Whilst every effort has been made to ensure that the content of this book is as technically accurate and as sound as possible, neither the author nor the publisher can accept responsibility for any injury or loss sustained as a result of the use of this material.

A & C Black uses paper produced with elemental chlorine-free pulp, harvested from managed sustainable forests.

Acknowledgements
Cover photography © Getty Images
Illustrations by Ed Dovey
Inside design by James Watson

Typeset in 10.75pt AGaramond

Printed and bound in Great Britain by Biddles Ltd, King's Lynn.

contents

part one PRE-SEASON

part two THE SEASON

preface

Ever wondered how to start a football club and run it yourself? Your ambition for a club can be brought to life, whether it's a club for family, friends, pub or youth club. This book tackles topics such as:

- how to form a team and enter it into a football league
- how to kit out your club and stay out of debt
- how to organise football matches.

Park football – this book tells it like it is, step-by-step. As you go through this book, the world of the Football Association and non-professional football will be de-mystified. Questions about how to get a football pitch and keep players happy are answered, and special attention will be given to... *THE THREE BIGGEST PIT-FALLS FOR CLUBS.*

While finding enough fit and available players is an ongoing issue for clubs at all levels, the three most common crises at amateur football clubs are:

- not enough people off-the-park to help in the running of the club
- not enough money to pay the club's bills
- a communications breakdown.

This book devotes whole chapters to each of these problems, with lots of practical ideas to help your club. No more do you need to know 'the right people' to discover how it's done – which was always a matter of luck. No more need you depend on experience being passed on by a league secretary – possibly inexperienced himself – and whose attention is split between dozens of clubs. This book puts such know-how in your own hands.

Nowadays, running even the smallest Sunday League club can cost hundreds of pounds annually. This book gives you the know-how to save money as well to raise it.

Best practice, the benefit of experience at the sharp end of football, money-savers, how to avoid the pitfalls and have a smooth-running club, this book has it all.

UEFA wants more attention at national and international level on amateur football. With over two million people taking part in amateur football in the UK alone, you're part of one of the great sports of the world. The privileged few may lead their team out at the great stadiums, but to run your own team for your friends, that is a dream you can live for real.

acknowledgements

No book is truly the work of one person. Particular thanks to all the league and club officials who said they didn't mind the things that really happened going into print.

To Chris, your company has been an education. To all the boys, girls, men and women whose teams have called upon me, I've learnt more from you than you ever learned from me.

Thanks to the coaches, and to the officials in the F.A., the County F.A.s and local authorities who provided insight; to all who offered encouragement – there are too many of you to name you all, but you know who you are – many thanks again.

terms and descriptions used in this book

Most football clubs are amateur in the true sense, players taking part at their own expense, for the love of the game. That's why I use terms such as amateur, non-professional and park football, not the derogatory-sounding 'non-league'.

To avoid repetition, I have used the terms 'he, him and his' generally to mean both sexes. No offence is intended in this. It is simple economy with words.

Football does mean sport for all. Whether your club will be a girls' team, boys' team, a mixed team of girls and boys, men's team, women's team, able-bodied or disabled players' team, a mixed team of youths and adults, or any other legal alternative – association football ought to have room for you. This book focuses on the organisation of 11-a-side football. Much of the information is also relevant to running mini-soccer for under-11s.

This book describes the way football is presently organised in England. Even so, from Scotland to Senegal differences should be minimal in the way association football is run, thanks to FIFA. So right where you are, this book has handy ideas for your club. It will help you understand how association football is run, whether you are going to play in a league, or only in cup competitions.

part one
PRE-SEASON

chapter 1

LOOKING AT THE TASK AHEAD

Are you thinking of running an extra team at your club? Are you planning to form a brand new club? Or are you taking over the reins at an established club? This chapter covers what needs to be done to form a brand new club. It will also put you in the picture about what running a club entails, to help if you are planning an extra team or to run an established club.

WHY SET UP YOUR OWN CLUB?

Why – when you could join one of the thousands upon thousands of clubs competing in thousands of local leagues up and down the country – set up a new one? It could be because you, your friends or family have nowhere to play football. It could be an ambition to build your own football club from scratch. Whatever the reason, I'm asking you to think about it now because when the going gets tough later, you will need to remind yourself of it.

WHO RUNS A CLUB?

As a rule, the person who runs a football club is the club secretary. Hardly anything happens without him. He is often the unsung hero of a club – the manager and players get more attention, but a club secretary does as much as anyone.

For instance, your players may think pre-season work starts and ends with football training. Not so. Not for the club secretary. His work starts long before the first ball is kicked. It goes on throughout the season. It continues after the very last final whistle. You'll find a shorter job description for the club secretary in Chapter 4, but almost every chapter of this book deals with subjects the club secretary is involved in.

SO WHERE DO WE START?

We begin by giving thought to three things:

- a snapshot of what is needed to see this through
- understanding the pressure on your time
- planning a meeting to get your club started (whether you like meetings or not, you'll have to have them sometimes).

true stories

This is where I came in...

Friends of mine occasionally played friendlies to which I was never invited against football teams I never knew existed. From that, make your own mind up about my ability.

Out of the blue, I heard a friend was starting a new league. Sounded like a good opportunity to get my friends' team into a league and get myself involved to boot. I asked the players if they wanted to form a club and join the league. They said yes. What happened next is told in this book...

THE CHILDREN ACT 1989

This is an important matter to raise. This legislation affects England and Wales, and if any of your players are under the age of 16 it is as well to know about it. In countries other than England and Wales you should ask your own authorities about their advice and rules for working with children.

You may just be taking a few kids down the park for a kick-around club each week, but in these days with more awareness of the ill-treatment of children by some people in positions of trust – and with more allegations against those in charge of children – you can save yourself lots of worry by being well-informed of the facts. This is good for their protection and for your protection too.

You will find useful information about the Children Act in Appendix I at the back of this book, together with sensible ideas for working with children. The F.A. has produced some advice for working with children too. You'll find the address of the F.A. in Appendix II.

WHAT'S NEEDED FOR THE JOB AHEAD – A SNAPSHOT

To start off a new club, these would be regarded as essentials:

- at least two of you to handle the paperwork, money and phone calls
- being in a position to sign enough players to put out a team regularly
- the ability to raise cash – hundreds of pounds – every year.

If you can do that – and this book tells you how – the rest should fall into place.

top tip

THE MOST VALUED POSSESSION OF A CLUB SECRETARY...

is the telephone. Without it you will be in difficulties. If you are away from the phone a lot, and you don't have a mobile phone, it is a good idea to get a telephone answer-machine, and if the machine is for 'club use' perhaps your club will pay for it. As a club secretary people will be trying to contact you every week – the other clubs, the League Secretary, confused players who have forgotten where to meet for the next game, maybe even referees – all will want to speak to you on the phone.

If being around to answer your phone is going to be difficult for you, then you will need someone to work with you – most especially to take those phone calls. Or the answering machine.

PRESSURE ON YOUR TIME

Even before you find a league to join, ask yourself this question: how long have you got till the next season starts? Most leagues have a deadline for teams to join – the deadline will be in the spring or summer depending on local factors – so the beginning of a new year is a good time to start planning. You and any helpers need to give yourselves time to sort out paperwork, obtain kit, equipment and

deadlines

There are always deadlines in association football. Some are set by the league you choose to play in, and some by the F.A. (that's usually the County F.A. for amateur clubs). You'll read a lot in this book about deadlines – there are so many of them. No matter how we feel about them, there'll be no getting away from them.

facilities, and find the money to pay for all of this. Most importantly, you need to know about your deadlines.

In the following pages I will paint a picture for you of how much time you need. So before we even talk about finding the right league for your team, even before finding players, let's get that picture clear. Here's a diary of how a year spent running a new club might work out for you.

IMAGINARY CLUB DIARY

JANUARY 1st: At party, make resolution with mates to start our own footy team.

FEBRUARY: Asking around mates, we've got fifteen lads interested in playing for us so far. We have a meeting for the whole team because we've worked out this is going to cost us more money than we thought. We decide to ask a pub to sponsor us.

MARCH: Find a suitable league to join.

APRIL: The league we want to join has sent us some forms to fill in. I agree to be Club Secretary (no-one else wants to do it). I look for a local pitch.

MAY: Got a deadline to return those forms to join the league for the new season: this means deciding on home and away colours, though we can't afford a kit yet! Friends sign the forms as Club Treasurer, Chairman and Manager. I return the forms so we can join the league, hoping our friends will not disappear before we kick a ball.

JUNE: Sent the booking form for the pitch to the local council before their deadline. Go to the league's Annual General Meeting. We pay fees to join the league by their deadline. No sponsor yet – a few of us lend cash to pay the bills.

JULY: The players ask about training, so we meet twice a week at a local park. I get my players to sign player registration forms to send to the league before the pre-season player-registration deadline. Go to the league's monthly meeting – wonder how I'll find the time every month.

AUGUST: The bill for the pitch arrives. Short of time, buy our home and away kits, nets for goals, corner flags, footballs, etc. We find a sponsor to pay the bills just in time. I phone clubs in the league to fix up a couple of pre-season friendly games.

SEPTEMBER: At last the season starts! Every week there are deadlines for making telephone calls about matches, for turning up at the ground, for phoning in match results and sending team-sheets into the league, for paying subscriptions – and meetings to go to each month.

OCTOBER-NOVEMBER-DECEMBER: Into a routine of deadlines – manage to stay on top of it to avoid league fines. Christmas means a couple of weeks off.

JANUARY-FEBRUARY: More of the same – only in bad weather. Seems a long time since that New Year resolution to form a team.

MARCH-APRIL: A struggle to complete fixtures put back by winter weather. Players are negotiating with partners and employers for a pass, so we raise a team. Order tickets for the league's dinner before deadline.

MAY: We haven't won anything this time, but we go as a team to the league dinner and party. Already forms have started to come so that we can play next season.

So you can see that to play in a league next season, work begins months before.

PLANNING YOUR FIRST MEETING TO GET YOUR CLUB STARTED

If you're the club secretary, a word in your ear. If there isn't a football to be kicked, it's a job-and-a-half to get your team to turn up for a meeting. But at this stage it's vital you find out that they really are behind you. So, call a meeting. And if you want to kick off a new season in August, try to hold your first meeting before April, as you will need to leave yourself plenty of time to set up the club.

BEFORE THE MEETING

Your players will probably ask you why you need them at a meeting. They'll expect you to take care of everything. Tell them:

- they need to find out what is happening in their club
- they need to find out if they will be able to give their time
- you can't run this club on your own – it's just too much work
- you'll need people to manage the team, the money, the kit, and more
- you need their ideas for raising money
- if they share in key decisions, they will be happier at the club

Of course some of these things you could do yourself, so how much you want to share the responsibility is up to you.

top tip

Find out where you can use a photocopier. Sooner or later you'll need one. Many corner shops have one. In some shops it can be as cheap as 5p a copy. Don't forget to ask for a receipt from the shop, and keep it in your expenses note-book, in order to claim your money back from your club.

If you have a computer or typewriter, great, it might enable you to print your own stationery, and cash book, and make your club letters look nicer. If you don't have one, perhaps someone else in your club could type up your letters for you, to make them look neat. Ask around your members for any help you need.

shopping list for the stationery shop

The club secretary's stationery
Paperwork needs organising if you have the job of club secretary. Visit a stationery shop to stock up. Here's a shopping list: buy whatever you can afford.

- handful of black ballpoint pens (the best colour for photocopying)
- an exercise book (for scribbling thoughts in)
- a note book (for writing the minutes of team meetings)
- a small note book for yourself (to keep a record of every penny you spend on the team. Why should anyone bankroll the team and not get their money back?)
- a packet of envelopes
- a dozen or more first class postage stamps
- an A4-size wallet/folder to keep everything in

The club treasurer's stationery
You will need a club treasurer. If you know who will be your treasurer already, ask him if he has stationery. If he doesn't, the club needs to buy his stationery too. I'll explain more about what the treasurer does in chapter 4 and chapter 6. He will need much the same stuff from the stationery shop as the secretary. He will also need the following things:-

- a receipt book
- a cash book (or book-keeping ledger)
- a pocket calculator

a fool's guide to calling a meeting

Find out the best place, time and day for a meeting with your club members, a time to suit all who should come. Then choose when and where.

If you want to meet in a public place like a pub or a cafe, ask the owner/landlord for permission.

Make sure everyone hears about where and when the meeting will happen. I would usually give my teams at least a week's notice – long enough to give them warning, not too long so they forget.

You could write them a simple letter. Photocopy it to give all your members a copy. (On the next page is a letter for you to copy.) Another idea: if you don't see the team yourself, ask friends to help you phone round everyone or to spread the message any other way.

So the day of the meeting comes around. And then – guess what? – you have your meeting but many of the players don't turn up. You may feel like quitting because some people don't show up for meetings. But don't panic – a lot of players never turn up unless there's a football to be kicked. It happens to professional clubs for off-field events. So the story goes, only four members of the 1990 England World Cup squad turned up to record their 'World in Motion' single.

You still want a meeting with your club, so try this suggestion – why not hold the meeting before or after a kick-around? BUT give your members notice – they may not like surprises.

top tip

Gremlins breed in back-logs of paperwork

By now you have probably formed the idea this is a job that needs administration skills. None of it is difficult work, but there is a lot of it. The key is to stay on top of the work by doing it as soon as it arrives – not letting a back-log of paperwork build up. That's how to stop a build-up of pressure on your time. And that's why it's best if at least two of you can do the work together: when one is busy or tired, the other can help. When gremlins get in the works, the football authorities will try to force a club back on track. Their preferred methods are fines, and, in the worst cases, bans. I'll explain about such fines later.

Given that players will be a lot happier when they know what's going on, why not send them a letter before your first team meeting? Here is an imaginary letter you could crib from:

WANNABE F.C. CLUB NEWS

Twelfth of Whenever

I want everyone connected with our club to know what's going on in the next few months. It's important that you know.

Introductions first. For those new to me, my name is .... I've agreed to act as club secretary until we hold elections. My commitment to you now is to get everything in place for the new season – the administration side, a team manager, and training in the summer. We'll have kick-arounds and friendlies till then.

First we need to have a meeting. We need to see as many of you as can come at:

PLACE: Bill's Cafe, Bloggs St.
DAY: Saturday 20th of Whenever
TIME: 2.30 p.m.

AGENDA FOR THE MEETING
1. Apologies (let me know if you can't come. My phone number is ....)
2. Before we have elections, we need to nominate and second:
        club chairperson
        club secretary
        club treasurer
        first-aider
3. We need to talk about how to make sure we have enough players
4. We need to discuss what day and time we want our games to kick off
5. Suggestions for:
        what league we want to join
        where our home pitch should be
        club colours for kit
        raising money
        a name for our club

6. We need to agree on
    date of our club's Annual General Meeting for proper elections
    time and place for training to start
    time and place of next club meeting

7. Any other business

Kind Regards
Joe Wannabe

AT THE MEETING

At your club meeting you might get responses such as: 'Hey, we'll solve all these problems, leave it to us.' (This translates as: 'We don't trust you. You're sacked.') Or: 'We can leave you to sort it all out, can't we?' (This translates as: 'We're bored. We're going to the pub.')

If you get strong co-operation and help from your members, count yourself fortunate. If you end up doing most of the work yourself – for little thanks – you will be walking in the footsteps of many club secretaries before you. The reward for you may be to see your smooth-running club go from strength to strength.

Still, having a few reliable people with you to help to run the club is ideal. You don't have to put pressure on players to take up the work for you. Instead, if players are unwilling, ask them to tell their friends and family that help is needed running the club.

Ask your team for a few ideas on football strip colours. When you make contact with local leagues, you could find out the colours worn by other clubs. That is probably a better time to make the final decision about your own colours.

WHAT DAY AND TIMES GAMES SHOULD KICK OFF

Ask members at your club meeting to tell you the best days and times for them to play, and how often they want the games – do they want games every week? They should give you choices for favoured kick-off times. Consider whether you could afford the time to organise a game every week.

Ask those questions, because:

- clubs that frequently turn up short of eleven players become an embarrassment to themselves;

- leagues work on the basis of agreed match-days and agreed kick-off times. Once you've joined a league the chances are it will be too late to change your mind about when you want to play;
- whatever time the team wants to play, you will have to book a pitch that is available at that time.

If it is already obvious to you where you will play, and what time you will kick off, fine. Otherwise, read on.

In most regions there are Saturday/Sunday morning/afternoon pitches to choose from. Some teams prefer to play weekday evenings (while the lighter nights last). That especially goes for school teams. Then there are floodlit pitches. Warn your players you may have to shop around for a suitable football pitch. Tell them there may be a trade-off between favourite kick-off times and the availability of favourite pitches.

CHOOSING A NAME FOR YOUR CLUB

At the meeting, ask for two or three suggestions for names for your club. County F.A.s are strict about ensuring that no two clubs in their county have a similar name. They will tell you if your club's name is not different enough. Two of my former clubs were told to change their names when they affiliated to the County F.A. – because another club had a similar name already. That's why in a big city, there may be only one club called, say, the Dog and Duck, though there may be a dozen such pubs. Your local County F.A. can give you a directory of existing clubs.

WRITING MINUTES OF THE MEETING

At the meeting use a notebook to take minutes on what's decided – to avoid confusion later. It's the club secretary's job to write the minutes. You can look back at your minute-book whenever you need to check your decisions. The more you take minutes, the more you will understand what needs to be written down and what can be left out.

At the meeting your team may well talk through many issues, including the ones suggested in that letter above. Here's a guide for where to find help:

WHERE TO FIND OUT MORE ABOUT...

- how to pick the coach and manager. You don't have to decide this yet. Your players may want some say in this, or you may want to leave the final decision on a manager up to your club's officers. These questions are discussed in detail in Chapter 4

- for an explanation of nominating officers and having proper elections at the Annual General Meeting, turn to Chapter 4: 'Building the structure of your club'
- for finding a league to join, see Chapter 2: 'Joining a local football league'
- for a pitch to play on, see Chapter 7: 'All about football pitches'
- for money-raising ideas, see Chapter 6: 'Balancing the books'
- for finding players for your club, see Chapter 5: 'Building your squad'
- for choosing a football strip for your club, see Chapter 8: 'All kitted out'.

And don't forget that your County F.A. is intended to be a ready source of advice for clubs on these sorts of issues.

NOW THE WORK REALLY STARTS...

Now, if you've agreed that your team should play in a league, the next step is for you to find the right one to join. That's what the next chapter is all about.

Remember that time is a factor. To kick off the new season next August, you will have to be ready for deadlines set by the league and by the County F.A. If you have to miss those deadlines you will probably be planning to join your new league the following year instead.

CHECKLIST

- decide whether you have enough time to plan for playing in a league next season
- call a club meeting to make key decisions
- get the stationery you will need.

chapter 2
JOINING A LOCAL FOOTBALL LEAGUE

This chapter explains how to enter your team into a football league. Even if you do not know a single person in any league, that need not get in your way.

You are already prepared in part if you had that first club meeting as set out in Chapter 1. From that meeting, you should know:

- the day and time your team prefers to play
- the approximate ages of your players
- your club's suggestions for team names
- your club's suggestions for football strip colours
- who has the job of contacting local leagues (probably your acting club secretary, in fact probably you).

FINDING A LEAGUE TO JOIN

If it is obvious to you which league you will join, fine. Otherwise, read on. If you are not in contact with a league, how do you find one? There are a few ways of finding leagues, including making a phone call to your local County F.A., and reading the sports pages of local newspapers. The first is probably the easiest.

TALKING TO THE COUNTY F.A. ABOUT LOCAL LEAGUES

The County F.A. can advise you on which leagues to approach, or they may try to place you in one. Your County F.A. have all the contact names and all the phone numbers you need for amateur leagues in your area. Ask them if they will put you in contact with secretaries of any Leagues you might be interested in. Get the phone numbers of two or three suitable leagues from them if possible. You may be interested in competitions catering for particular groups, such as army leagues or church leagues. Your County F.A. will be able to tell you about any such leagues.

There are other competitions that are not affiliated to the F.A., which therefore may have no details of them, and you may find them only by word of mouth. For instance, leagues for Asian players are popular in England, and some of these have chosen to preserve their independence from the F.A.

top tip

Finding your local County F.A.

I have listed all the local County F.A. headquarters in Appendix II at the back of this book. At the time of going to press, every effort has been made to ensure these details are up to date. If your County F.A. has changed address, then you could do one of two things:

1) ring the F.A. Headquarters in London – they will have an up to date list of contact details for the County F.A.s in England. This information is also on their web-site;

2) look in your local Yellow Pages under Sports Clubs and Associations or in your local phone directory, but note that the entry will rarely be called 'County F.A.' It should be entered under the name of your region (e.g., 'Manchester County F.A.'; 'Middlesex County F.A.'), so look in the phone book under the name of your city or district.

USING LOCAL NEWSPAPERS TO FIND OUT ABOUT LOCAL LEAGUES

You can learn about amateur leagues in your locality from the sports pages of your local newspapers. They usually have a page or two devoted to amateur football teams, including their league tables, fixtures and results, and occasional photographs. Those tables will show that some leagues have a lot of teams, but others only a small number. You should be able to find a league that suits your players.

WHO WANTS TO PLAY IN SMALLER LEAGUES?

Bigger leagues like to play every week, while smaller ones, made up of, say, only 10 teams, meet a demand for teams who want a game every two or three weeks. What if players with families want to ration their appearances? Or what about those who occasionally have to work Saturday/Sunday shifts – can they re-roster their working days to suit match fixtures? It may be that a small league playing once a fortnight would suit such a team best.

WHO WANTS TO PLAY IN LARGER LEAGUES?

Or you might have a young team with time on their hands who want to play and train as often as possible. It you have a squad with a lot of spare time, it may suit them to play in a large league with more teams to play against – where there will be games almost every week.

So you can find out a lot from the local newspaper. See how many teams there are in each division: this should give you an idea of how many games they are expected to play in a season. See too if the newspaper says on what days games are played. Make a note of the name of any league that sounds like it might be right for you. Then you are ready to ask the County F.A. to put you in touch with the league secretaries of those leagues.

GETTING IN TOUCH WITH LOCAL LEAGUES

Tell league secretaries about your team, what age your players are, what standard of football you want to play at, what day and time your team can turn up for games. When you first make contact with a league secretary ask about the usual kick-off time in his league. Read this true story to see why.

true stories

'You what?'

I visited a league's meeting of its club secretaries one September. This was about three weeks before their season kicked off. The man seated right in front of me turned to the man next to him and asked what time games kicked off. 'Ten-thirty' he replied. 'You what?' the first man said. He sat there a while deep in thought, then turned to someone else and asked again what time the games kicked off. 'Ten-thirty,' came the answer. The first man said, 'You what? My lads all work till one o'clock on Saturdays.' The meeting then had a big open discussion about whether all the other teams could play this team's games at a later hour.

This situation should never have happened, it being September before the man learned the kick-off time from his league secretary. Never be afraid to ask your league secretary even blindingly obvious questions. You can save yourself a lot of embarrassment.

It may be a good idea to speak to more than one league before you find the right one for you, and this is perfectly all right. There may be big differences between, say, a teenage boys' league, or a men's Sunday league.

Each league secretary will tell you about the present situation for letting new teams join his league. They may be pleased to take on an extra team, or they may feel it's not the right time for their league to grow in size.

Consult other people in your club. One consideration may be whether you aim to become part of the Pyramid of Football, especially if you have experience at a higher level.

THE PYRAMID OF FOOTBALL

Most teams are content to play for local honour. But you may wonder how high you can aim. There is a ladder for aspiring teams to climb – ultimately reaching up to the professional game. This ladder is the Pyramid of Football, or to give it its proper names, the national league system or the national game.

One team to climb it in recent times was Wimbledon, from non-professional to top-flight in a decade. This 'dream' doesn't happen in every country. For instance, leagues are 'closed' in many European countries, and in such countries amateur clubs cannot rise to the top.

Of course the higher up clubs go, the tougher the requirements, not only to do with playing and extra paperwork. Issues include having a private ground with facilities for spectators, or at least ground-sharing. Other similarities with professional clubs include longer journeys to away games, opposing fans segregated more often, even security guards having to be present.

The higher you go, the more clubs are constituted as Limited Companies – a rare find in lower leagues. That's why at the top of the amateur Pyramid – the Conference League – boards of directors and wealthy chairmen play a bigger part, using their riches in a push for promotion to the professional Football League. At some of the smallest Sunday league clubs, chairmen sometimes have no role at all. Worlds apart.

At the top of the Pyramid, many players are not amateurs in the true sense. Many are part-time semi-professionals, some even professional, so money is a bigger issue.

More of the wealthy clubs near the top of the non-professional Pyramid are in the south of England. Less wealthy chairmen elsewhere may be being realistic about the task facing a club wishing to go all the way and join professional football.

Most leagues are not part of this Pyramid. Of over 40,000 clubs in England, fewer than 1,000 are in the Pyramid. Aspiring clubs can always apply to join the Pyramid in the future, and those in it don't all have a plan for turning professional! Ring your County F.A. for details about the local Pyramid structure, such as which local leagues feed teams into it. Newer clubs may need to be established a while before they can join a league in the Pyramid. Don't be afraid to ask the league secretary of any league you intend to join if it is connected in any way to the local part of the Pyramid.

To decide how different leagues should be linked for promotion and relegation, the F.A. has a 'Joint Liaison Committee'. Later in this chapter I'll say more about cup competitions for teams towards the top of the Pyramid.

SO YOU'VE DECIDED WHICH LEAGUE TO JOIN...?

When you've found the right league for you, ask its league secretary if you could apply to join. At this point, one thing he might ask you to think about is: how much time you have left before you join his league.

time

I'm repeating myself here, but any league should have a deadline for you joining. This is because they need to do their paperwork too. The league also need to publish their new fixture list in good time for the new season, so latecomers will not normally be accepted.

I would suggest you do try to make contact with a league secretary by April if not sooner. This will give him time to advise you on how to iron out any details prior to your joining the league.

The deadline for completing the formalities of joining many leagues is in June. Ask your league secretary when your deadline is.

APPLYING TO JOIN MEANS... FORMS TO FILL IN

If the league secretary sounds positive about your club joining, ask him to send you application forms so that your team can join for the next season. In the following pages I will go through typical forms in more detail. For now, you need to get these three documents most of all:

- a 'League Registration Form'
- a 'County F.A. Affiliation Form' (sometimes called 'County F.A. Form A')
- a copy of your 'League Code of Rules' (sometimes called 'League Constitution')

If you have not received all of these by May, ask your league secretary to send them to you as soon as possible. These are the most important forms to start off with. Any league would tell you that you haven't joined before the formalities are completed.

GETTING HELP ON THE LEARNING CURVE

If the league publishes any kind of information pack to assist local club secretaries, ask the league secretary for a copy now.

The F.A. has recently begun to hold courses around the country on 'Effective Club Administration'. Some of these are aimed at clubs nearer the top of the Pyramid, but I have been told by one of the organisers that teams of all levels should find them useful. Your County F.A. should have more details.

Our own league held one-day training events for club secretaries. We would talk them through much the same issues you find in this book. If you are fortunate enough to be in a league that holds such an event, get down there with a few team-mates. What you and they learn now should spare you time and effort later.

WHAT ARE THE FORMS TO FILL IN?

In these pages I have provided a list of forms. It's not as fearsome as it first seems. I'll take you through the information you'll need to write on the forms. (I haven't put the exact deadlines or costs in pounds and pence because these will vary from league to league. But in Chapter 6: 'Balancing the books' I'll give you some examples of what you might expect the cost of joining a league to be.)

important note

You will be asked to fill in various forms in the year you join, and to fill them in again every year. Registering your club is an annual job. Every club, no matter how established, does it, even the professional clubs you support.

top tip

When filling in the forms, the really important things are:

- if you don't know an answer to a question, don't send the form in blank! Instead, ring up the league secretary and ask his advice. (He'll probably send it straight back to you if you don't fill it in properly.)
- don't miss those deadlines for sending the forms back. Missing deadlines could cause your club to be left out of the league's plans.

Forms you may expect to see include the following:

FORM	WHERE TO GET IT FROM	ANY COST?	ANY DEADLINE?
County F.A. Affiliation (you cannot play without this)	County F.A. unless your league secretary sends it to you – check with him whether to return it via the league or directly to the County F.A.	YES	YES
County F.A. public liability insurance deal (see Chapter 5)	DITTO	YES	YES
Player insurance (see chapter 5)	VARIOUS	YES	YES
County F.A. Competition Registration (see later in this chapter)	County F.A.	YES	YES
League Registration	League secretary	YES	YES
League Cup Registration – if your league holds its own League Cup competition – may be optional	League secretary	YES	YES

FORM	WHERE TO GET IT FROM	ANY COST?	ANY DEADLINE?
League Rules The league secretary will send you a copy of the League Rules. It should need signatures of more than one member of your club. Then you keep a copy and send the signed original back to the league secretary. This is to show all the clubs are signed up to the same rules.	League secretary	NO (The only cost should be the cost of making a photocopy of the whole document after it has been signed This is the copy your club keeps.)	YES

TIMING IS IMPORTANT

A word about your County F.A. Affiliation Form. You will be sending this completed form and affiliation fee either to your league secretary or to your County F.A., according to the preference of your league secretary. Some league secretaries prefer to gather and send all of their clubs' County F.A. Affiliation Forms in one batch to the F.A., and they do so in order to know when all the forms are in.

Within a few weeks the County F.A. replies to your Affiliation Form by sending you a note of your affiliation number. Tell your league secretary this number (each year). Don't delay. Until he has all the clubs' affiliation numbers he cannot register his league with the County F.A. This means latecomers might have to lose out. He has to do this every year. Hard to believe, but it is true. In my old league, the league secretary has been forced to wait for late affiliation numbers from clubs. In those years the County F.A. left our league out of its list of local leagues in its published directory.

WHAT THE FORMS WILL ASK FOR

Before you fill in the forms you will need to decide a fair few things. For instance:

COUNTY F.A. AFFILIATION FORM

You will normally need to write these things on the County F.A. Form:

- the name of your club
- the present number of members (that includes the players)
- name, address and phone number of club secretary (probably you)
- name, address and phone number of club treasurer
- the address of your home pitch
- where your changing rooms will be
- the name of the league
- team kit colours

The County F.A. will ask that you keep records of membership, money and minutes of meetings, and that you have a proper Annual General Meeting for your club.

LEAGUE REGISTRATION

Your own league may ask, in addition to the above, for:

- both home and away team kit colours
- name, address and phone number not only of the club secretary but also of the team manager, club treasurer, the holders of the club's bank account and two or three people nominated to attend the monthly league meeting

WHERE TO GET HELP

Chances are you don't know many details yet. For help on this see the relevant chapter:

- for help with money or accounts, see Chapter 6: 'Balancing the books';
- to know about choosing a team kit, look in Chapter 8: 'All kitted out';
- for a pitch and changing rooms, look in Chapter 7: 'All about football pitches';
- for appointing club officials and keeping membership records and so on, look in Chapter 4: 'Building the structure of your club'.

when is your club a member of the league?

When you have sent the forms in, especially the County F.A. Affiliation Form and the league registration Form, filled in correctly and before the deadlines, the league secretary will have to do his own paperwork (including sending to the County F.A. a form listing all the clubs in his league).

Next the league secretary should put a motion on the agenda of his league's Annual General Meeting about letting your club join the league. (The AGM will probably be in June.) You, as club secretary, will be expected to go to the AGM.

At the meeting the representatives of all the clubs in the league will be asked to vote on permitting new teams such as yours to join the league. When the league secretary puts your club's name forward at the AGM, you can usually expect the vote to be just a formality, because there may have been discussion at previous meetings. Once this vote is carried your club will become a member of that league – now you will have league fixtures to play next season.

If your club is already a member of the league, no vote is needed for you to play next season. Normally, only new clubs need a vote.

FIXTURE LISTS

You really feel like your club has arrived when you see your team's name on your first fixture list. At amateur level we pore over our fixtures before the season starts – just the same as we pore over the fixtures of the professional club we support. I'll say more about the fixture lists in the next chapter.

WHAT ELSE DOES THE LEAGUE DO?

Now that you have an idea how much there is for you to do, you probably wonder what on earth the league does for you. As a league official I answered so many questions about what the league does in return for your membership fees that I'm devoting most of the next chapter to it.

CAN WE ENTER MORE THAN ONE TEAM?

I have assumed you are entering one team only, to save repeating in every chapter that what needs doing for one team needs doing for each of your teams. But you can usually enter more than one team into the same league, so long as not more than one team is in the same division. Even if your teams were promoted or relegated into the same division, your league would act to keep them in separate divisions. Apart from that, you can have as many teams as you want.

If you do enter extra teams, you must write something like 'second team' or 'B team' on your affiliation forms – otherwise the F.A. may get confused by applications for teams with the same name.

Many clubs do have several teams, with some of those teams even playing in different leagues, never mind different divisions of the same league. This is typically true of school teams, but most famously of professional clubs, with their senior, reserve, women's and youth teams, for example. I can remember from my schooldays that about ten teams represented our school – more than some professional clubs.

People expect schools to provide sport for their children, but often don't know the burden on teachers and helpers who organise the number of games involved. For the younger children's games the burden can be greater since the younger ones must play smaller-sided mini-soccer instead of 11-a-side – that means two teams often have to be organised instead of only one, to ensure places for all the children who want to play. Many schools still don't have football teams until the day someone will organise them, because of the extra work involved.

You should consider how much time and effort you can devote to a football club – each team needs someone to do the work of secretary, treasurer, coach and manager. That work is outlined in Chapter 4: 'Building the structure of your club'.

Then there is the expense – for example, it costs several hundred pounds a year to run a typical park football team, despite reductions off some County F.A. fees for second and third (etc.) teams. I'll say more about that in Chapter 6: 'Balancing the books'.

Don't forget too that any league ultimately has the authority – which can be exercised at the Annual General Meeting – over how many clubs are wanted in that league.

JOINING OTHER COMPETITIONS

In addition to being in your league you may wish to join other competitions, such as cup tournaments run by your County F.A. Do speak to your league secretary before you join any county cup competitions. He may have a view on how you can fit county cup games into your fixture list. He may be concerned about fixture congestion should your club progress to the later rounds of a cup tournament. To make up for this, many leagues run their own cup competition instead – they can integrate their own league cup fixtures into their own league's fixture list.

NATIONAL COMPETITIONS

The F.A. runs seven national cup competitions. Those open to the most teams are the F.A. Youth Cup, the F.A. County Youth Cup, the F.A. Women's Cup and the F.A. Sunday Cup.

For more details about any of these competitions and to obtain application forms contact the F.A. Headquarters in London. The address is in Appendix II at the back of this book. The usual time to obtain these forms is February each year, with the forms to be returned to the F.A. by April. This would enable teams to join in the competition in the following season.

THREE NATIONAL F.A. TOURNAMENTS FOR THE PYRAMID

It is easy to get confused between the three national cup competitions for the Pyramid run by the F.A. Two of these competitions are for the clubs near the top of the football Pyramid but outside the professional leagues. The other is the F.A. Cup.

THE F.A. TROPHY

About 180 teams enter this one. They come from the Conference and the leagues directly below it in the Pyramid. Sometimes only the top two divisions of each of these leagues are allowed to enter the F.A. Trophy, to keep the numbers down and the standard up.

THE F.A. VASE

Around 450 teams enter this competition. This brings smaller clubs in who have to learn quickly to take on extra duties about crowd control, dealing with the press and looking after guests, not to mention the extra administration. This competition attracts the better-equipped teams from further down the Pyramid.

THE F.A. CUP

Nearly 600 teams enter the F.A. Cup, the most famous national club competition in the world, including the professional clubs. Conference teams usually enter in the third and fourth qualifying round. Divisions 2 and 3 enter in the first round proper.

WHAT CAN SUCH COMPETITIONS DO FOR SMALLER CLUBS?

One of the attractions of such competitions for smaller clubs, apart from the excitement and prestige, is money – the sponsors have cash prizes for the victors in every round.

These competitions provide extra motivation for teams in the wider base of leagues at the bottom of the Pyramid to be ambitious.

From time to time the F.A. may re-organise the Pyramid, which can mean changes as to which teams can enter these competitions. F.A. rules cover everything from player eligibility (meaning who is allowed to play) to the travelling expenses that are allowed.

LOCAL COMPETITIONS WHERE MORE CLUBS TAKE PART

There's no need to feel left out if you can see no prospect of your club playing in these national F.A. tournaments in the near future. All over the country, each County F.A. has several county cup competitions for the different levels of ability of teams at local level – entering these tournaments is voluntary. In such cup tournaments, the more senior the competition the greater the responsibilities your club will have to deal with. For instance, many County F.A. cup tournament rules require you to provide refreshments for visiting clubs, particularly where they have travelled over considerable distances. Your County F.A. will be able to advise you on this.

CHECKLIST

- make contact with league secretaries
- get the necessary forms to fill in
- apply to join a league
- apply to join any other competitions
- pay fees.

chapter 3
DEALING WITH THE AUTHORITIES

This chapter explains the role of the following authorities:

- the league your club plays in;
- the Football Association and the Women's F.A.;
- the County F.A.

THE LEAGUE YOUR CLUB PLAYS IN
THE LEAGUE MANAGEMENT COMMITTEE
The league you play in will have an Annual General Meeting which you, as club secretary, will probably be expected to attend. It may not seem that interesting, but it is where you vote for the following people to form the League Management Committee, which has authority over your club:

- league chairperson
- league secretary
- league treasurer.

EXTRA JOBS ON THE LEAGUE MANAGEMENT COMMITTEE
In some leagues, to share the league secretary's workload, each division also has its own division secretary, and you may come across the following additional officers:

- fixtures officer – to set dates for all the games
- referees officer – to appoint referees to games
- F.A. liaison officer – to talk with the County F.A. about general issues
- news officer – to prepare a league newsletter, to pass results and news to local press
- fund-raiser – anyone who is good at raising money.

Quite often two or three people end up with all the work of running the league. Most leagues have vacancies for committed people to share the work, but normally none of them get paid for it.

Usually the League Management Committee will consist of people who used to run clubs in your league. This shouldn't mean there is any favouritism going on. In any case, it's all democratic – you can vote for the people you want in charge at your league's Annual General Meeting.

The Management Committee holds its own meetings. It is independent from the next tier of authority, your League Council.

THE LEAGUE COUNCIL

Your League Council is of great importance. It is made up of representatives from each club in your league. That probably means you, as club secretary, will be involved, with your club's vote.

This Council normally meets once a month. You might sometimes hear the League Council Meeting called 'the League Meeting'. On your application to join your league, you will have to enter the names of two or three people from your club who can go to this meeting.

At professional level, it is customary for the club chairmen to be the ones who attend their League's Council Meeting and vote on their club's behalf. For instance, you may have read criticism in the newspapers of club chairmen using their power in professional leagues by casting their votes at their Council Meeting to stop their league being cut in size – fewer matches means less gate receipts.

At amateur level, it is more often the club secretary who goes to the League Council Meeting and votes on the club's behalf. At least one person should turn up from your club every time – that much is normally compulsory. (Some leagues do not have a Council. Instead they have a larger Management Committee with plenty of clubs represented on it.)

the point of all those meetings

If meetings bore you, bear in mind that here is a structure for when you need action; a structure so that you know who is in charge and where you stand – after all, no-one would want decisions that affect your club made by faceless people who no-one elected. So this set-up, unwieldy as it may seem, means every club has a say.

The other great use of League Council meetings is that they are like a doctor's surgery. Teams go in with their problems and other officials sit down and work it out together.

SUB-COMMITTEES

In many leagues a sub-committee will be formed to handle matters such as discipline. In fact it is ideal for a league to have a Discipline Sub-committee, because separating the executive from the law-enforcers is normally seen as a good thing for justice – that's why, in other areas of life, the government and the judiciary are separate from each other, for example.

WHO'S IN CHARGE?

Some become confused over who has the greater authority: the League Council, which makes decisions at its monthly meetings, or the Management Committee, which makes day-to-day decisions, or a sub-committee with disciplinary powers. The League Council ultimately has the power, through the Annual General Meeting, to remove Management Committee members. In practice, it is left to the Management Committee to wield power in most day-to-day decisions.

Confusion may stem from the fact that in some leagues the Management Committee may also carry on the business of disciplining players and clubs. Even where there is a Discipline Sub-Committee, the Management Committee will normally still have the power to fine clubs for simple things such as failing to send in their team-sheet on time.

WHAT TO DO WHEN YOUR CLUB CANNOT ATTEND LEAGUE COUNCIL MEETINGS

If your club's usual representative (yes, probably yourself) cannot go to the League Council meeting, here's what you should do:

- Try to get someone else to go. (That should be one of the other names you've already given as 'official representatives' when you completed your registration papers for their league.) If that fails…
- Phone the league secretary to send your official apologies for not being able to attend. (Leagues usually fine clubs who fail to turn up without any explanation or apologies.) Finally…
- Make sure you have a representative at the next meeting. (Some leagues would fine any club missing from two meetings on the trot, even if apologies were received.)

where are the decisions made?

Decisions on all kinds of matters are made almost daily in running a league, some by the Management Committee alone, some by the League Council, and some by the league's Annual General Meeting, which is a meeting of the Council and Management Committee with special powers. I'll give you a flavour of who normally gets to decide what.

The **Management Committee** (unless they delegate to sub-committees) have authority on matters such as:

- overall control of dates for match fixtures
- disputes between clubs on matters such as signing players or abandonment of games
- disciplinary measures for clubs or players who break rules
- how much to charge clubs for membership
- appointment of referees to games (as occurs in many leagues).

Unless you stand for election, you won't have to be on the Management Committee.

The **League Council** may inspect the league accounts and decide on issues as they crop up throughout the year, such as:

- how many teams should comprise each division of the league in future
- whether to hold new competitions or scrap existing competitions
- choosing venues for special matches such as cup ties.

As club secretary, you will probably be your club's representative on the Council.

The **Annual General Meeting** votes on matters such as:

- electing the members of the Management Committee for the next year
- changes in the rules of the league
- allowing new clubs to join the league
- fixing dates for the season to kick off and to finish by.

As club secretary, you will probably be expected to be at the league's AGM.

A **Special General Meeting** can also be called at less notice, with similar powers to those wielded by the Annual General Meeting – to sort out urgent issues.

The **County F.A.**, which is covered in more detail later in this chapter, decides on matters such as:

- punishments for players who have been cautioned by match referees
- punishments for clubs that fail to fulfil obligations (such as not paying their bills)
- supervising the standard of referees.

WHAT DOES THE MANAGEMENT COMMITTEE DO DURING THE SEASON?

Aside from taking the decisions referred to above, the Management Committee does a lot of day-to-day work. Except where some of these powers are delegated to sub-committees, their work includes:

- Dealing with other authorities. This may mean liaising with the County F.A., attracting County F.A. referees to your league, and possibly appointing referees to matches.
- Publicity. The Management Committee may be publishing a league newsletter and forwarding weekly league details to local newspapers.
- 'Special events'. The Committee probably has to make arrangements for special matches such as cup finals, not to mention organising the annual awards presentation.
- General administration. There is always the business of gathering monies (subscriptions, fines) from clubs and keeping the finance and paperwork of the league in order.
- League records. The Committee will be keeping up-to-date records of players' registrations, match results, league tables, accounts, minutes of meetings.

Mostly, however, members of the Management Committee spend a lot of time (normally unpaid) on the phone or writing letters to help clubs, such as over a dispute or a breakdown of communications affecting fixtures. You can see why it is normally handy for a league to set up sub-committees for arranging, say, social occasions, or organising fixtures, appointing referees or resolving disputes.

Further insight into the work of the Management Committee can be gained from some of the 'True Stories' in this book.

When I listen to members of clubs talking about the football authorities, it is usually a complaint about the attitude of the authorities. So you may wonder what attitude you should expect from your league Management Committee or County F.A.

WHAT IS THE ATTITUDE OF THE AUTHORITIES?

Firm but fair: that's what you should expect the authorities to be. The reputations of the game's governing bodies have suffered in recent years – people have accused them of being inflexible and showing favouritism.

When a Management Committee I had been involved with had been in charge of our league for a few years, we joked: 'We used to think the people who ran football were the worst bunch of stiff-necked, jack-booted, hide-bound, stuffy-nosed dictators you could meet... Now we know they are.'

We set out to be nothing like that, but that was how some clubs saw us. The truth was, with one or two teams trying to postpone games to gain an advantage, and some not paying their dues when others did, we were always just a step away from the season collapsing in chaos and matches unplayed. We had to be firm, and make sure the same rules applied to everyone. Only when we were in charge of our league were our eyes opened about what the authorities have to deal with. The true stories opposite may raise some eyebrows.

As a league official I hated dishing out fines to clubs – it's no way to make yourself popular. But I began to see the good officials do in holding organised football together – just.

APPEALS

So what do you do when the league gives you a fine or a ban and you don't agree with it? Turn to Chapter 18: 'The match – discipline and sportsmanship' to read about appeals.

FIXTURE LISTS

As mentioned earlier, another thing the Management Committee deals with is fixture lists.

THE STANDARD ARRANGEMENTS

It is important that the business of arranging fixtures is clear. Normally the league secretary will send your club the fixture list for the new season about a month before the season starts. In some leagues, the league secretary may then allow you about a week to request any changes to the fixtures – for example, if you know in

true stories

Can we speak in private?

Some teams want to bend the rules to gain an advantage over some other team. You may not believe this one – but it did happen.

On one occasion a team asked to meet the Management Committee in private. We agreed. They had just had players banned by the County F.A. after a stormy match. We thought they wanted to smooth over recent events. We were taken by surprise. They asked for our permission to let them secretly play their banned players under false names. They feared that without them in their next few games, their team might get a good hiding. They claimed other clubs were doing the same behind our backs, saying, 'You know it goes on.'

To cap it all, they said the reason they had asked for a meeting was that they wouldn't want us to think them dishonest in their dealings with us! You couldn't make it up.

On another occasion a team tried to get a game postponed at short notice because they couldn't put their best team out.

There is only one way to deal with such things – and that is to know the rule book and to stick to it, come what may, whatever sweet voice whispers in your ear, and no matter who thinks you're being an inflexible dictator (league officials get called this and worse – they develop thick skins).

The point is that if you use rules made up out of thin air – instead of the ones all the teams signed up to in the constitution before the season kicked-off – you've had it. And once the people in charge have lost respect, they can't get it back. So we stick to the rules. League officials don't have a quiet life. But then they took a position of authority, so it wouldn't be fitting if they did have a quiet life, would it?

advance of a particular problem with certain dates, such as a wedding day. After that the fixture list is fixed. If you want to know how 'fixed' is 'fixed' turn to Chapter 20: 'Game on, game off'.

In most leagues, as soon as time runs out for you to object to dates in your fixture list the league secretary – or in some leagues the referees officer – will then set about contacting his pool of referees. He will arrange with them which referee is going to cover which game for the first few months, if not for the whole season.

With the referees booked the league secretary will become very reluctant to consider any requests for fixtures to be moved, because that would mean reorganising the referees too. Referees don't like to be messed about with respect to their diaries. I will deal with circumstances in which fixtures might be rearranged in the 'Game on, game off' chapter.

When matches get called off, due to circumstances such as the weather, it is the league secretary who will usually have the final say on a new date for the game to be played.

LESS COMMON FIXTURE ARRANGEMENTS

I have come across leagues where the organisation is less formal. In one league, all the club secretaries would get together before the season in a big meeting to arrange their own fixture lists – the result is a mad scramble lasting hours, as each team arranges with every other team. Leagues that do this claim that it enables clubs to organise around the most suitable dates for home and away fixtures. The major criticism of this sort of arrangement is it lacks leadership and is apt to collapse in total disorganisation as teams clash over their preference for dates for matches.

FINDING OUT INFORMATION ABOUT YOUR LEAGUE

There are various means of obtaining information about your league, including the following.

NEWSLETTERS

Communication between the authorities and clubs is vital, but often neglected. Ideally, your league will publish and post (or e-mail) a newsletter, probably monthly, to remind clubs of fixtures, to give them news of recent results and league tables, to remind them of meetings their representatives have to attend, forms that have to be filled in, and anything else that matters.

LEAGUE COUNCIL MEETINGS

When the league in which I have been involved as an official has been short of the manpower to get a newsletter prepared, we have stressed even more the importance of club representatives' attendance at the monthly League Council meeting. This is the best way of getting information across anyway, because questions can be asked and answered there.

LETTERS AND PHONE CALLS

As an alternative, the league secretary may ring or write about any outstanding duties on your club's part. If you are in doubt about whether you are doing every-thing right, then by far the best thing to do is give the league secretary a call your-self, and ask him if in fact all your dealings with the league are in order. This includes signing players, submitting team sheets on time, paying bills, or making important telephone calls.

Of course it is in your club's interest to respond to all of the league secretary's requests as quickly as possible. When your own workload in your club does get heavier please bear in mind that the league secretary isn't just spending time on your club, but on every club in the league.

THE LEAGUE RULE BOOK

Being part of a league will go most smoothly if you familiarise yourself with the rules. That's why you should read your league's constitution or 'Rule Book'. Every league should have one. It's usually about 15 pages long. I have come across an F.A. league with a one-page constitution. The reason for this was: 'We don't go a bundle on paperwork. We all get on pretty well, so we like to keep it informal.' But it leaves that league with no authority for resolving all kinds of problems. You should expect to see a full set of rules.

Read it well. Most situations that arise during the season should be catered for in it. The whole reason that all the clubs sign it every year – before the start of every season – is so that all agree to playing under the same rules. By rules I don't mean only the Laws of Association Football as policed by the referee in a match; I mean the rules for the day-to-day business of running a football league. It's your League Constitution. If you don't like it, you have the opportunity to suggest changes at your league's Annual General Meeting.

ONE STRUCTURE FOR THE GAME

A similar structure, with Management Committee and Council, is used in leagues at all levels of the game. It may seem bureaucratic for any modern organisation, but traditional thinking is that it's right that each club has a say in how its league is run.

As for the F.A., this is run by the F.A. Council and the Executive Committee (a more impressive name for a Management Committee). The F.A. Council itself is a bit different, since the F.A. is not a league – it is a governing body. There are 92 seats on the F.A. Council but these are not all held by the 92 clubs in the top four divisions. The seats are held by a mixture of people elected to represent the Premier League and Football League, and the County Associations, not to mention universities, schools and certain services needed by the game. It meets about six times a year to decide on footballing matters. In theory, the F.A. Council is the more powerful body because it votes on policy, but in practice the Executive Committee (like the Management Committee) runs things.

Now that you know about the league structure, you will want to know also about where the F.A. comes in. I would stress that as a club secretary you will deal with your league secretary more than with your County F.A. Your league secretary is in charge of the day-to-day running of your league.

THE FOOTBALL ASSOCIATION

It is the Football Association, not County F.A.s, which deals directly with:
- men's professional football;
- the top men's Pyramid leagues;
- national and local women's football.

WOMEN'S FOOTBALL

Information on women's football is available from the Women's Football Alliance, which also has a regional structure. (The contact details for the Women's F.A. are in Appendix II at the end of this book.) Since the organisation of association football follows a pattern, the following section on the ordinary County F.A. applies in most respects to the Women's F.A.

In England there are about 1,700 women's clubs – that's about 34,000 women playing. (World-wide, you can make that about 30 million girls and women, according to FIFA.)

THE COUNTY F.A.

For the rest of English football, your Football Association contact is your County F.A. That includes, as well as men's football, schools' football because the English Schools F.A. is represented at County F.A. level.

The County F.A. in your area is a branch of England's Football Association. It's like a tree, a huge structure governing the whole of association football in this country. The County F.A.s are the branches we usually deal with at amateur level.

There are 43 County F.A.s. Under their wing are the hundreds of local leagues and their many referees. Very little happens in organised football without the F.A. giving permission somewhere along the line. In England alone, there are some 40,000 clubs affiliated through the County F.A.s. Those clubs have over two million registered players.

In addition, your County F.A. has the job of bringing national F.A. projects to grass roots level, projects such as the 'Let's kick racism out of football' campaign.

AREN'T SOME LEAGUES OUTSIDE THE F.A.?

There are leagues that have nothing to do with the F.A. Sometimes this is because the teams want to have less paperwork and save money, and feel they can trust each other to run their own affairs. Some exist this way for a number of years. Sooner or later most of them decide to affiliate to the F.A. and do things 'by the book'. Here are three reasons why:

- some local authorities may bar you from the use of playing fields – perhaps they are concerned about whether their insurance covers them against accidents at 'unofficial matches';
- County F.A. referees will normally refuse to officiate at non-F.A. games – again the insurance issue worries them. This means 'unofficial leagues' have to persuade anybody they can get to referee their games;
- local newspapers may refuse to print 'unofficial league' results – they may only give space to leagues affiliated to the F.A.

THE INSURANCE QUESTION

There are legal implications for 'unofficial leagues': a referee normally has insurance cover in respect of an incident in a game resulting in harm to someone, but that insurance may be invalid when he or she takes charge of a non-affiliated game. No referee wants to be in that position, especially following the recent case of the lawsuit that concerned a rugby match where an injury received in a collapsed scrum was blamed on the match referee. I'll say more about insurance in Chapter 5: 'Building your squad' and Chapter 6: 'Balancing the books'.

'ISN'T THE F.A. AN UNFAIR MONOPOLY?'

I've heard the complaint that the F.A. is an unfair monopoly, a bit of a Mafia. This is not fair criticism – it's not a wicked cartel established for the sole sake of taking money from you; it's a way to keep the game together in one structure from grass roots to professional level. It's for everyone's good that there should be proper order and a proper structure for football in our country. The whole world is never going to agree with every decision made by the F.A. – we all have our opinions about sport, and it's right we should – but we all need a structure to develop the game.

To play in an F.A. affiliated league, your club needs to affiliate to the F.A., not just your league – the process for this was described in Chapter 2: 'Joining a local football league'.

I should add that while affiliating to the F.A. is a good thing, it is not like waving a magic wand. For example, the F.A. has a shortage of referees at grass roots level – they need to recruit and keep far more referees. Even if you have regular referees, you may not have assistant referees, or linesmen as they used to be called. There is more about this in Chapter 17: 'The match – referees and laws of the game'.

WHEN WILL WE COME INTO CONTACT WITH THE COUNTY F.A.?

You can ring your County F.A. for advice on many things. But it's generally when things go wrong – such as when a player is booked or sent off – that the County F.A. gets in touch with clubs.

COUNTY F.A. INSPECTIONS

However, the County F.A. has the power, like your league does, to demand to inspect your club's paperwork at any time. Inspections do not seem to happen too often at the level of park football.

The County F.A. also demands that your club holds at least one meeting a year where members, too, can look at your account books. An Annual General Meeting is a good time for this.

F.A. DISCIPLINE

However, the most likely occasion you will hear from the County F.A. is when a referee gives one of your players a yellow or a red card. You, as club secretary, will receive from the County F.A. a notice of your player's punishment. I'm going to tell you how to deal with matters such as F.A. punishments in Chapter 18: 'The match – discipline and sportsmanship'.

You will deal with other authorities too. See the following chapters:

AGENCIES HIRING OUT YOUR FOOTBALL PITCH
See Chapter 7: 'All about football pitches'.

REFEREES
See Chapter 17: 'The match – referees and the laws of the game'.

THE BANK
See Chapter 6: 'Balancing the books'.

THE LAW
Hopefully you will have no need to meet either the police or the courts but, just in case an incident in football brings you into contact with them, a brief section on both is included in Chapter 18: 'The match – discipline and sportsmanship'.

THE CHAIN OF COMMAND IN ASSOCIATION FOOTBALL

The last word on the authorities, for the sake of completeness, is to explain how football is structured as a world-wide game.

- **LOCAL:** For most clubs, the County F.A. is the top authority for most of their concerns.
- **NATIONAL:** The national authority is your F.A., the English Football Association. It has branches such as the Women's Football Alliance and County F.A.s, and for schools' football the English Schools F.A. If you are in Scotland, you have the Scottish Football Association, while in Wales there's the Football Association of Wales. Across the water, there is the Northern Ireland Football Association and the Football Association of Ireland in the Irish Republic. (Wherever in the world you are reading this, for details of how to contact your country's F.A., see Appendix II at the back of this book.)
- **CONFEDERATIONS:** The Confederations are higher authorities than the national F.A. bodies mentioned above. In charge in Europe is the European football authority, UEFA (Union des Associations Européennes de Football). The English F.A. is a full member of UEFA, which is one of six confederations that cover the world's continents. They answer to FIFA (Federation Internationale de Football Association).
- **THE HIGHEST AUTHORITY:** So top of the tree is the world-wide football authority, FIFA. Just as your club needs to affiliate to its County F.A., and your County F.A. is a branch of the national F.A., so your national F.A. is affiliated to FIFA. That goes for England, Scotland, Wales and all. More than 200

countries are affiliated to FIFA. You can see how and why a similar structure runs through all of association football.

HOW THIS AFFECTS YOUR CLUB

Your club will be affected by decisions made at the highest level, such as changes to the Laws of the Game. This information is 'cascaded', as they call it, down from the top. That means that if FIFA, the top authority, decides to change a law in the game, such as when it decided goalkeepers should be banned from picking up back-passes, you will hear it from your County F.A. You might read about it first in the newspapers, but sometimes press reports are only half accurate, so you should check the paperwork the County F.A. send you to make sure you have it right.

In fact, unless you play in those leagues nearer the top of the Pyramid of Football, you should expect that the County F.A. is the highest football authority your club would ever need to deal with. And even then, the authority with which you will have most contact should be your own league.

CHECKLIST

- make sure club representatives attend the league's AGM.
- make sure club representatives attend League Council meetings.

chapter 4

BUILDING THE STRUCTURE OF YOUR CLUB

The previous chapter showed how football leagues are normally organised. Now let's see how clubs are commonly organised. A 'structure' for a club means having rules and people doing jobs.

Organising this is a low-key job. Just as professional football clubs do, amateur clubs have jobs to be done. How their club officers do their jobs is vital to overcome the most common crises at clubs. They are:

- not enough people off-the-park to help in the running of the club;
- not enough money to pay the club's bills;
- a communications breakdown.

This chapter is of most use to anyone forming a new club from scratch. If you are taking over a club that's been around for years – and what follows is familiar – why not use this chapter as a check-up on the health of your club? After reading it, you should have a clearer idea of how you want your club run. For a start, see the suggested club rules. There's no need to follow all my suggestions to the letter. Make any changes you and your club think fitting.

TIMING (AGAIN)

When planning how to structure your club, the first questions, as so often, are:

- How long till the season starts?
- How long do you have to do the paperwork to join a league for the new season?

If your season starts around September, you need to get through the business of this chapter by June. That's why June is a good month for your Annual General Meeting (or AGM), as suggested in Chapter 1. The AGM is where you should normally appoint your club's officers and agree on your Club Rules. If you are later than June, you should plan to hold your AGM pronto.

PLANNING AN AGM

Since people need time beforehand to think about the issues that come up at an AGM – like voting for people who will run their club – let members have at least 21 days' warning that there's going to be an AGM. For a simple guide to organising a meeting see Chapter 1.

WHERE TO FIND HELP ON POINTS RAISED AT AGMs

In the following pages you will see a suggested agenda for your AGM, and a template for your Club Rules. One of the main issues involved is...

CHOOSING YOUR CLUB OFFICERS

You will find job descriptions for club officers in this chapter. You may wish to mention these job descriptions to your members at the AGM – people want to know what they are letting themselves in for when they take on a job. You don't have to have players as club officers. Tell friends and family that club officers are needed. Ask your members to do the same. There may be someone out there willing to get involved in your club.

You can see a list of officers in the Club Rules on the following pages. Your AGM can vote on whether you want more or fewer officers running your club.

GIVING NOTICE OF YOUR CLUB'S AGM

You should send (or hand out) a letter to everyone in your club. Every year, at your AGM you have the following issues on the agenda – every year you vote to keep or change the rules, and to keep or change the officers. Your letter might go something like this:

WANNABE F.C. – OPEN LETTER TO ALL

Twelfth of Whenever

It's time for a meeting for everyone, the ANNUAL GENERAL MEETING. It might last an hour or two.

DAY:
TIME:
PLACE:

AGENDA FOR THE MEETING

1. Apologies (let me know if you can't come. My phone number is ....)
2. (If your club has had an AGM before, the minutes of the last AGM will be read out.)
3. A report on our club's development so far.
4. A report on the club's finances – and how we can raise money to pay for the club.
5. We need a discussion and a vote on our suggested Club Rules. Attached is a copy of them. If anyone wants to suggest changes to these rules, you must propose your changes, and someone else has to second them. The meeting can vote to make changes.
6. We need to nominate who should be elected to the jobs on our club's general committee. If you want to stand for election, someone must propose your name and someone else has to second it, before a vote. The jobs for elections are:

    club chairperson
    club secretary
    club treasurer
    players' representative

We also want to appoint a qualified first-aider, and a resources officer to look after club kit and equipment.
7. According to the proposed rules, this meeting will not elect a team manager. The general committee you elect will have the final say on a manager, but we will want to hear the views of the meeting.
8. Do we put a limit on the size of our squad, or do we leave that up to the manager?
9. Personal accident insurance for players – how much can we afford?
10. We need to decide what is the best way to get messages round all our members – especially urgent messages.
11. Any other business – your chance to raise questions that concern you.

That's all. See you there.

                                  Kind regards,
                                  Joe Wannabe

SAMPLE RULE BOOK

'..' F.C. RULE BOOK

NAME OF THE CLUB
1 The club's name shall be '.........................' Football Club' (hereinafter 'the Club').

AIMS OF THE CLUB
2 The Club's aims shall be to:
i) affiliate to the Football Association ('the F.A.');
ii) promote the footballing interests of its members, including: the provision of training and competitive association football, promoting fitness and discipline and nurturing talent;
iii) have such social and fund-raising activities as the Committee considers appropriate. (N.B. If your team has another object, such as charity work, it should be set out here.)

MEMBERSHIP OF THE CLUB
3 MEMBERSHIP BOOK. The secretary shall keep a register of playing members and non-playing members of the Club.

4 Any person shall be deemed a member who pays due monies, and signs a statement in the Membership Book agreeing to abide by the Club Rules; and any such person who is also registered to play football for the Club shall be deemed a playing member.

(SIZE OF SQUAD: If you want to limit the size of the squad, it should be set out here: i.e. 'Membership of playing members shall be limited to .... playing members.' CONDITIONS: If you have any other conditions for members, such as a minimum age, it should be set out here (e.g. '16 shall be the minimum age for playing members'.)

5 RESIGNATIONS. To resign or transfer away from the Club a member must normally give written notice to the club secretary and complete payment of all his Club dues. The club secretary shall inform the league secretary in writing of when a member's resignation from the club is received in writing; and of when payment of the member's club dues is complete. The name of any player who has resigned or been expelled from the Club shall be marked accordingly in the Membership Book.

ANNUAL GENERAL MEETING (AGM) OF THE CLUB

6 The Club shall hold an AGM not later than .... (put a suitable date). Seven members shall be a quorum. The secretary shall make best endeavours to give 21 days' notice of the AGM to all members by any such means as are available to him.

7 The AGM may:
i) receive the treasurer's financial report and secretary's annual report;
ii) consider appointing an independent qualified accountant to examine the accounts;
iii) overturn any decision of the general committee and undertake any other business;
iv) vote to amend and/or approve the Club Rules;
v) elect each officer of the General Committee, except for the team manager;
vi) elect officers to be signatories to the Club's bank account.

8 Every member present may cast one vote on all matters. The chair shall have a casting vote in the event of any tied vote. Candidates for election shall be proposed, seconded and voted for. The candidate with most votes shall be elected. Candidates may be re-elected in further years. Any elections shall be with immediate effect for one year.

THE GENERAL COMMITTEE OF THE CLUB

9 The Club's business shall be administered by a General Committee ('the Committee') comprising the following officers: chairperson, secretary, treasurer, team manager and players' representative. At least two of the said officers shall be appointed by the Committee as delegates to attend League Council Meetings. At least two of the said officers shall be signatories to the Club's bank account. When required a vice-chair may be appointed for one meeting by a vote of the officers. (N.B. If you want any more officers, it should be set out here.)

10 The appointment of any person as an officer shall cease immediately upon receipt of any decision of the F.A. to suspend such a person from taking part in any activity relating to association football.

11 The Committee shall normally meet monthly. Three members shall be a quorum. Decisions shall be made by a simple vote. The chair shall have a casting vote.

12 POWERS. The powers of the Committee shall include the powers to:

i) appoint and dismiss the team manager;

ii) suspend or expel any member whose conduct it considers detrimental to the good name of the Club;

iii) dismiss from the General Committee a member absent from three consecutive meetings without an explanation it considers satisfactory;

iv) appoint persons to unfilled roles on the Committee between AGMs;

v) appoint a Club Discipline Sub-Committee and other such sub-committees as may from time to time be deemed necessary; and require reports of such sub-committees to be made to the Committee;

vi) decide on interpretation of the Club Rules, and on any other club matters not governed by the Club Rules. Such decisions may be amended at an AGM or an Extraordinary General Meeting (EGM);

vii) exclude any officer from voting at Committee Meetings on any issue that directly affects him.

13 MINUTE BOOK. The decisions of all club meetings, including the Committee, shall be written in a Minute Book.

14 DELEGATES. The Club's delegates to the League Council will be responsible for:

i) finding out the time and place of Council meetings;

ii) ensuring a delegate, or other club representative, attends Council meetings;

iii) forwarding their own apologies to the league secretary in advance in the event that none shall be able to attend a Council meeting;

iv) dealing with business on the Club's behalf at the Council meeting;

v) reporting back to the General Committee on the business of the Council.

EXTRAORDINARY GENERAL MEETING (EGM) OF THE CLUB

15 An EGM shall have the same powers as an AGM. Seven members shall be a quorum. The secretary shall make his best endeavours to give seven days' notice of the time, place and the purpose of such meeting to all members by any such means as are available to him. An EGM may be called:

i) by the Committee; and/or

ii) upon the written request to the club secretary of any four members.

THE CLUB RULE BOOK

16 CLUB RULE BOOK. A copy of this Club Rule Book (the 'Club Rules') shall be available on request to any member.

17 In the case of the F.A.'s disapproval of any part of the Club Rules, the Committee may call an EGM to make suitable amendments to the Club Rules.

18 Amendments may be made to the Club Rules, subject to the following conditions:
i) that such amendment is made by an AGM, or by an EGM called for the purpose;
ii) that such amendment is voted for by at least two-thirds of the members present at such AGM or EGM;
iii) that such amendment is approved by the F.A., and such amendment comes into force on a date 14 days or more after the date of the F.A.'s approval.

19 The Club Rules shall be governed by the rules and regulations of any league or competition of which the Club is part where they apply and which are in use for the time being. The latter shall prevail in the event of any conflict between them, subject to the rules and regulations of the F.A.

20 The Club Rules shall be governed by the rules and regulations of the F.A. in use for the time being where they apply. The latter shall prevail in the event of any conflict between them.

THE CLUB FINANCES

21 The Club's finances shall be administered by the club treasurer. He shall present the books of account for inspection at each official Club meeting.

22 Any property, assets and liabilities of the Club shall be deemed to be jointly owned by the members, and entrusted to the care of the Committee. Any member who leaves the Club prior to the disbanding of the Club forfeits his part in any such property and assets. In the event of the disbanding of the Club, an EGM shall vote on how to dispose of any such property, assets and liabilities, together with all records.

23 BANK ACCOUNT. The club shall have a bank account at .... bank. Any cheque must be signed by at least two of the authorised signatories.

24 CASH BOOK. The Committee shall be responsible for keeping proper books of accounts, including records of all monies received and all payments made.

25 The Club's book of accounts may be checked annually by any suitably qualified person who is independent of the Club.

26 RECEIPTS. Any officer of the Club may sign receipts for monies received. Such an officer must notify the treasurer of any such receipt. Receipts must be given for all monies received, except that receipts need not be issued for match subscriptions where payments of such match subscriptions are recorded separately.

MATCH SUBSCRIPTIONS OF PLAYING MEMBERS

27 The rate of match subscriptions for playing members shall be set by the Committee. They may include different subscription rates for:

i) full match played;

ii) part of match played;

iii) no match played (many clubs don't charge when the player does not play).

28 A written record of each player's payments of match subscriptions shall be kept.

29 Where a playing member's match subscription is overdue by at least two weeks, and without an explanation regarded as satisfactory by the Committee, such a player may be suspended from playing for the Club until such a time as such a player's due match subscriptions are paid in full. The County F.A. may be notified of such suspension.

ANNUAL SUBSCRIPTIONS OF ALL MEMBERS

30 In addition to match subscriptions, the rate of any annual subscriptions to the Club for playing members and non-playing members shall be set by the Committee. Non-playing members who are officers of the Club, or have served as officers of the Club, are not required to pay a subscription.

31 A written record of all payments shall be kept by the club treasurer.

32 Payments of annual subscriptions must be completed not later than the deadline of .... (give a suitable date, e.g. 1st October), subject to the following. Any person becoming a member after this date may pay his annual subscription within six weeks of becoming a member and may be offered a partial discount.

33 In the event of non-payment of any member's annual subscription by the deadline set out above, and without an explanation considered satisfactory by the Committee, such a person's current membership shall be regarded as expired, and his name shall be struck from the Membership Book. Such a person may seek membership anew.

CLUB CARE AND CONDUCT

34 The officers of the Club, in their personal capacity and in their capacity as officers, do not assume any duty of care to club members training and playing football. In the context of training and playing football, all members playing will exercise all care that is reasonable in the prevailing circumstances to avoid inflicting injury to fellow players.

35 All members will respect the match referee's duty of care towards the safety of players, and in that regard will obey all referee's requests that are reasonable in the prevailing circumstances.

36 In the context of club matters, all members will conduct themselves in a way fitting to keep the good name of the Club. They will also abide by such code of conduct as the Club may draw up.

DATE OF COMING INTO FORCE

37 These Club Rules shall come into force on the twenty-first day after the day of their approval at a club meeting. This is subject to approval by the F.A., as represented by the County F.A. except where otherwise notified by the F.A.

38 DATE OF RULES. This version of the Club Rules was approved by the Club meeting held on (DATE) ....

Signed .... (Club Secretary)

Signed .... (a witness present at said Club meeting)

NOTES ON CLUB RULES

You may wish to request from your County F.A. their own suggested Club Rules.

The reason for having this suggested Club Rule Book (sometimes also called a constitution) is this: where there's money changing hands, and where there are people in positions of power over other people, there should be rules in everyone's interest.

Any clubs that require more sophisticated Club Rules, such as clubs that own assets, should also consult their County F.A. Your County F.A. will expect you to send them a copy of your Club Rule Book. You could send it to them with their 'County F.A. Affiliation Form' (see the previous chapter). They will tell you if anything is not to their liking.

A quorum is the smallest number of members needed at a meeting for it to count as an official meeting. In your Club Rules, you can make any number a quorum as you see fit.

You have the author's permission to copy the rules for your own club's use. Adapt them as you see fit.

NOTES ON SUBSCRIPTIONS

No two clubs I know ask members for the same subscriptions. Some ask for annual and match subscriptions. Some have only annual subscriptions or only match subscriptions. It's up to your club to decide what it needs in your Club Rules. By the way, charging non-playing members a subscription is really only common where the club can offer non-playing members facilities to enjoy; many clubs may wish to put in their rules that non-playing members will not have a subscription to pay. This is especially so if non-playing members do the unpaid work of running the club. I will explain more about subscriptions later in Chapter 6: 'Balancing the books'.

SPECIAL RULES FOR SIGNING PLAYERS

You may also have something in your Club Rules about who can play for the team. For example, a factory football team may want only factory staff as players. The whole of the next chapter is given over to questions about signing players for your squad.

LIMITED COMPANIES

There's no pressure on a typical park team to become a Limited Company, and it's not usually something to worry about if your club is a park team for friends, a youth club or anything like that. Most clubs are simply clubs for the benefit of their members, so Club Rules are a simple thing.

It can be more complicated for a senior club, which may be formed as a Limited Company with a board of directors. Clubs that want to be Limited Companies should see the F.A. Handbook for rules on this, and may also wish to take an accountant's or solicitor's advice. It would mean more paperwork and responsibility.

WHAT CAN I EXPECT TO HAPPEN AT THE CLUB AGM?

At your club's AGM it may be obvious who is suited to the jobs of the officers. In any club there is usually a small number of people talented in dealing with paperwork, so people are bound to put their names forward. Of course it's not always possible to persuade people to take on a role, especially when no-one is getting paid.

Some might ask you for an idea of what being a club official means. That's why on the following pages I've put a summary of the work to be shared between the officers, and suggestions for who does what business at the club.

WORST-CASE SCENARIO

If at the end of the AGM no-one has come forward to help run the club and you are left on your own to do all the work, you have three choices:

- lean on someone (nicely) to help you; or
- put off the idea of joining a league for a year; or
- carry on – on your own – running the club.

I don't believe it's good for anyone's health to have the whole weight of the club to carry around alone. But if you do carry on alone, you might ask the AGM to elect you to all of the posts on your own. Here is an alternative, however.

WORST-CASE SCENARIO RESCUE PLAN

A more sensible way forward, if you are left to do everything alone, is to consider changing your plans this way:

- look for a league with a small number of teams – fewer games to organise;
- ask the league secretary if you can join a year later instead;
- just play friendlies for a year;
- spend the year looking for two or three people who can share the work at the club.

You should encourage your members to take an interest in the matter of electing your club's officers, because the grim truth is that a lot of your members may simply assume that they can leave all this to someone else: all they want to do is kick a football. Remind them that the health of their club matters as much off the pitch, and that ensuring the club is run well and by the right people is in everyone's interest. After all, it's everyone's club, not the Committee's. Frankly, members get the club they deserve.

For more thoughts about handling a situation where one person's shoulders carry too much of the burden, see Chapter 21: 'Crisis at the top'.

SHARING THE WORK-LOAD

Let's assume all goes well at your AGM and that you will be appointed as a club officer with other club officers to work with. This means you can split the work up. Experience and common sense will suggest that this split of duties between several persons will be best for a club:

- chairperson
- vice-chairperson
- secretary
- treasurer
- resources officer
- first-aider
- team-manager/coach
- team-captain
- players' representative on the General Committee.

Some clubs go further. They get their AGM to appoint extra officers such as these:

- child protection officer (see the suggestion in Appendix I of this book)
- social events organiser
- assistant secretary or general organiser
- fund-raiser
- their club's own assistant referees – to be available to run the line in matches.

It's up to your club to decide what its needs are. At clubs with more than one team – say, a youth team and a senior team – each team has its own committee comprising the officers listed above, to share the work. As ambitious clubs rise through the Pyramid, they may find they also need a fixtures secretary, a publicity officer to do their club's own match programmes, someone to organise hospitality for visiting teams – and so it goes on.

That split is based on the club being simply an association for the benefit of its members, rather than a Limited Company. Following are typical job descriptions for the roles listed.

THE CHAIRPERSON'S WORK

His work can include:

- ensuring that meetings are kept in order and address the issues that matter to

your club;
- making sure all the other club officers do their jobs;
- having a casting vote at club meetings;
- possibly acting as delegate to attend League Council Meetings;
- possibly acting as a signatory to the club's bank account;
- at clubs higher up the Pyramid a chairman may have a role of attracting investors.

THE CLUB SECRETARY'S WORK

The club secretary, more than anyone, needs to know all the business of the club, every duty to the league, to the County F.A., to other teams, to match officials and to your players. To help him through the playing season there is Chapter 13: 'A club secretary's weekly routine'. The secretary's work includes the following, explained in detail in the chapters ahead:

PLANNING:
keeping members informed of where and when to turn up for games and meetings.

PAPERWORK:
writing the minutes of club meetings; communication with the authorities, by letter or phone, fax or email, including signing and registering players; communication with other clubs, usually by phone; keeping club records such as copies of team sheets; almost certainly acting as a signatory to the club's bank account; making an annual report (about how the club is coming along) to the club AGM.

SOME CLUB DOCUMENTS:
The County F.A. expects the club secretary to make sure the club has:
- a Membership Book (see below);
- a Rule Book (such as the example of Club Rules earlier in this chapter);
- a Minute Book (your record of who was at your club's meetings and the decisions they made);
- a Cash Book (your treasurer's record of the club's money – paid and received).

If your club charges admission to matches, you need to keep a separate record of that 'gate money'. Most clubs never have that responsibility!

MEMBERSHIP BOOK:
This is sometimes called a Members' Register. It is a list of your club's players and

any other members. In your club's Membership Book, it's wise to write something like this on the first page: 'By signing this Membership Book, a member indicates his consent to abide by the Club Rules.' All members should sign under this statement. If players do not sign anything to say they will abide by the Club Rules, the Rules may be worthless. You should list all playing and non-playing members in the book, alongside these details for all of them:

- name;
- address;
- phone number;
- league registration number (you will know your players' league registration numbers when your league secretary confirms which players you have signed. I will deal with this in the next chapter.);
- if any children are members, you will need further details about them. See Appendix I for more on this.

OTHER DUTIES:
attending club General Committee meetings;almost certainly acting for the club at League Council Meetings and the League AGM.

THE CLUB TREASURER'S WORK
Typically, the other crucial role in the running of a football club's off-the-field business is that of club treasurer. His duties may include the following, which are covered in detail in Chapter 6: 'Balancing the books'.

PLANNING:
making sure there is enough money in the bank at the right time to pay the bills.

FUND-RAISING:
including seeking a sponsor and other ways of fund-raising.

HANDLING MONEY:
including dealing with petty cash, paying cash into the club bank account, almost certainly being a signatory to the club's bank account, collecting annual subscriptions and match subscriptions from members.

PAPERWORK:
involves keeping records of members' subscriptions, keeping receipts, etc., and keeping the books of the club's income and expenditure (the 'Cash Book'), mak-

ing a financial statement to the club's AGM, and acting with the club secretary to pay bills.

OTHER DUTIES:
may include attending club General Committee meetings and possibly being a delegate attending League Council Meetings.

THE PLAYERS' REPRESENTATIVE
Having a players' representative on the General Committee means there is someone players can talk to confidentially, and who will speak up for them. Often players are afraid to speak their mind to the manager or other club officers, for fear of losing their place in the team.

what if our club officers change?

During a season, it may be necessary for a change of faces on the club's General Committee. If so, you need to inform your league secretary of who has stood down, and who replaced them. If the club secretary or club chairman changes, the County F.A. want to know too. Also inform them of changes of such officers' addresses and phone numbers.

FIRST-AIDER
This is another essential role at any football club. At every match your club should have a qualified first-aider. Ask in a team meeting if anyone is qualified in first-aid. If no-one is qualified, ask if a friend of a friend is willing to be the team's first-aider.

If you can't find anyone, you should send a couple of members of your club on a first-aid course. Ask your club to pay for the course for them. Ask your County F.A. who should know about the F.A.'s first-aid courses. Or find a course by looking up the Red Cross or St John's Ambulance, for example, in the phone book.

FIRST-AID KIT
Your club needs to provide your first-aider with a first-aid kit unless they are kind enough to bring their own. For more about what is needed see Chapter 8: 'All kitted out' and Appendix I. For more about first-aid in general, see Chapter 16: 'Match day – getting ready for kick-off'.

THE TEAM CAPTAIN

Most clubs let the team manager choose his own captain – often a very personal choice – and it is something that can wait till the start of the season. The team captain is usually someone who can keep a cool head in a crisis, someone who the referee can deal with and who can clearly pass the manager's instructions on to other players.

THE TEAM MANAGER

Amateur clubs have a surprising range of ways of managing the team, governed either by choice or necessity. Here we'll cover the pros and cons of them. This is just the kind of issue that needs to be sorted out pre-season. There's not much worse in the build-up to matches than being unsure of who is in charge of the team.

MANAGERIAL SET UP 1: THE GAFFER

In England, during the last 50 years or so, it has been typical to have one person in charge of team selection, tactics and team-talks. If he is a 'track-suit' manager he will also take charge of training sessions. If he is a 'suit' manager, he will more likely let someone else take training, while he saves his decisions and team talks for match day. (For ideas for training sessions, see Chapter 11: 'Pre-season training and friendlies'.)

MANAGERIAL SET UP 2: THE COLLECTIVE DECISION

Before this, however, many clubs picked their team round the board-room table. Even in modern times the manager of the Welsh national team has (reputedly) been required to submit his team selection to the Council for approval.

There is danger, however, if no one person has control over the team. In the famous Liverpool boot-room, debate was vigorous but the manager's word was final. A casting vote in an odd-numbered group may be 'the final say', but it doesn't add up to an overall vision.

RESOURCES OFFICER'S WORK

If it is a good idea to appoint extra officers, a resources officer would be top of my list. His job would be to look after such matters as:

- ensuring that your club gets all the kit and equipment it needs;
- ensuring you have enough transport for your whole team to away games;
- making sure someone washes the kit after each game;
- making sure the club's kit and equipment are available for each game,

including the whole kit (shirts, shorts and socks), the match-balls, the first-aid kit, and possibly goalnets and goalposts.

You will find more on this in Chapter 8: 'All kitted out'. A resources officer could take a large burden off the secretary's shoulders. If you don't appoint a resources officer, you might add all the resources stuff to the club secretary's job description. At most clubs I know the secretary still takes most of this burden. The reality is that willing hands are always at a premium.

PLANNING FOR EXTRA OFFICERS

Of course, if you do appoint extra officers you need to agree whether they should be on the General Committee or not. If you decide such extra officers should be on the club's General Committee, you need to get the officers attending the AGM to put this in the list of officers in your Club Rules (see section 4 of the Rules) so that everything is above board.

BUT IT'S UP TO YOUR CLUB

What I've suggested above is not set in stone. For instance, there's no reason why you can't have, say, two people taking care of the secretary's work together, so long as one of them is the official contact for the authorities, and so long as the two of them have a close working relationship. You can't afford a communications break-down at the heart of the club. Such mishaps can too easily result in troublesome fines.

Other aspects of building your club are club kit and equipment and money matters. These will be covered in other chapters.

CHECKLIST

- set a date for your club's AGM
- give your players/members advance notice of your AGM
- write a draft of your club Rule Book for your AGM to vote on
- find out who could do the various jobs for your club.

chapter 5

BUILDING YOUR PLAYING SQUAD

There is a bit of politics in squad-building. The bigger a squad gets the more people get left on the sidelines. Is your team meant to be a get-together for you and your friends, or an attempt to build the best amateur side you can? The pros and cons below should help you weigh up the answer that suits your club. It is a question you should discuss in a club meeting and with the manager. You'll want a happy balance between having enough players to fulfil your fixtures and on the other hand not so many that it means some players don't get a decent run of games.

HOW BIG A SQUAD DO YOU NEED?

There is no single answer to how many players you should have. It is fair to say that if you have fewer than 16 you may struggle to put a team out every week. But there are pros and cons to large and small squads.

SMALL SQUADS
PROS: If you are a close-knit group of friends who want to have your own team, then you would probably see a large squad as a threat – after all there are still only 11 starting places. A small squad can mean that all get their fair share of appearances in the team.

CONS: Small squads can struggle if a few players get injured, get a Saturday job, have family commitments, for example. Getting 11 players out every week can be a headache. That is not to mention difficulties in persuading substitutes to turn up. Having fewer players in the squad also means fewer subscriptions, which means difficulty in paying the club's bills.

LARGE SQUADS

PROS: Whatever difficulty arises, with a large squad you should normally be able to start a match with 11 players. What's more, a large membership means more subscriptions, and that means more money to pay the club's bills.

CONS: The danger in a squad of more than 20 players is that a few never seem to get a full match, or a decent run of games. These players may begin to think they were only signed for their money. They usually get told they are 'important squad players' but it doesn't stop them getting upset.

true stories

Down

It was close to the end of the season. In one league only the bottom team was relegated. The next-to-bottom team had a Saturday morning relegation dogfight away to the bottom team.

But all was not well with the travelling club. They had made their own trap for themselves by signing new players every month in search of the perfect 11, inflating the size of their squad, and pushing more and more players onto the sidelines. The one thing they weren't expecting was to turn up for this do-or-die match with fewer than 11 players. Perhaps they hadn't realised how serious it is when squad members feel disaffected at being left out week after week. On this day when they needed these squad members to make up their numbers, they were horrified to find a lack of interest.

The squad that assembled at the meeting place was too small. They waited. Club members were despatched in cars to rouse fringe players.

But the clock was ticking – players should have been at the ground at 10 a.m. for a 10.30 kick-off. It was 10.45 when at last the club got eleven players assembled at the ground. But the referee, refusing to let the match finish later than planned, had already gone home, and had exercised his right – match abandoned.

The home team claimed their three points – as was their right. The visiting team appealed desperately to the league – to no avail. The rules are the rules. The three points were awarded to their opponents. They were relegated by just one point weeks later – effectively a double punishment.

The moral is, look after the so-called 'fringe' players in your squad. Players see themselves as players, not 'fringe' players. Hurt their pride, and you may be sealing your club's fate.

DO WE NEED PLAYERS FOR SPECIFIC POSTIONS?

Another common question about squad-building is: are you as a club happy that you have players who can fill all the positions from goalkeeper to striker? Of course, before signing players to strengthen your squad, see how this fits in with your club's idea about the size of its squad.

As for who are the 'right' players, that's a discussion I'll save till Chapter 11: 'Pre-season training and friendlies'.

we cannot find enough players to form a club

'We cannot find enough players to form a club.'

A question that often comes up: what can you do if your squad-building still leaves you a few players' short? Here are some solutions.

If you live in or near a city or a town it is of course easier to recruit players than if you live in a small village or a remote area. In the latter case, it may be worth ringing up local centres of employment (such as hotels or schools) and asking if any of their employees would be interested in taking part in a local team. (If you're very fortunate, you might even end up with a sponsor this way.)

Or you may wish to ring your County F.A. Unsigned players sometimes ask their County F.A. to find them a new club. Yours could be the club that signs these new players. (This could work the other way of course – if your efforts to form a club fail, you could ask the County F.A. to find teams for you and your friends to join.)

There are many ways to find players. Word of mouth can be surprisingly effective, as friends and cousins come out of the woodwork. There are many places to advertise. Here are a few:

■ ask permission to put a notice on the board of a sports club or gymnasium;

■ or place an advert in a shop window;

■ or place a small notice in a local newspaper – in some papers this is free.

Ideas such as club weekends away may create interest – see later in this chapter for more details.

RULES FOR SIGNING PLAYERS

You won't be surprised by now to know there are rules about signing players. This is true just as much for a Premier League club as for a Sunday League club. There are different kinds of rules. Most park clubs need to know only about registering and transferring players, but the F.A. also has rules for trainees, scholars and players under contracts. Rules concerning trainees and scholars are mainly intended for professional clubs, and are therefore outside the scope of this book.

CONTRACTS

It's not just professional clubs that have players under contract. There are many players on contracts in the Pyramid too. In park football, contracts are virtually unheard of – and many park leagues have a rule preventing their clubs from having players on contracts. So a park club will simply register and transfer players (and in this chapter I will explain how that works). They need have no worries about contracts.

In England, if you are a club where players may be signed on contracts, you will deal with the national Football Association directly. The F.A. deals with about 10,000 of these contracts every year. For registering players under contract and for transferring them, such a club needs to get 'Form G' and 'Form H' from the national F.A. Contact details are in Appendix II at the back of this book. F.A. Rules 18 and 20 clarify the procedure. At park level you might never have to fill in either of these forms.

Higher up the Pyramid, there is an issue that crops up for clubs near the borders within the UK, such as the border between England and Wales. Simply stated, when players on contracts move from a club on one side of the border to a club on the other side, international clearance is required from FIFA, just as for professionals who transfer from one country to another. For players who play for two clubs regularly, one each side of the border, this clearance is needed each time they play for 'the other team' across the border. Paperwork hell, perhaps, but apparently the authorities take it seriously.

CLUB RULES

If you want, your club could adopt special rules restricting who can join, so long as those rules are lawful. For teams higher up, however, the F.A. will expect an 'open' policy on signing players. So if you get far, you will find you cannot be an 'exclusive' club for your own interest group any more. Some special rules on membership are:

- a factory team might limit its membership to factory workers;
- an ethnic minority team may allow only players who share their background;
- a veterans team may exclude players under the age of 35;
- a disabled team might exclude persons without a disability.

As I've said, it's up to your club to make sure such rules are applied fairly. These things also depend on the permission of the County F.A. and the rules of any league or competition you enter. So let's look at their rules.

LEAGUE RULES

It follows from the above notes on club rules that you could join a league for a particular social group (such as an ethnic minority league). Most adult leagues don't have special membership rules.

GENERAL LEAGUE RULES

Your league's Code of Rules should include a couple of pages of rules about signing players. You need to get to know your own league's rules. Typically, the main points would be:

- A player can be signed for only one club in your league at a time (although he may sign for clubs in other leagues).
- If a club will not let a player transfer to another club, the player can appeal to the league for help. If the club still objects, the league will rule on the matter.
- The club has to keep records of who their players are. The league will do the same too.
- If a club plays a 'ringer' (ineligible player) in its team, and gets caught, the league usually has the power to award the points to the other team.
- Male and female players may not be allowed to play in the same match, except in under-7 to under-11 games.
- For leagues and competitions involving younger children, none of these may be more than two years older or younger than each other, and there needs to be a set age range, such as for under-7, under-8, and so on up to under-11. The English F.A. intends that rule to apply right up to under-14 by the year 2005.
- There will probably be a transfer deadline before the end of the season.

Another standard rule of most leagues is that you must put out your strongest available team.

PROCEDURE FOR REGISTERING PLAYERS IN A LEAGUE

You will need to understand the procedure for registering your players. At the time of writing this is a local matter for most leagues. In a few years, though, the English F.A. intends to bring in a National Player Registration Scheme, making it possible for computers to record the registration of all 3 million players in England. This has yet to take shape – and I understand that many County F.A.s are not yet linked by computer.

These comments are restricted to the present situation. To be helpful I have divided the business of registering players into two stages: pre-season; and during the season.

SIGNING PLAYERS IN PRE-SEASON

Before a playing season, if your club was already playing the season before, your league will already have a list of your members. They may send you, as club secretary, a copy of the list of your team's members, with instructions for you to indicate which members are still with your club, and which, if any, have left your club.

If you are signing new players or you are a new club registering your squad for the first time, first you will need your League's Player Registration Forms for your players. (Leagues normally have their own forms.) The league secretary should have sent you such forms. If you don't have any, ring him and ask him to mail some. In some leagues, you need one form for each player who signs for your club: in other leagues you put the details of all your players on a single sheet.

What to fill in: see the typical form on the next page. The player signing fills in parts marked with an X. You as the club official fill in parts marked with a Y.

The counterfoil: the league secretary normally fills in all the details on the counterfoil, and the reference number at the top of the page.

So a player registration form in an amateur league may look like this. (This won't be the actual form you fill in, but similar.)

LOCAL DUDE'S LEAGUE

PLAYER'S REFERENCE NUMBER   (to be completed by league)
PLAYER REGISTRATION FORM   (to be filled by player and club)

PASSPORT
PHOTOGRAPH
OF PLAYER

Name of club   X...
Player's previous clubs   X...
Players surname   X...
First or other names   X...
Date of birth   X...
Player's home address   X...
      ....
      ....

Player's telephone number   X...
If player is under age of 16
telephone number
of parent or guardian   X...

SIGNATURES
Signature of player   X.................... Date X............................
If player is under age of 16
signature of parent or guardian   X.................... Date X............................

Signature of club official   X.................... Date X............................

(Send the completed form to the league secretary.)

COUNTERFOIL (to be completed by league and returned to club)

REGISTRATION OF A PLAYER IN THE LOCAL DUDE'S LEAGUE

I certify that today I registered ....(player's name)
as a player of ....Football Club (name of club)

Signature of league official   X...
Date   X...

Player's Reference Number   X...

PASSPORT PHOTOGRAPHS

It is standard in more and more amateur leagues to incorporate a photograph of the player on the registration form. If you are meant to put a photograph with the form, don't ignore it. Leagues would not normally accept registration forms that are incomplete.

Photographs were introduced to registration forms so that players could be correctly identified if ever league or match officials were asked to investigate an incident in a match where it is important to know whether any particular player was involved. It also enables officials to ensure that banned players aren't playing in matches. No-one likes accusations, but if one is made it is good to have a way of checking it.

SIGNING PLAYERS DURING THE SEASON

There will usually be a transfer deadline before the end of the season. After this deadline, no players can transfer until the season has ended.

Send the Player Registration Forms in to the league secretary in good time. A common rule says that seven days must pass after registration before a new player can take part in matches. Leagues typically charge a small administration fee (say, a pound) for registering players.

WHAT TO DO WITH YOUR COMPLETED PLAYER REGISTRATION FORMS

Before you send off your forms, it is a great idea to photocopy each of them. They contain important information you need for your club records. You can save yourself having to ask for the information twice by copying the forms. Keep the copies with your Membership Book. After players have left your club, you should not keep the forms any longer than is necessary.

To save on postage, send in a lot of registration forms together during pre-season. There will be a deadline for registering players in time for the first match of the season. This deadline will vary from league to league.

INVALID PLAYER REGISTRATION FORMS

Check that everything is in order. In our league, if we found forms completed in pencil instead of ink, or we couldn't read the writing, or if any part of a form was not filled in properly, we would send the form back to the club to fill in properly.

The point about filling the form in properly is very important. Until a Player's Registration Form is officially registered by the league secretary, your player is not registered, and he cannot play for your team, not in any league match.

SO HOW DO YOU KNOW WHEN YOUR PLAYER CAN PLAY?

You know your player is registered in time to play in a match:

1. when the league secretary returns the counterfoils (from the Player Registration Forms) to you as club secretary; or if he writes to confirm your players have been registered;

2. but if the counterfoils or letter have not arrived, ring the league secretary and ask him if your player is registered so that you know if you can play him;

3. in most league constitutions there is a third way, where in emergencies you can send a postal registration (but don't sign players this way until you have checked that your league's constitution permits it). This means:

- the time of the post-mark on the envelope must be before the time of the kick-off of the match the player plays in;
- this player cannot play another game until the league confirms his registration in writing;
- you can normally only submit a registration form for one player at a time this way.

When you receive the counterfoils (or a letter from your league secretary confirming your players' registrations) there is one more job to do: copy the players' League Registration Numbers next to the players' names in your club's Membership Book.

DO WE NEED A CLUB MEMBERSHIP FORM TOO?

You do not normally need to have a club registration form. The completed League Registration Form makes a player a member of your club. Some clubs also have their own extra club membership form, along the same lines as the League Registration Form. This can be made more useful if it includes extra information such as details of a contact in case of emergencies – information you should obtain in any case. Where children are part of your club, such information is essential. A club registration form could also include a line saying, 'I consent to abide by the Club Rules.'

INSURANCE FOR PLAYERS

One subject often overlooked in the past was buying accident insurance for players. In some leagues this was compulsory; in others it was left up to each club.

In the past, too, even many professionals were not insured. In England the F.A. did not force players to buy insurance, and even their own union, the Professional Footballers Association, did not make it compulsory for their members. This is changing. The English F.A. has spoken about personal accident insurance becoming compulsory for all players. Two types of insurance are especially important.

PERSONAL ACCIDENT INSURANCE

This matters because injury might make a player unable to work for weeks or months, leaving him short of earnings. Insurance might compensate him. Without insurance, how can a player be helped financially? Of course, you might arrange a benefit event to raise funds for the injured player, or you might even try to sue the other player if one caused the injury. But having insurance is a sensible protection.

PUBLIC LIABILITY INSURANCE

This matters because a player from another club might try to sue one of your players for an injury he suffered while playing against your club, to make one of you liable for a massive compensation bill. Insurance might save your player or your club from being liable for such a bill.

MAKING THE PLAYERS DISCUSS INSURANCE

Insurance is not an easy subject to raise with players because it is, frankly, short on laughs. But here's a tip. Put insurance on the agenda of your AGM – one time when people expect to discuss business. Research a few different insurance deals beforehand, and ask the club to vote on which deal they will pay for. You may find your County F.A. offers a competitive deal.

PERSONAL ACCIDENT INSURANCE DEALS

These usually have a scale so that the more you pay, the more you stand to get from a claim. Insurance can be bought on the high street as well as from the F.A. Shop around.

Work out how much extra your club will have to raise from your players depending on different deals. A £300 compensation deal could mean about £15 from each player or an extra 50p each week on top of their subscriptions. Talk to your club treasurer and your members about what your club can afford. Given that you get what you pay for, typical high street insurance deals for amateur clubs have ranged from £50 to over £300 to cover all players for a year.

Insurance should not only cover injuries sustained in matches. Insuring your players for their journeys to and from matches is important, so check on this when you buy your club's insurance.

You may have to submit a list of your club members to the insurers. Whether you have to or not, ask the insurance company if your club's new signings later in the season will be covered by the insurance deal. Ask the insurers if you will need to inform them when new players sign for your club, to make sure they are covered.

Having insurance means premiums have to be paid. There are many deals on the market, but you get what you pay for. Cheap deals mean smaller pay-outs. For instance, say you want personal accident insurance to pay an injured player a couple of hundred pounds a week while he is off work, such a deal might well cost your club over £1,000 in premiums each year. Most clubs buy deals for only a few hundred pounds, so would expect much smaller pay-outs. Can you afford a better deal? Can you afford not to buy a better deal? Those are the questions your club must answer.

Professionals in sport pay large premiums for their insurance – a professional footballer may pay several thousand pounds each year to insure against serious injury. And as he gets older his premiums will be greater. As he picks up injuries some insurers may not let him insure this or that part of his body, a situation players think unfair.

top tip

When you have negotiated an insurance deal for your players, copy the section that tells you the pay-outs for different injuries. Give all your players a copy of this – it's important that they are not in the dark about what they can expect if a serious injury changes their life.

Tell players that if they want to be insured for larger sums of money, they should consider paying for their own extra insurance.

THE SMALL PRINT AND 'RINGERS'

The small print is something you should read on any kind of insurance policy. For instance, public liability insurance might not cover an ineligible player taking to the field as a 'ringer' if he is involved in an incident. A ringer is someone playing for a club he is not a member of.

In the year 2000, an amateur player in Cheshire was sued over an injury he caused in a tackle. The player he hurt was a 'ringer' (an ineligible player) and the club's insurance did not cover ringers. The risk in such situations is that neither one club's public liability insurance nor the other club's personal accident insurance would pay up. However, the ringer sued the player who hurt him. It was reported that the court ordered the player who injured him to pay him £20,000.

All the more reason why clubs should never field ineligible players, and for members to read the small print on the insurance policies.

TEAM SPIRIT

Building team spirit calls for imagination. The best way for players to become comfortable with each other is to play football. It's the only thing that suits everyone. But what more can you do to build team spirit?

There is more to this than going to the pub. For teams with time on their hands, usually younger teams, weekends away can be cheap and fun. They give you the chance to find out what kind of characters there are in your squad.

A weekend away is a good step in inviting new players to join your squad – it gives club officials a chance to make their mind up about new players who may want to join. After such a weekend, one man joined a friend's team and became their leading goalscorer.

A WEEKEND IN THE COUNTRY
To take his team to a cottage in the countryside, one club secretary only had to charge players £15 each. That covered petrol, food and renting a cottage. (They managed to borrow a van.) They spent a whole weekend playing football on a local park, getting to know each other.

A WEEKEND AT THE SEASIDE
With hotel bills, this cost the same team a little more, and while there was more fun, there was less football. It was a better weekend for building team spirit... until the distraction of bumping into a women's rugby team also on a weekend break!

ARE THE EXTRA EVENTS WORTH IT?
How much effort you put into team-building is down to choice. For some, all they want is a team that plays. Even this can do a power of good. The country's administrators have tuned in to the idea that football is a good thing for communities. Police and politicians have argued for years about how to keep restless teenage boys out of trouble. Now they've realised that being part of a football team gives a youngster self-respect, as well as being good for his health. A key fact is that disaffected teenage boys often have few interests – but football is usually one of them.

POSITIVE MESSAGES

The powers-that-be have also realised that football is a great platform for giving young people messages about such things as healthy eating, exercise, self-control and discipline, no-smoking, anti-drugs, anti-racism, and playing their part in a team. These positive messages stand a better chance of reaching someone who takes pride in his place in the football team – where there is some street credibility.

Some professional clubs have built-in classrooms in their stadiums. 'Learning through football' is a big success in schools, and midnight football leagues help keep teenagers from hanging around on street corners. Professional footballers now spend more time visiting schools and youth clubs – messages brought by someone children will listen to get heard better.

SOCIAL INCLUSION

So bringing young players into your team may do some good – and, as your team benefits, society may too. The government wants football to help reduce anti-social behaviour, provide a source of discipline, and a distraction from crime, and promote social inclusion.

For more about what your local professional club can do for local youths, ring the club and ask to speak to someone about their 'Football in the Community' scheme.

CHECKLIST

- get Player Registration Forms from your league secretary
- keep copies of the completed forms
- return the forms to the league
- find out about accident insurance deals
- give players details of their accident insurance.

chapter 6
BALANCING THE BOOKS

Handling your club's money is a subject that prompts so many clubs to cry for help. There are whole books on managing money – see Appendix III at the back of this book for titles. This chapter, hardly containing more than the minimum necessary information, is designed with park teams in mind, although in certain respects it is applicable to senior clubs too.

YOUR CLUB TREASURER

You need a safe pair of hands to act as club treasurer – the custodian of your club's cash. I am assuming that you are the club secretary and you have someone else to be treasurer. But the secretary needs to know what the treasurer does too. Here's a reminder.

THE TREASURER'S WORK
The treasurer's duties, as listed in Chapter 4, include:
- looking after petty-cash
- collecting subscriptions from members
- keeping receipts, and issuing receipts
- keeping the books of the club's income and expenditure
- almost certainly acting as a signatory to the club's bank account
- making sure there is enough money to pay the bills
- acting with the club secretary to pay bills
- making a simple statement of club finances each year.

YOUR TREASURER NEEDS HIS STATIONERY
One thing that makes the treasurer's job easier is having the right kind of sta-

tionery. In Chapter 1 there was a list of stationery the club secretary needs, and which the treasurer should have too. The treasurer will need these additional items from the stationery shop:

- a receipt book – to give a receipt to any person who gives the club some money
- a Cash Book – this is explained later in this chapter
- a calculator
- something to keep petty cash in – separate from his own money.

BUDGETING – HOW MUCH DOES A FOOTBALL CLUB COST TO RUN?

Before your club is launched, figure out how much it will cost to run. I've seen enough clubs go bust to recognise a key question: will your club have enough money to finish what it's starting? Here's how to find the answer.

The answer for a typical grass roots club is between £400 and £900 every season, depending on where you live and what you need to buy. The biggest differences tend be in different charges for hiring football pitches. See Chapter 7: 'All about football pitches' for more on this.

For a brand new club there's more to pay before your first season because of start-from-scratch kit and equipment you will need. Chapter 8: 'All kitted out' goes through money-savers for kit and equipment. But if you were to pay shop prices for everything, they would cost a lot more.

THINGS YOU MAY PAY FOR AS A BRAND NEW CLUB

If you buy everything new at shop prices here are typical costs:

£400	**complete home strip (numbered shirts, shorts, socks)**
£400	**complete change strip**
£70	**two match-quality footballs**
£15	**football pump and two adaptors**
£15	**first-aid kit**

So far that could give us a setting-up cost of £900.

Some clubs pay for these additional things (some don't because they are provided with the pitch they rent):

£80	a pair of nets
£10	tent-pegs for nets
£450	a pair of full-size goals (posts)
£30	four regulation-size corner flags

So for certain clubs, that could add another £570 or so onto the setting-up cost. Little extras add up: you might well spend a further £40 or more on a roll of gaffer tape, hammer for tent-pegs, stud-key, spare goalkeeper's gloves, spare pair of shin-pads, referee's whistle, and an A–Z map (or book) of your district.

That means as a new club you could expect shop prices for all these things to add up to between £1,000 and £1,500. Later I'll show you where to find the bargains, but don't relax yet, because...

BILLS YOU MIGHT PAY EVERY SEASON

£250	home football pitch fee
£30	County F.A. affiliation fee
£15	any County Cup registration fee
£10	County F.A. public liability insurance
£300	personal accident insurance for whole club
£75	league registration fee/subscription
£300	referees' fees for the whole season
£35	a replacement match ball
£3	registration fees for new players (often as little as £1 per player)
£???	fines (see later in this chapter)

DON'T FORGET ADMINISTRATION COSTS

You might need to claim expenses from your club for phone calls, stationery, postage, any photocopying. Typically, these might add up to £20 per season.

So we would have an average annual cost of around £1,000 for a team.

GRAND TOTAL FOR SETTING UP A NEW CLUB AND PLAYING A SEASON
Add all the costs together and you will find the costs of setting up a new club and playing a season will be over £2,000, at shop prices. You can see your club is going to need a fair bit of money coming in. I have known teams without much money who scrimped and saved on cheap match-balls, and doing without accident insurance. Obviously that's not the sort of advice you expect to read here. Later in this chapter I will talk about ways of raising money. When I set up a brand new club a few years ago, our costs for the first season were less than £500, including having to buy new nets. Most of that was raised with one fund-raising event. Money-saving ideas we used are explained in detail in Chapter 8. They include:

- how to get a cheaper football strip. We bought our first complete strip for £80 (second-hand). I've known teams get a free strip (see Chapter 8);
- how to make DIY corner flags;
- how to find cut-price footballs;
- how to find a pitch where goalposts are provided for you (see Chapter 7).

A CLUB'S ANNUAL EXPENSES

Time now to explain the bills you can expect to pay, season after season after season...

MATCH FEES

Some leagues now cover your 'match expenses' for you. By 'match expenses' they mean payments to match officials and costs of hiring your pitch. Such leagues cover these costs by charging their clubs more for joining their league, with an arrangement under which clubs share their pitches and their referees. However, this may not be the arrangement in your situation. The following is what you may have to pay every year.

COUNTY F.A. AFFILIATION FEE:
This varies. Here are approximate prices:

Senior Clubs (this includes professional clubs)	£40
Junior Clubs (these are adult clubs)	£30
Associate Clubs (such as in new leagues)	£25
Youth Clubs (all players are under 18 years of age)	£10

If your club has more than one team, your County F.A. may have a reduced rate for your second and third (etc.) teams to join. However, if your teams play on different days they may be required to register separately – each paying full price.

ANY COUNTY CUP REGISTRATION FEE

This varies. For many County competitions the fee is still less than £20. Do speak to your league secretary before you join any County Cup competitions. He may have a view on how you can fit County Cup games into your fixture list. He may also be concerned about fixture congestion if you progress to the later stages of a Cup competition.

COUNTY F.A. PUBLIC LIABILITY INSURANCE

This has usually been less than £10, purchased from the County F.A. It's the premium for a good deal of insurance. You don't have to buy this insurance from your County F.A.: you can buy it on the high street, or sometimes from a 'pitch agency', but the County F.A. deal is cheap and convenient in my view. I don't know anyone who goes to the high street instead. Your County F.A. may refuse to affiliate clubs without public liability insurance, more so in the case of senior and junior clubs, less so associate clubs. This insurance will not cover your players against accidents.

PERSONAL ACCIDENT INSURANCE FOR YOUR PLAYERS

On the high street this might range from £50 to over £300 to cover all your club's players for a year – for matches and for travelling. See Chapter 5: 'Building your squad' for more on this. The English F.A. has also been considering bringing in a new civil liability scheme for all clubs.

LEAGUE REGISTRATION FEE AND SUBSCRIPTIONS

You might be surprised to know how much a league costs to run. Some leagues are sponsored, some not. So a fee of around £100 a year per club is not unusual. To spread the cost, you may find your league asks for less as your registration fee, and more over the season in regular subscriptions. Subscriptions may work out at less than £5 per match. Ask your league secretary what fees you pay to your league.

ANY LEAGUE CUP REGISTRATION FEE

As explained in Chapter 2, your league may run its own cup competition. If it does the entry fee may be very reasonable.

FEE FOR HIRING FOOTBALL PITCH

This may cost you anything between £100 and £1,000 per season. It depends on where you are in the country, and who you hire the pitch from. More on this in Chapter 7.

MATCH OFFICIAL'S FEES

It is standard practice that the home club pays the referee his match fee. The fee is presently approaching £20 per game but it varies from competition to competition. Your league secretary will tell you how much to pay the referees in your league. So if we assume you might have 15 home games a season, that would mean around £300 per season. If you play in a higher-level Pyramid league, with assistant referees to pay too, budget for more.

SETTING UP A BANK ACCOUNT

Next, let's talk about getting a structure in place to handle money, beginning with the club having its own bank account. In a league each football club should have its own bank account. Some leagues overlook this – unwisely.

A bank can tell you about their various accounts. From time to time, banks set up special accounts for clubs, societies and charities – such as a Treasurer's Account. These schemes do come and go, and such special accounts may not necessarily offer much more than an ordinary current account anyway. The benefits may include the bank providing an annual financial statement for you.

If all you need is to pay money in to the bank and draw it out when you want, that's what an ordinary current account lets you do.

WHAT TO EXPECT AT THE BANK

It's not a big deal to set up an account for a football club. Visit a bank, tell one of their staff that you want to start an account for a sports club. Tell them whether your club will be handling just a few hundred pounds each year, or whether it will handle much more than that.

Tell the bank that you want this account to be set up in the name of your club, not in the name of any individual person, but that you would want two or three people to be authorised to sign the club's cheques. Perhaps add that you would be happier if a cheque always needs to be signed by two people (more on this below).

You will normally have to take away some paperwork – usually called a Bank Mandate – to complete. For this you may need to know about the following things.

OVERDRAFTS

Most banks will let you set up an overdraft facility, allowing you to go into debt to pay your bills. Don't be afraid to ask at the bank to agree to an overdraft facility right now – before your club gets into debt. Don't forget your bills add up to several hundred pounds a year. So be frank with the bank about how big an overdraft you expect to use.

Do ask the bank what charges there may be for using an overdraft facility, such as interest you have to pay them. Don't forget the bank will charge your club a nasty sum of money if your bank account goes into debt without an agreed overdraft facility – or into more debt than the overdraft you agreed with them.

SIGNATURES ON THE CHEQUES

On the Bank Mandate form, you should be able to say who will be signatories to the account. That means who has the right to sign the cheques. At a meeting of your club, such as the Annual General Meeting, ask for a vote on who gets to write their signatures on the cheques. If this doesn't happen, it is up to your General Committee to agree on. It normally makes most sense for the club secretary and the treasurer to sign the cheques. Sometimes the chairman or resources officer would be signatories too.

Needing two signatures on cheques can prevent one person going off and using the chequebook on his own. If you think it couldn't happen at your club, read the 'True Story' on the next page

TELLING THE BANK WHEN YOU CHANGE CLUB OFFICERS

Sooner or later, your club will have new officers, who may need to become signatories to the club bank account. You have to fill out another Bank Mandate to make these changes.

MONEY TO START THE ACCOUNT

Don't worry yet about having much in the way of funds. The important thing is to set up the account anyway. Banks will usually let you start a new account by putting just one pound in it.

KEEPING CLUB ACCOUNTS

Keeping proper accounts is not difficult. It involves 'vouchers' and a 'Cash Book'.

true stories

A good egg

One of the clubs in our league was in turmoil. The club secretary left under a cloud – a crying shame: we all thought him a good egg. His team had been struggling. I rang to see how things were but he stopped returning my calls. We realised the pressure was getting to him, but when someone doesn't return your calls, it becomes difficult to help.

At the end of the season he left the club. After some pestering he handed over the club's paperwork to the members, including the chequebook and the account book. The club did have a treasurer, but he hadn't been keeper of the money. The first time the treasurer thought anything was wrong with the accounts was when he saw this paperwork. He expected to see a few hundred pounds in the account – his own records told him the lads had been paying their subscriptions every week. There was less than a hundred. The Cash Book had no record of this money coming and going, so it looked difficult to argue where it might have gone. Then there was the chequebook.

This chequebook only needed one signature – the club secretary's. One stub in the club chequebook showed a cheque was paid to a furniture shop. I am sure the secretary's idea was to pay that money back – otherwise why write on the stub the details of the furniture shop? But with the shortfall in the money, it looked bad – the club didn't even have enough money to pay its bills.

The club had a traumatic summer. They got no more money from the club secretary. They even thought about going to see a solicitor. All this could have been avoided if the cheques needed two signatures.

VOUCHERS

You are required to keep any bills and receipts – file them in a safe place. This is evidence that the figures in the Cash Book are correct. Accountants call any such bits of paper 'vouchers'.

CASH BOOK

The County F.A. will expect your club to keep a Cash Book, meaning simple accounts. In its basic form this means writing down every amount of money the club gets in and when, and every amount it pays for anything and when. It might look like this:

DATE	ITEM	PAID OUT	RECEIVED	NOTES
	TOTALS			

top tip

Add up the totals in your Cash Book regularly. Once a month check that the club has money left to pay for things. At the same time the club secretary and treasurer should check what bills the club will have to pay – big or small amounts. If you let paperwork pile up, it is harder to plan the club's finances.

As you fill in the Cash Book it may look something like this:

DATE	ITEM	PAID OUT	RECEIVED	NOTES
21/05/04	Hiring pitch	£300		Shown on bank statement
27/05/04	League registration	£20		Shown on bank statement
27/05/04	County F.A. affiliation	£23.50		Shown on bank statement
01/06/04	Sponsored swim		£141	Shown on bank statement
01/07/04	Players' annual subscriptions		£260	Shown on bank statement
13/07/04	Pub sponsorship		£400	Shown on bank statement
14/06/04	New kit	£400		Shown on bank statement
04/09/04	This week's subscriptions		£33	Paid into bank 07/09/04
04/09/04	This week's match fees	£15		Paid in cash
05/09/04	New match ball	£35		Shown on bank statement
	TOTALS	£793.50	£834	

That's a simple Cash Book. You could buy a ready-made Cash Book – often called a 'book-keeping ledger' – from stationery shops for a couple of pounds.

BEING OPEN TO SCRUTINY

Members of a club have a right to know how the club's money is spent – how much information depends on the size of your club. Here we distinguish between clubs that own 'assets' and clubs that don't. Having assets is usually taken to mean owning, say, a club building, a club vehicle or a significant amount of money – not a few bits and bobs such as footballs. The Inland Revenue can advise on the status of assets if you're not sure.

STATEMENTS FOR CLUBS WITH NO ASSETS

Many park football teams do not own any assets worth speaking of. In their case, F.A. rules are light, saying that what a club with no assets has to do is to draw up a statement of receipts and payments each year. It is common sense to assume the treasurer will do this job. The F.A. do not demand that you get an accountant to do it (even though an accountant could do an annual examination of the club's books, if you wish).

The end of each playing season is as good a time as any to do a statement of receipts and payments. You could use it for the statement of the club's finances at your club's AGM. All you really need to do for this is to write down these things for all to see:

- how much money the club received in the last year;
- how much money the club spent in the last year;
- how much money the club has left.

It's a good idea to add a note about how much money you would guess the club will need to spend in the next year.

The treasurer should be able to answer any members' questions about the club's money at the AGM.

At the time of writing, the F.A. Handbook (section 34) asks you only to keep a record of money received and spent. If you want more information about this, ask your County F.A. to send you a format for 'A Receipt and Payments Statement'. The F.A. is likely to change their preferred format for this from time to time. You should keep your records for at least six years.

ADDING EXTRA INFORMATION TO THE STATEMENT

To give your club useful information – and for the treasurer to show he knows his stuff – he could include in his statement a few lines about assets and liabilities. Here's how.

ASSETS: I have already said that a park football team may own no assets worth speaking of. You could argue that everything it owns, including the kit, does have a value. A really on-the-ball treasurer could therefore present a list of such property to the AGM. Here's a simple way to do this:

- write down a list of all the kit and equipment the club has bought (Chapters 8 and 9 should help);
- write down how much each of them cost;
- write down your best guess at how much money you'd get for them if you tried to sell them second-hand now;
- write down a guess of when the various bits and bobs will need to be replaced;
- write your best guess for how much you expect all the replacements to cost.

LIABILITIES: Any club may have some bills or loans it has not paid up on yet (by the time of the AGM). Such bills and loans are called 'liabilities'. It makes sense to put the total of any unpaid bills in your statement.

And there you have it – a statement of the club's receipts and payments. This may prove useful in planning your future fund-raising. In any case, your club's members have a right to know such things. After all, the members of the General Committee are effectively the club's caretakers, not its owners.

STATEMENTS FOR CLUBS WITH SOME ASSETS

The F.A. say that they expect clubs which own assets to get someone with a suitable accountancy qualification to prepare 'A Financial Statement'. If you are not sure how to set this out, ask your County F.A. for a copy of a format for this.

MAKING ACCOUNTS AVAILABLE FOR INSPECTIONS

The treasurer should take his books to every club meeting so that any club member who asks can see the accounts for themselves. If the treasurer shows himself to be open in this way, he may get a better hearing from the members whenever he needs to ask them to raise money.

The County F.A. may ask to see a copy of your Receipt and Payments Statement at any time – that's their right. In some regions they don't ask park clubs too often.

Your League Management Committee also have the right to see your club's books of accounts any time they ask – this is once a year in many leagues, such as at the AGM. They may ask your club to tell them how much money is in your club account. This is to reassure them that none of their clubs could go bust half-way through the next season. Hopefully, by the end of this chapter, you'll know how to keep any park club afloat.

DO YOU NEED THE ACCOUNTS CHECKED?

I have known one County F.A. to write that each club should have an annual 'audit'. A trained accountant may disagree. A typical park football club should normally not need such heavy-handed paperwork as an 'audit' – it is only an association for the benefit of its members. See below for what an audit can mean.

If your club's annual 'turnover' is less than £10,000, it should be satisfactory to follow the steps described on previous pages. ('Turnover' means how much money your club handles each year. It does not mean any profit.)

If your club turns over more than £10,000 in a year, it may be appropriate to have what they call an 'independent examination'. This means that an accountant looks over the accounts to see if they match up with the club's records of income and expenditure. It's not a big deal and you may be able to find yourself a friendly accountant who will do it for nothing – a friend of a friend...

If anyone does suggest you need an actual audit, as in some County F.A. papers I read, they should be aware that an audit is a much more complicated business and it is not usually appropriate until there is a turnover of about £350,000. The audit involves a pattern of tests that a body of chartered accountants can approve. I'd be surprised if anyone wants this for a park football club.

TAX

Don't take my word for this, but if you worry about whether a small club needs to pay any tax, you may find the Inland Revenue not interested in hearing from such a club – unless it is perhaps turning over a regular profit. They wouldn't want to waste their time. What's more, park teams often have no assets to speak of. Do ask the Inland Revenue by all means, but you may find that such a park football club may not have to pay much regard to tax matters.

LIMITED COMPANIES

For the more ambitious clubs that have become Limited Companies, usually nearer the top of the Pyramid, there is more work to be done to comply with The Companies Act. This will of course cost money. If this affects your club, advice should be available from your County F.A. and from a solicitor or accountant.

CHARITIES

If your club is one of the few that has become a registered charity, this means you have extra financial responsibilities. The Charities Commission publishes various guides, such as 'Accounting for Charities with an income of less than £10,000 per annum', 'Charities and Insurance', and 'Responsibilities of Charity Trustees'. The Charities Commission can also provide advice on accounting for registered charities. Contact details for the Charities Commission are in Appendix IV.

It's not enough to be open to scrutiny of course. You'll have seen from the story 'A good egg' how easily a club's finances could get in a mess for want of a better system. Your club's finances need most of all to be properly organised.

A SYSTEM FOR PAYING BILLS

One thing about a club's bills is that they will normally be sent to the club secretary, but the treasurer is usually the one in control of the purse-strings. So it is simple common-sense that the club secretary and the treasurer need to be able to meet and talk regularly so that:

- the secretary can show the treasurer the bills, and
- the treasurer can make a note of all the deadlines for paying bills, and
- the treasurer can tell the secretary if there is enough money to pay the bills, so that
- they can decide which are the most important bills to pay first, and then
- they can both sign the cheques, and
- they can make sure the payment is sent off before any deadline – particularly to avoid fines.

HANDLING CASH

A club treasurer will probably handle cash regularly, especially collecting players' match subscriptions. Here are a few simple safeguards.

When you have finished collecting cash – whether at a training session, a match or a fund-raising venture – here's what to do:

- two people should count the cash together
- that means counting the cash twice
- write down on a piece of paper the total money received
- both people should sign and date the piece of paper once they agree the figure is correct

- the piece of paper should be put with other such papers in a safe place
- the total should also be written in the Cash Book
- the money should be put in the bank as soon as is convenient

This may seem a bit time-consuming but it is the most basic of checks to make sure that money cannot disappear without trace.

HANDLING CHEQUES

Whenever someone gives you a cheque to boost club funds, however large or small, ask them to do two things:

- make sure they write the correct name for the club bank account
- ensure that the cheque is crossed with the words 'account payee only' – this means it can only be paid into a bank account.

FINES

When a league punishes a club, it has to think carefully – not being able to pay fines is one cause of grass roots clubs going bust. Of course it is ironic, since the point of these fines is to persuade clubs to organise better.

They are a heavy-handed way to sort out sometimes small problems. But for league secretaries running time-consuming leagues for no reward, fines will be a simple and sharp way of keeping careless clubs in line with the rest.

Clubs hate fines. Some have even written to the Prime Minister and the Minister for Sport in the hope that pressure from on high will save them from paying fines. This doesn't work. The government is unlikely to interfere in the running of your League. Appeal processes should be run by your league and County F.A. Your league's constitution should have rules on this which you could get to know.

Chapter 14: 'How to avoid fines' should be of some help. One way to avoid fines is for the treasurer to take a positively nosy interest in the running of the club, remind the secretary to meet deadlines with paperwork, and offer a hand if there is any overdue paper work. The treasurer won't like signing cheques to pay for mistakes, which makes him a good choice to keep an eye on things.

If the club secretary tells the club treasurer he has received notification of a fine, then they should act quickly together. They should first check what the fine is for. There are two kinds of fines: clubs' fines and players' fines.

CLUB FINES

Fines against the club are normally the ones the club treasurer should be concerned with. Most of these would be levied by your league for paperwork not being done on time, for missing League Council Meetings, or because league fees have not been paid on time. Your league will decide how much to fine clubs. A badly run club can run up hundreds of pounds in fines for these little faults. Some clubs go bust over it. The usual stumbling block is to do with deadlines.

If the club has been fined by the league or the County F.A., you have two choices:
1. pay the fine immediately (a delay could mean another fine); or

true stories

Tears are not enough

One club was in the middle of its first ever season as a league club. On the field they were flying high. Off the field the organisation was hopeless – and one person seemed to do the work of both secretary and treasurer.

The annual cost of league membership to any club was about £75. As a league we phased payments over the season to ease the burden on clubs. We expected clubs to make payments at monthly League Council Meetings. This team did not. Sometimes they didn't turn up for the meeting. The club secretary was scarcely available. We listened to excuses about forgetting to bring the money, or about the league's messages not being passed on, or about needing to get the money organised. All the other clubs were paying to keep the league going but this one club wasn't.

Near the end of the season, our league's secretary and chairman decided to go in person to the home of their club secretary to discuss how his club might pay.

When they saw him in his own home the club secretary, a teenage lad, burst into tears. Straight away he confessed that on Saturday mornings his players had given him their subscriptions, and on Saturday nights he had gone out and spent it.

The truth was out, and now the situation could be dealt with. On top of the money they owed, the club was fined for not having any system for looking after its own business properly. New officers were put in place at the club, they raised the money to pay their debts, and afterwards everyone got on with a normal footballing existence again.

The club survived the trauma, and we were all pleased that they did. A year later they won a national tournament.

It taught us that clubs should have two separate people to be secretary and treasurer, and that they should have a good system for checking on each other where money is concerned.

2. appeal against the fine immediately (a delay may mean your appeal can't be heard); there will be a pretty short time limit for appealing.

PLAYERS' FINES
When a player is booked or sent off by a referee, the club secretary will be sent notice of an 'administration fee' by the County F.A. You may ask the player or the club to pay this fee, which stands at £6 at the time of writing. (Children do not pay – their club does.) If, on top of the fee, there is a County F.A. fine for an adult player who has been booked or sent off, then that is a fine that the player must pay. (Again, children do not pay – their club does.) If the player does not pay up on time it could get your club into trouble with the County F.A. (See Chapter 18: 'The match – discipline and sportsmanship'.)

DEADLINES
The importance of meeting deadlines simply can't be overstated. The glue that holds the administration of football together is deadlines, and fines for missing them. For example, if your County F.A. Registration Form is sent to the County F.A. late, the County F.A. may fine your club, typically £15.

PLANNING AHEAD

Once you have an idea of how much money your club must spend in the next year, you can plan ahead to keep your club afloat. Planning is straightforward:
1. make a list of bills you expect to pay
2. work out how much you expect the club to pay
3. make a note of when you must pay the bills
4. work out how to raise the money
5. set aside funds for unexpected costs
6. make sure any debts do not become bigger than your club's bank overdraft facility.

RAISING MONEY

Once you know how much you need to raise, you need to get on with the job of raising it. Here is a quick run-through of some of the most popular ideas. Many of the ideas that follow are used at amateur and some professional clubs. It's up to you and your club to decide which ideas suit your club best.

SUBSCRIPTIONS

Decide on whether your members should pay subscriptions for being part of the club. Paying to play is the mark of amateur sport.

This can cause arguments. I know men who would think nothing of paying £100 a year for membership of a gym but complain about paying half of that to play football. The answer to that is football costs a lot of money to run nowadays.

Clubs can charge their members in different ways. Some charge a flat membership fee every year. Some have a pay-as-you play scheme – that is, 'match subscriptions'. Some spread the cost by having a combination of an annual membership fee and match subscriptions. Some clubs charge more than others. To help you to decide what sums are right for your club, here are some typical charges:

TYPICAL PLAYERS' SUBSCRIPTION FEES

ANNUAL SUBSCRIPTIONS	
Playing members	**£20**
Non-playing members	**£15**

Some clubs don't charge their non-playing members because they are often the ones doing the work of running the club for no financial reward.

MATCH SUBSCRIPTIONS	
Full match played	**£3**
Part of a match played	**£1.50**
No match played	**£0**

NON-PAYMENT OF SUBSCRIPTIONS

An idea in the suggested Club Rules (see Chapter 4) is to suspend players who aren't paying their due subscriptions. This could be controversial, though not as controversial as some players never paying, leaving their mates to pick up the tab for running the club. This happens at many a club.

Consider how you would approach players who say every week, 'I forgot to bring my money. I'll bring it next week.' Your Annual General Meeting should decide whether to have a rule for suspending players in your Club Rules.

COLLECTING MATCH SUBSCRIPTIONS

The club will probably leave the job of collecting match subscriptions to the treasurer. Here are some suggestions.

Most clubs I know collect subscriptions in the dressing room after the match. (I have never known a groundsman to object.)

One team I know gets the money in like this: the treasurer happens to be the biggest man in the club: he stands in front of the door of the dressing room – he doesn't like to let anyone out without squaring with him over their match subscription. (He does stop short of false imprisonment!)

In one hand he has a pen and a bag for the money, in the other hand the Membership Book to record what people pay. He marks out the pages of his register like this:

| | game 1 | game 1 | game 2 | game 2 | game 3 | game 3 | game 4 | game 4 |
PLAYER	**PLAYED**	**PAID**	**PLAYED**	**PAID**	**PLAYED**	**PAID**	**PLAYED**	**PAID**
J.Bloggs	1	£3	1	£3	1	£3	1	£3
I. Claudius	1	£3	1	£3	1	£3	1	£3
A. Wannabe	1	£3	1	£3	1	£3	1	£3
I. Aye	½	£1.50	1	£3	1	£3	1	£3
P. Knutt	1	£3	1	£3	1	£3	1	£3
Y. Turnip	1	£3	½	£1.50	1	£3	1	£3
B. Last	1	£3	1	£3	½	£1.50	1	£3
R. Nutter	1	£3	½	£1.50	1	£3		
A. Fowler	1	£0	1	£0	suspend			
U. Watt	½	£1.50			1	£3	½	£1.50
O. Eck	½	£1.50	1	£3			1	£3
D. Mob	½	£1.50	1	£3	1	£3	1	£3
J. Cloth	1	£3	1	£3	1	£3	½	£1.50
T. Boy			½	£1.50	½	£1.50	1	£3

This is a good way of keeping track of payments. You can see that the table shows which players played a full game and paid the full subscription, and which players played half or part of a game and paid half-price.

The Membership Book is a good place to record all of this, if only because the F.A. requires clubs to keep a members register anyway. It takes only a few minutes to fill in the book while players hand over their money. This plan could bring in £33 per match. Of course, when the team is at home, £15 or so may go to pay the referee, and the rest would go towards club funds.

SUBSCRIPTIONS AT TRAINING SESSIONS

Some clubs also ask players for money at each training session. A pound might not be unreasonable. It all adds to club funds. Again you should keep a record in the book of any money received. Even if you don't write down who has paid, you should record in the book how much money has been collected.

BUSINESS SPONSORS

Another popular source of money is sponsorship. If anyone in your club knows someone in charge at a business, it would be a good idea if he asked if they would be interested in sponsoring your football team. In approaching a business, make yourselves look credible. You don't know how many requests for money businesses get. You could be competing with people you've never met. You can improve your chances by sending them well-presented information along the following lines.

Write a covering letter to the business. It could be more effective if you address your letter to the right person. If you don't know who to write to, ring up and ask. Keep the letter brief, printed on a very few sheets of paper, and lay it out nicely. You need to get a few points across about your club and what it could mean to the sponsor.

Tell them a little bit about the history of your club, because they may not have heard of you before. If your club has achieved anything, mention it. Businesses love to be associated with success. Don't be afraid to come right out and say how much money you need – that includes saying exactly what the money is to be spent on, such as a new kit, or paying for a football pitch. It saves the potential sponsor time if you get to the point.

WHAT YOU CAN DO FOR THE SPONSOR

Of course, the sponsor should know what they get out of sponsoring you. It's hardly ever money for nothing. They may be happy to have their name on your shirts. (Chapter 8 explains about getting sponsors' names printed on shirts.) They may want more than that, for example want your club to do something for the image of their business. Tell them what you can honestly do. And tell them how you will keep them in touch – so that they can see they are getting their money's worth.

Don't be afraid to try – a lot of businessmen are keen to 'give something back to society'. In fact there is nothing to prevent you from writing to anyone else you think could sponsor a football team. It is up to you to come up with those ideas. Most football teams are pleased to find a local pub to sponsor them.

PUB SPONSORS

Grass roots teams all over the country play with the name of a local pub on their shirts. How much money the club gets for this can vary between a couple of hundred pounds and thousands. Of course, the sponsor still wants to know what he gets out of it. In the case of pub sponsors, it might be expected that both teams go back to the pub after the match. Many landlords will offer free sandwiches if they know a couple of teams will spend money on drinks. Drinking alcohol straight after a match is no good at all for your fitness. But I admit it can attract a return for your club coffers. As for other money-raisers, here's a selection.

SPONSORED ATHLETICS EVENTS

Sponsored athletics events are a tried and trusted money-spinner. But how can you make sure more than two or three fitness fanatics will turn up? You may need to be a master of the gentle art of persuasion to get the team to turn up.

The other thing is this: the people you ask to sponsor you have to feel that your cause is worthy. How will you persuade them to reach into their pockets for a football team? If you promise to give half the proceeds to a charity and half to the football club, would that in fact raise more money for both causes?

Whether you do a sponsored swim, walk or run, or sponsored play football in fancy dress, as with everything good organisation is the key. You should give everyone taking part a sheet for sponsors to fill in. Don't forget to make sure that everyone should hand in those sheets to the club treasurer. He will need to make sure all the money comes in and goes where it was intended.

BUCKET COLLECTIONS

Amateur clubs with private grounds sometimes pass a bucket round the crowd for loose change and raise quite a bit this way. However, if you have to hire your ground the hire rules may state that you cannot collect money at the ground. This is a typical rule at pitches hired out by local councils.

What's more, local councils have bylaws about asking for money. If you want to do a bucket-collection in public you should ring your local council and ask how you apply to them for a licence for a street-collection. Anyone collecting without a licence might be in trouble with the law.

THROWING A PARTY

A friend of mine is terrific at organising a party. He would hire a decent venue for a reasonable price, get a DJ friend of his to bring his decks and lights and supply the music at a bargain rate, hold a meeting with all his team-mates at which he would get them to buy or make food – all of them would get a different job to do – so as to provide a big spread, and to top it off he would get hundreds of people you never saw before to come. He would always pick a good time for a party, such as Christmas or the end of the student year.

And the place would be packed for a few pounds admission each. You've either got it or you ain't. Again and again he would raise hundreds and hundreds of pounds. Since that team was formed he has really kept it afloat financially. He always finds the actual work of organising his parties tough, but I don't know any-one who could do it better.

SUPPORTERS' CLUB

If your club has a fair-sized following, might they be willing to band together and form a supporters' club? The best supporters' clubs get involved in raising money, and if they do give such help, it would be good for their voice to be heard too. That's why some amateur clubs have a fans' forum.

CHARITABLE SOURCES OF MONEY

If you ask your public library for books listing charities, you may be handed a book as thick as the phone directory. There are far more agencies willing to sup-port deserving causes than most people realise. For this reason there is informa-tion on this in Appendix IV at the back of this book. This includes charitable funding for ground improvements.

WHAT CAN WE DO IF OUR CLUB IS GOING INTO DEBT?

Even well-run clubs occasionally find themselves short of money. If you find your club is going into debt, help could be available from the bank, your club and your league.

THE BANK

First, check that your debts are not bigger than any overdraft facility you agreed with your bank. If they are, phone the bank to see if they will agree to give you a bigger overdraft facility. One problem with unauthorised debts is that the banks add to your debt by punishing you with extra bank charges. If they say no to a bigger overdraft, the next step is even more urgent.

top tip

During the season is a tough time to raise funds because you are always busy with games to arrange. But the best time for the club treasurer to build up a war chest of spare money is in fact during the playing season. Here's why:

1. It's the best time because this is also when you see the players most regularly – so you can get them involved in fund-raising.

2. You normally need the money before the summer – to pay for your pitch for next season, to affiliate to your league and F.A., and so on.

3. Often the end of the season is too late to begin raising money. This is the time of year when everyone looks forward to a break. And before you know it, you don't see your members again till near the start of the next season. Getting everyone together to take part in raising money is more difficult. Fund-raising becomes a lonely, up-hill task. Suddenly the spectre of debt looms large.

A CLUB MEETING

The club's General Committee should meet as soon as it is convenient to talk about what needs to be done to boost the money in the club's coffers, and the players should be told too. You could go through the money-raising ideas mentioned here. Members should discuss what you can do to save money. For instance, is your club losing money because of league fines?

One club in our league had been fined a few times for not sending its match team sheets to the league. The fines came at a time when they had no money to pay the bills. But month after month, requests for the team sheets met with no response. So the fine got bigger. And bigger. And there were other bills to pay. Eventually a few members of the club had to meet together to put their house in order.

TALK TO THE LEAGUE SECRETARY

If it looks like your club has debts it cannot pay, then also call the league secretary. Some leagues have a fund for clubs in financial trouble. This might tide a club over for a while. What's more, the league secretary may be able to offer advice. He has probably seen this situation before. It is in the league's interest to see you stay afloat to complete your fixtures, so there should be no need to keep any problems a secret from your league secretary.

true stories

The suspended sentence

One of the worst moments for myself as a grass roots league official was after we dished out a suspended fine of £100 to a club. The offence was abuse of another league official by a crowd of the club's players. We didn't fine a particular player – we fined the club. But since the fine was suspended we simply asked to be given a cheque that would be kept locked away until the period of suspension was over. We were not going to pay the cheque into the league account unless there was a repeat of the misbehaviour.

Then the cheque arrived. It was not from a football team's chequebook. It was from a married couple's chequebook. The husband was the team manager. I felt terrible. I felt we were not punishing the club members who had caused the trouble. This married couple had decided to take the burden of the fine on themselves. It was very good of them to do this, but it missed the point of the punishment.

Then it became clear that the club didn't have a bank account. This was their only way of giving us the cheque.

There was no repeat offence, and I was pleased when we destroyed that cheque at the end of the period of the suspension, a very relieved man. I'd have found it tough taking that money from that household. But had we found the club guilty of a similar offence during the suspension period we would have had to consider cashing the cheque. Ever since, I've felt more strongly that it is better for all concerned if a club keeps its own bank account with funds in it.

Ironically, years later it came to light that to impose a bond on a club for their good behaviour is against F.A rules. So in this case, that Management Committee unknowingly did wrong too.

A SURVIVAL PLAN FOR LARGER NON-PROFESSIONAL CLUBS

Clubs higher up the Pyramid often may have larger debts. If so, such clubs do well to make progress in all these ways:

- letting supporters take a greater role in the running of the club
- persuading creditors, such as banks, to show special goodwill

- finding new financial backers
- finding short-term help from charitable sources of funding
- agreeing to adopt improvements in administration as a condition of funding
- cost-cutting.

Some clubs near the top of the Pyramid even try some of the same ways that professional clubs use to raise money – that is through share issues, selling players, selling club merchandise, attracting media interest – not to mention gate receipts of course.

CHECKLIST

- get your club to appoint a trustworthy treasurer
- estimate how much it will cost to start your club
- estimate how much it will cost for the team to play for a season
- set up a club bank account
- have two or more signatories to the bank account
- start using a Cash Book and a receipt book
- have fund-raising ideas
- raise money
- make a note of when you must pay bills
- set aside funds for unexpected costs.

chapter 7

ALL ABOUT FOOTBALL PITCHES

This chapter sets out to help anyone in this fix: they have spotted a football pitch and want permission to play there; but no-one knows who owns the pitch; there's no sign erected at the ground to say who owns it; it's not listed in the Yellow Pages; and no-one is playing there who could be asked about it.

FINDING A FOOTBALL PITCH

Your league secretary should know of pitches in your area. So should your County F.A. In some regions, football pitches can be found on almost every green space – no problem. What's more, many schools and universities have their own playing fields.

In other regions, football pitches are almost invisible. So many parks and pitches were sold off in the eighties and nineties – about 10,000 – half belonging to schools, half to local authorities. Apparently the headmaster of the school attended by England striker Robbie Fowler used to drive young Fowler three miles after school to a football pitch.

PITCH AGENCIES

Who might have football pitches ready and waiting for use? The answer could be: 'pitch agencies'. Getting in touch with the pitch agencies is important for these reasons:

■ to find out where their football pitches are
■ to find out how much they cost
■ to book a pitch as your home ground.

Pitch agencies and their grounds mostly fall into these kinds:

■ local council pitches (this is where 70 per cent of organised football takes place)
■ school and university playing fields

- youth association playing fields
- artificial surfaces at sports centres
- private football grounds.

TRACKING DOWN THE PITCH AGENCIES

The first task is usually to get the telephone number of the pitch agencies. It's surprising to find that some sports grounds do not advertise their owner or display a contact number. Detective work may be in order.

Here are suggestions for finding a telephone number or address of a pitch agency or other organisations (including youth associations and private football grounds) to find out who leases out their grounds:

1. Is there a board near the ground entrance with a telephone number? If so, that should be the number you want. If not…

2. Are there any staff at the ground, such as ground staff in their office, or reception staff at a sports centre? If so, ask them if they have the telephone number of the people who hire out the pitch.

3. If you see a match going on at a local pitch, you could go over to ask the club secretary, if he's there, who he books the pitch from. However, you will probably find during a game is not the best time to ask questions. To get the information you want, you may be hanging around a while.

4. If you suspect that the pitch you want belongs to a local council, you can't do much better than ringing up the council directly. It could be a borough, city, county or parish council, depending on where you live. If you don't know the relevant number, it should be listed in the telephone directory under the name of your region (e.g., 'Birmingham City Council'), not just 'Council'. In the Yellow Pages, it should be listed under 'Local Government'. When you ring the council, ask them to put you through to the office that deals with booking sports grounds or recreation facilities. This department could go under almost any name, such as 'Leisure Services Directorate' or 'Leisure and Recreation Department' or 'Sports Centres' or 'Parks and Open Spaces'. It's a good idea to ask for a list of local council pitches in any case, to see the choice on offer.

5. A local school, college or university may be willing to lease out its pitches. You should be able to ask at their office. (Their pitches can be quite expensive, hired out to bring in extra money. At schools you should also check if the goals are the right size for your league – because schools for younger children use smaller-size goals.)

6. If none of the above works for you, look in the Yellow Pages under a heading such as 'Sports Grounds & Stadia'. You will normally find some football grounds listed there. Lists in telephone directories almost never list every ground, so if the number is not there, don't give up.

7. Ask your County F.A. if they have a list of local pitches.

8. Ask your league secretary for details of pitch agencies used by his league.

CHOOSING YOUR HOME GROUND

The first consideration when choosing a football pitch is price, then quality. Once you have tracked down a pitch agency, ask them about prices of their pitches. Ask them to send you a pitch booking form too.

The cost of hiring a football pitch varies widely. Even council pitches differ hugely in price. At the cheap end, some council pitches in Lancashire have been hired for use 'every other weekend' for less than £100, a very good, flat deal for the whole season. At the expensive end, some London councils hire out pitches for upwards of £500 for block-bookings of 13 games or so. Even within a region prices vary a great deal. Here is a likely order from the cheapest to the dearest:

- local council pitches
- school and university playing fields
- youth association playing fields
- artificial surfaces (such as plastic pitches)
- private football grounds with floodlights.

In any case, a few hundred pounds may be needed. You can expect the bill in the summer months. This couldn't be a worse time of year from the club's point of view – the most difficult time to raise money. Part of the solution is to plan a budget for your club as suggested in Chapter 6: 'Balancing the books'.

PITCH ACCESSIBILITY

When deciding what pitch to book, also look at accessibility:

- a pitch available for the days and times you need
- convenience of locality
- the route
- car parking
- access designed for persons with disabilities (if required).

DAYS AND TIMES

Some pitches are open both mornings and afternoons, some only in the afternoons. Some are open Saturdays and Sundays, some only Sundays. Some are available midweek.

This is important because any league you join probably expects you to play your matches at the same time and on the same day as all the other teams. Before you book a pitch, ask the pitch agency if their pitch will be open when your league needs. If it will not, you may have to look for a different pitch – unless there's a chance of your league letting you play home games at a different time to other clubs. Ask your league secretary about this.

EVENING GAMES

As for games in the evenings, without floodlights you will only expect light enough nights in August, September, April and May. If your league's fixtures have evening games, ask your pitch agency if their pitches can be used for matches in the evenings.

MONTHS

Check that the pitches you may wish to play on will be open throughout your league's season. For instance, some council pitches are open from August to March. Others are open from September to April. In the summer they mostly turn into athletics and cricket pitches. (Your league secretary may already have arranged fixtures around the months when council pitches in the area are open. But check with pitch agencies about what months you will have access to your pitch.)

LOCALITY

While most teams prefer somewhere local for a home ground, some teams travel miles to their own home pitch. In some cases this is because there are no other pitches in the locality, but usually it is a matter of preference – choosing the best pitch within reach.

THE ROUTE

Questions to consider include: is there decent public transport, or can you drive to your ground easily? A situation to avoid is players of either team failing to reach the ground on time where the route is a traffic nightmare, blighted by regular jams, roadworks or flooding.

CAR PARKING

Check that there is space at the ground for teams to park cars, or you may be forced to park half-a-mile away and walk the rest of the way in all weathers.

FACILITIES

At one ground I know, teams are forced to change into their kit on a wind-swept, freezing pitch – at best on the car-seat, using the open car door for a wind-shield and for a little privacy. This is enough to put many off playing the game. So let's consider these key factors in choosing a pitch:

- changing rooms
- goalposts
- playing surfaces.

CHANGING ROOMS

How much would you and your players be prepared to put up with? How about: no changing rooms at the ground itself, changing rooms without showers, changing rooms without hot water, one big room that all the teams share, instead of separate rooms for teams, no lockers?

I've seen changing rooms with the worst of the above and others with decent facilities. The price you pay for your pitch will depend in part on the facilities. Ask your club treasurer what your club can afford.

GOALPOSTS

Goalposts are probably the most important issue to ask about before you pay a penny. Park teams see this wide variety of facilities:

- pitches with goalposts and nets left up permanently
- pitches with goalposts (but no nets) left up permanently
- pitches where the goalposts are left out by the groundsman for teams to put up and take down themselves (but without nets)
- pitches where you have to bring your own goalposts and nets.

Ask the pitch agency about the situation with goalposts at their ground, since goalposts are expensive, not to mention time-consuming to move. Aim for a pitch with goalposts provided. If you must supply your own goalposts, there may be a hut to store them in or a fence to chain them to. Details of how to get your own goalposts are in Chapter 8.

PLAYING SURFACES

It is surprising how much the quality of pitches varies. Some are wide, some narrow. Some have clear, straight, white markings, some have faint and uneven markings. Some are flat, some on a slope and full of divots.

It's worth finding out how a pitch stands up to the weather. It may be rock solid in August, but come the rain and the snow you'll notice how some pitches drain incredibly well, while others turn into a mud-bath overnight. One I know is regularly waterlogged in winter. This means a lot of games get postponed, and a fixture pile-up happens. A team that used that pitch gave up home advantage and played all its games away to complete one season.

You could find out more by asking teams you see on local pitches. They will tell you what it is like in bad weather. They may moan that the problem is too many teams using their pitch and ruining it. But it is not up to them who uses the pitch – unless they own it.

All pitches can be closed due to the weather, but some more often than others. Some have a reputation for being closed by their owners at the first spot of drizzle. Such pitches are usually in beautiful condition and so are tempting – but pitches are usually beautiful when teams cannot get on them.

ARTIFICIAL SURFACES

There are alternative surfaces to muddy fields, such as 'plastic pitches'. Many players dislike them. A lot of these surfaces are of the cheaper kind, and have these problems:

- they may be worse than natural pitches with regard to wear and tear on your joints, especially your knees
- falling on these surfaces can result in burns and grazes – nastier than on grass
- bad drainage
- surface water may make the pitch treacherous, if not unplayable (calling them 'all weather pitches' does not mean they are safe in all weathers)
- the ball bounces much higher and rolls away much faster than on grass.

The most expensive artificial surfaces are a big improvement over the cheaper ones. If you can afford it, hire the best. An additional advantage is that these artificial surfaces are often surrounded by floodlights at very modern sports centres – this can make them ideal for training matches during the dark winter nights.

The only other advantage of them over natural pitches, in my view, is to the home team, who will be used to a strange bounce and the speed at which the ball runs, while the away team may struggle to get used to it. I think that that is taking home advantage a bit far.

Most of us don't expect a surface like Wembley, but it's just as well to open your eyes. How much time you spend on finding a pitch depends on how fussy you are. Once your club has made up its mind about a home ground, you should return the booking form as quickly as possible.

true stories

The geese

When I started out in amateur football, looking for the right pitch took up several days. I was fussy. One I had heard of was in a picturesque riverside location – and it was local. Cautious by nature, I went to see it with my own eyes – after all I'd never looked at it before.

I arrived on a fair day, saw the fine scenery... and geese droppings all over the pitch. The pitch was white, I kid you not. A few geese were having a stroll in one half of the pitch.

A few ground staff were there, so I asked about the pitch and the geese droppings. They were apologetic, but assured me the droppings would be cleared before the season started. They explained that a local man owned the pitch and the geese, but they had an agreement with him about where the geese were allowed to roam. They were optimistic that this agreement would be respected for the season – after all, he was leasing out his land, not his geese.

I was taking no chances. I booked a different pitch. A few months later I was passing and decided to see how the other pitch was looking during the season. It was still white.

Moral: before you book a pitch, try to see it for yourself.

BOOKING YOUR PITCH

You may have to book your pitch as early as May or June. Local councils, for example, may be faced with many more teams than pitches, so it is in your interests to submit your booking form to the pitch agency as early as possible. First come, first served is normally the rule. Ensure you don't lose out, or you could find your team playing all your games away from home. Worse, you might be punished by your league for the want of a home pitch.

Ask the pitch agency when you should pay the bill. This differs from area to area so that you may pay a fee for the whole season, or a fee for each game, depending on the pitch agency.

Even a club lower down the amateur leagues can find itself at quality private grounds in cup matches. For a competition run by your own league, your league secretary will probably take responsibility for booking a venue for the final.

USING YOUR FOOTBALL PITCH

There is a section on looking after your football ground generally in Chapter 19:

true stories

The unhappy groundsman's fixture list

It was a rearranged game. The teams turned up on time on a fine Saturday morning. Then the groundsman came to have a word. He wanted to know what we were doing here. He was quite a brusque man at the best of times, but we could tell that today he was in an especially bad mood. He said we had no game today. He showed us his blackboard at the changing room entrance where he would write the day's fixtures – our game was not down. He pointed out the fixture list in his office – our game was not down. It was a rearranged game.

Our club secretary apologised – he had not passed on to him the details of our rearranged match. As far as the groundsman was concerned we shouldn't have been there. We pointed out all the empty pitches there, waiting for someone to use them. But to him it was the principle of the thing. He had to know how many pitches to prepare every day. And he didn't like surprises at his ground.

It ended as a stand-up row between the groundsman and our secretary in front of everyone. Eventually the groundsman backed down – after all, we'd paid our fee to use the pitch – but he was not a happy man. For us it was far from the pre-match preparation we'd planned.

Moral: your groundsman may not like surprises, so if he needs a fixture list, remember to pass on details of rearranged home games too.

'They think it's all over… it isn't'.

At some grounds you may be given your own keys to the changing rooms when you hire the pitch.

Find out whether you have to hand a list of your home fixtures to the ground staff or to the pitch agency before the season starts. This is so that the ground staff know when to prepare a pitch for you. If you have to hand in a list of your home fixtures, don't forget to send details of home cup matches and home rearranged matches during the season.

MOVING FROM YOUR HOME GROUND DURING THE SEASON

Half-way through a season, a club may decide to move from their soggy pitch. If you decide to move mid-season, you need to do these things:

- find a new ground before you leave your old ground
- check that you will be able to book the new ground mid-season
- check with the owner of your present ground if you can get a refund and if you

can leave with no further obligations (it all depends on what it says in the contract you signed with them)

- ask your league secretary for permission to change grounds
- book the new ground and go through all the usual steps, such as giving a copy of your fixtures to your new groundsman
- tell all the other clubs in your league how to get to your new ground.

PRIVATE FOOTBALL GROUNDS

If yours is a club of a higher amateur level where you need your own private ground, perhaps with floodlights and stands, then associated issues are insurance, safety certificates, local bylaws, quite apart from bills and any wages to pay. A helpful guide is Home Office Circular 34/2000: 'Guidance on Football Related Legislation'. For details of this, write to: Home Office, Action Against Crime and Disorder Unit, Room 541, 50 Queen Anne's Gate, London, SW1H 9AT.

There are general business issues, but this book is not the place to discuss business plans and practices. For these, you may wish to seek out suitably experienced colleagues, appropriate courses or books to assist you. There are also questions of maintaining the playing surface and the cost of doing so. The Football Foundation can offer helpful guidance in this situation.

Clubs with private grounds have always had to address issues such as the upkeep of their playing surface. Drainage work, for example, can cost thousands of pounds. There is a great need for funding for ground improvements. This is not only an issue for high-flying clubs but for many in rural areas that have to make and maintain their own football fields.

GROUND GRADING

A pressing issue for high-flying non-professional clubs is the improvement of stands and facilities for the comfort and the safety of the public. This is where 'ground grading' comes in. It means that club facilities are assessed by leagues and by the F.A. to decide whether they are suitable for the higher levels of the Pyramid. Teams are often told to undertake expensive ground redevelopment work, such as installing floodlights, or else play at a lower level. In some cases, the standard of changing rooms has been sufficient reason for the football authorities to bar a club from moving up to a higher level of league. Such demands on clubs have forced some to sell their grounds to stay in business. Some, for all their efforts, cannot get planning permission from their local authorities for their floodlights of choice.

Some clubs, having sold their grounds to survive, ground-share with clubs of a similar level. This brings problems of its own. That's why some clubs keep their old grounds and drop to a lower level of league (where floodlights, for example, are not compulsory).

The main factor is safety, which is why ground grading is here for good. So whatever your ground needs, be it a top-line brand of floodlights to win planning approval, or a mega-batch of weed-killer to stop your pitch being coated with a snowy layer of daisies, you may want to know about funding. You'll find a list of British funding sources for ground improvements in Appendix IV at the back of this book.

No-one can anticipate every problem. I heard of one urban pitch where players feared the discarded needles of drug-addicts. In rural areas you may worry more about sheep that refuse to leave the field of play, or goats nibbling your car aerials.

The F.A.'s 'National Facilities Plan for Football' says that poor playing surfaces and run-down and inadequate changing rooms have damaged the game. The report blames the state of grounds on the amount of games played on pitches and the lack of money spent putting them right.

The Football Taskforce reported to the Government that all grounds should have marked pitches where the grass is regularly cut; and facilities should always include separate changing rooms for each team, with locks on the doors, heating and lighting, hot and cold running water and showers, working toilets and drinking water. Equal facilities should be available separately on site for men's and women's teams.

The Football Foundation should make much of this possible over the years to come. It has been given the job of improving pitches and changing facilities around the country. The Government is reportedly stopping the playing-fields sell-off too.

INSURANCE

Pitches and facilities take a lot of wear and tear. At some grounds – not all – you may be asked to pay for extra insurance against a claim related to the ground. So if you have to pay, ring your County F.A. to see if any financial help is available.

CHECKLIST

- find a football pitch where you can play your home games
- make contact with the agency that lets out the pitch to teams
- ask the questions set out below
- send your booking form to the pitch agency
- pay your bill on time.

A DOZEN QUESTIONS YOU SHOULD ASK

Here are questions to ask pitch agencies about the football grounds they run:

1. Do they have pitches with goalposts provided?
2. Do they provide nets, or will your club have to bring its own?
3. Will their pitch be available on the days and times you want to play?
4. What months do they open and close their pitches for the season?
5. Are evening games permitted?
6. What changing facilities do they have?
7. Where is car parking permitted?
8. Do you need to give your home fixtures list to the groundsman or to the pitch agency ?
9. How will you find out if the ground is closed due to the weather?
10. Ask them to send you a list of their pitches and prices.
11. Ask them to send you an application form to hire their pitch.
12. Ask them when you need to pay for the pitch.

chapter 8
ALL KITTED OUT

This chapter first runs through kit and equipment any club would expect to use, and also gives a list of extra stuff for your kit-bag – but if you choose to do without this stuff, you shouldn't get into great trouble over it! (You may just one day wish you had it.

There's always the question of cost: how to get kitted out without breaking the bank. Here's a sample of typical prices for some of the essential kit and equipment:

- new football kit £400
- footballs £30 each
- goal-nets £75.

Given that there are other things to pay for, from registration fees to pitch-hire, money-saving ideas have their place. You can pay less. This chapter shows how.

You should then be in a better position to work out how much money your club needs to raise. There's more on this subject in Chapter 6. You will need to discuss with your club treasurer how much you can afford to spend on kit (and everything else). Some clubs have a considerable amount of property, so much that it's worth insuring. Most clubs own only bits and bobs and, as expensive as it all is, do not consider insurance worthwhile, not even insurance of the football strip itself.

A TELEPHONE

First on the list of essential equipment: a telephone for the club secretary. Without a telephone much can go wrong. (This will be a recurring theme in the second half of this book – things go wrong if messages get lost between the club secretary and the clubs in his league.) Land-lines are less likely to malfunction than mobile phones, and so are more important. If no-one is around to take phone-calls in the evenings you will also want an answering-machine for your telephone. Also, giving people your mobile phone number gives extra reassurance that people can get hold of you when they need to.

A mobile phone at the football ground can be a godsend too. Being able to use one takes pressure off in those moments when players or referee are late due to a traffic jam.

FOOTBALL KIT

Each player will need to bring their own shin-pads and boots. Here's what your club's team kit should include:

A COMPLETE FOOTBALL STRIP

Your team should have two complete sets of football strip – one strip for home, and one change strip for away games. 'Complete' normally means:

- at least thirteen shirts, numbered 2 to 14 (the colour of the shirts must not be black, or any colour so dark it could be mistaken for black – e.g., very dark blue – so that players cannot be mistaken for match officials, which can be confusing in incidents such as offside decisions);
- 1 goalkeeper's shirt, of a different colour, numbered 1
- fourteen sets of shorts
- fourteen sets of socks.

Before you place the order for your new strip, here are some of the things to bear in mind:

- You need to order kit of the right size: a big centre-half may not be impressed by being asked to squeeze into a 36 chest and a 28 waist.
- If your shirts are not numbered, then the referee may make a report to the County F.A. against your team – after all, his job is difficult enough already. You could be fined by your league or County F.A. over it.
- If finances are a bit tight at your club, find ways to buy cheaper kits (see following pages).

TEAM COLOURS

Bear in mind the views of your players when you choose colours. It may not go down well if a team made up entirely of Manchester City supporters are asked to play in red. A new team might also want to ensure their kit is not in the same basic colours as those of other teams in their league. So when you join a league

true stories

'Ref! Foul!'

There is a league where one team played in blue shirts with yellow stripes... and another in yellow with thin blue stripes. Both teams had blue shorts and socks. Never had 'away colours' been so important. There was a day when both teams turned up only with home kits. The teams had to play each other regardless. The referee did a great job, but when he saw three pairs of blue socks go into the same tackle together, how could he be sure who had fouled whom, or who touched the ball?

Choose colours well – for home and away.

do ask the league secretary for a list of the other teams' colours straight away. This will help you to choose something distinctive not only for your home strip but for your change strip too – and for socks in particular.

OPTIONS FOR BUYING A TEAM STRIP

The following ideas for buying a team strip are in order of expense, high to low.

CUSTOM-MADE: MOST EXPENSIVE

In the Yellow Pages, under a heading such as 'Sportswear Manufacturers', a large number of firms are listed who can make unique football kits to order. Before you order, ask them to send you a catalogue so you can see different colours and shirt designs – because some modern shirts are so fanciful as to be embarrassing.

As well as choosing colours, decide whether you want any design on the shirts, such as a club badge. Perhaps someone in your club could design a badge for your team, and the manufacturers could incorporate it in the shirt design.

Do you have a sponsor's name to go on the shirts? Give the manufacturers this detail when you place your order. BUT – if you won't know till much later the details of a sponsor (if you find a sponsor at all) don't delay your kit order; you still need the kit in time for the season. The fact is, the manufacturers can add details such as sponsors' names to the shirts later, although it may save money if you get any details printed on the shirt when it is first manufactured.

Your County F.A. can give you a copy of the rules on the size of the lettering. It's a good idea to check that the sponsor's name on shirts isn't bigger than permitted – before you pay for them.

SHOP-READY TEAM STRIPS

Specialist team strip retailers stock a wide range of ready-made team kits. They advertise in football magazines, but they should be in the Yellow Pages under a heading such as 'Sports Goods Shops', where you may find a large range of shops listed. Many of them only stock Premiership replica kits and shirts without numbers, instead of full team strips. You need a shop that specialises in kitting out teams, with shirts numbered from 2 to 14, normally a specialist shop.

Ask for a catalogue, or to see the goods – before you pay a penny. A description of a shirt over the phone, 'It's blue', does not tell the whole story about some of the terrible trimmings and patterns printed into modern shirts.

It should also be possible to order replacement shirts with a chosen number printed on the back. One team-mate of mine, of a larger build, bought his own extra-large shirt. Bear in mind, if you choose a very fancy, fashionable kit you won't be able to find an exact replacement shirt once it is out of fashion and out of stock.

You can usually get end-of-the-season (May and June) bargains – 'end-of-the-line' sets of kit going cheap to make room for new stock.

WARNING: if you ask a specialist shop to customise your shirt with a badge and a sponsor's name, the bill may add up to more than a customised shirt ordered direct from a manufacturer. There's no surprise here – the shops need to mark up the price to make their profit. So check that the price includes numbering and lettering on the shirts before you place your order.

SPECIAL DEALS: LESS EXPENSIVE

Many leagues have their own arrangements with local suppliers of kits. If you join such a league you may be obliged to go to this supplier for any new kits. But you may get a discount of, say, 10 to 20 per cent. Ask your league secretary if there is such a deal.

SHOP BARGAINS: EVEN LESS EXPENSIVE

Take care – you need to add up the whole cost carefully. In shops selling sports clothing, you may find two kinds of shirts going cheap – racks of cheap, plain football shirts; or out-of-date replica shirts of professional clubs on sale to clear.

The good news about these is the price – sometimes as low as £5 per shirt. The bad news is they won't have shirt numbers on – so before you rush out and buy the whole rack from the shop, find out a price for putting shirt numbers on. You may need to make a call to the specialist kit shops or manufacturers. Expect to pay at least a couple of pounds for each number printed. Shop around and you will find prices vary a lot. I knew a team in an out-of-date Premier League strip. It saved them a small fortune.

Three warnings about shop bargains

- cheap often means small: shirt and shorts sizes are important – don't forget to take account of those members of your team with size 48 chests;
- cheap may also mean poor quality – if shirts look flimsy and likely to tear easily, you are best looking for quality instead;
- if there are fewer than thirteen identical shirts, don't waste your money.

SECOND-HAND: CHEAP

A new club has mounting bills in its first season – so this option is worth serious thought. I kitted out the first club I formed with a complete home kit – shirts, shorts and socks – for just £80, all second-hand. The team didn't like those shirts a lot, not least because they bore the name of a sponsor none of us had heard of. But this money-saver ensured we joined our league on time.

Local newspapers are one of the sources for finding second-hand kits. Turn to the classified advertisements or 'small ads' and you should find a section listing sports clothing or equipment. Over a few weeks you may see a lot of second-hand football kits on offer – especially in the summer. The prices vary a lot. Some of these second-hand kits may be of good quality – because some clubs replace their shirts every couple of years, or maybe one is winding-up.

If you ask the club secretaries in your league, there is a good chance that one of their clubs may have an old kit they do not need any more. (I knew a team that got started this way. The kit was old and looked it, but complete, and it was free. It meant that the team could start playing.)

Before buying a second-hand kit, count that everything is there, especially all the numbered shirts. Missing old shirts are hard to replace because designs change. To replace shorts or socks with the right colour may be easier, although even these can be difficult to match exactly (unless you dye them all together).

CHEAP BUT DRASTIC

It is perfectly legal – just not very desirable – to buy thirteen matching T-shirts from the bargain rail, and write numbers on the back with a marker pen. Cheap shorts and socks can be bought in the sales.

KIT-SHARING

One money-saver I've been party to has seen two teams sharing one away kit because it was the only way both could afford one. However, this works only if both teams can get their hands on the change strip when they need it. Because of this potential problem, league secretaries may disapprove.

FREE KITS

Not every team can expect to receive free kits – but some schools and special cases may. Donors may be professional football clubs that run 'Football in the Community' schemes. (More so the Premier League clubs, which have greater resources.) No-one has an automatic right to such help, but if you feel your club is a special case it's worth asking. Phone up your nearest professional football club and ask to be put in touch with their 'Football in the Community' staff. You never know, you may end up playing in a replica kit of your local professional club.

true stories

Making the most of what you've got

One team I came across included a couple of players who were starring in a rock band enjoying top-twenty hits. No names, sorry. They wrote to a well-known kit manufacturer asking if it would like to do anything in connection with their team. The kit manufacturer was very pleased to be associated with the famous musicians – and gave the lads a free kit for their whole team! No kidding.

So if you can think of some reason why a kit manufacturer might like to be associated with your club, there's no harm in sending a nice letter...

GOALKEEPER'S KIT-BAG

Most goalkeepers these days prefer to wear goalkeeper's gloves, available from a sports shop. A cap to shield the eyes from the sun is another popular item. Some goalkeepers prefer to buy their own gloves and caps.

Ask your players if any of them has a spare pair of goalkeeper's gloves. You may want your club to buy a spare pair for those days when your usual keeper – and his gloves – are missing. Gloves are not compulsory, but generally if you ask another player to play in goal at short notice, they would expect you to produce gloves for them to wear.

MATCH BALLS

Apart from the footballs you use in training or for kick-arounds, you need match-quality footballs – and they can be expensive. They come in different sizes: the required size for adults is size 5, and there are smaller-sized footballs for children. The referee can report the home team to the County F.A. if they do not bring two match-quality footballs to a game.

As good quality footballs are not cheap here are some tips:

- You might be surprised how much prices vary for identical brands of football in different shops. Shop around to save money.
- The best time to buy footballs is usually in the weeks just after the end of the professional season in May and June. Sports shops usually have a sale then, to make room for their summer stock.
- If you have spare funds, do stock up on match balls whenever prices are low, because every season you will need to replace lost or damaged footballs.
- You will save a small fortune if you take simple steps to prevent the loss of footballs. Use a thick, indelible marker pen to write the name of your club on all your footballs.

The reason for this last tip is simple: at the end of a game one muddy football resembles another, and it is surprisingly easy for the visiting team innocently to take your spare match ball home. I have known teams lose several footballs a season this way at great cost. (Better still, after the warm-up put spare footballs in a bag, so that no-one starts kicking them about.)

FOOTBALL PUMP AND ADAPTOR

Any sports shop should be able to sell you these for no more than a few pounds. I recommend buying a spare adaptor since they snap easily.

A PAIR OF NETS FOR GOALS

You may be fortunate and play in an area where the people who hire the pitch out to you also supply you with nets on the goals. In London, for example, the pitches are expensive but normally are supplied with posts and nets. However, in many regions each team must own its nets. Ask your pitch agency if they supply the nets.

If you have to buy, you will need a pair of nets – the home team has to provide the nets for both ends of the pitch. Nets come in different qualities at different prices. The stronger and thicker the netting, the more pricey. Nowadays you could be paying over £80 for a pair.

In the Yellow Pages, look under headings such as 'Sports Goods Shops' or 'Sports Goods Manufacturers'. If you have no success in finding a supplier in your area, ring your County F.A. who should be able to advise you.

One money-saver for nets is the second-hand route. In the classified ads of local newspapers there may be nets sold by defunct teams. However, old nets may well have holes and shabby repair jobs.

The referee may report a club that provides poor quality nets – that is, nets that have holes, or nets not properly tied to the goal, or not properly pegged into the ground to prevent the ball escaping through the back of the net when a goal is scored.

NET-TIES

Ties for the nets are easily forgotten but essential – especially if you provide your own nets. A cheap roll of string may do. You will need a penknife or a pair of scissors to cut the string – ever tried untying tiny knots in string when it's wet and below zero?

TENT-PEGS

If you have to provide your own nets, then you will need pegs too. Thin tent-pegs bought from a camping shop usually hold the foot of the net to the ground nicely. Ask your team if they have any spare tent-pegs. (Many people have a mouldy old tent and a bag of pegs.)

Stock up on spare pegs in advance of matches. Bear in mind that you must peg the nets in both goals. In addition, after the match, when your players collect the pegs, they will invariably leave one or two behind. By the end of the season you may not have enough to peg the nets down properly. I have seen bags and stones used to hold nets down. Some people would deem this dangerous.

A PAIR OF GOALPOSTS

To save money, I strongly recommend you seek a pitch where goalposts are provided. You can read more about this in Chapter 7: 'All about football pitches'. If you must buy ready-made goalposts from a manufacturer, you may not see much change out of £500. Prices will vary for children's and adults' sizes of goals. By shopping around, you might find a bargain.

For full-size goals in adult games (and usually for over-11s) the space in the goal must be 8 feet (2.44 metres) high and 24 feet (7.32 metres) wide. For children's (usually under-11s) games, the goals may be smaller. You will find the specific rules about the sizes of goals in Law 1 of FIFA's Laws of the Game.

HAVING GOALPOSTS MADE

Having posts made for you does not necessarily come a lot cheaper. They can be made of wood or metal, but if you are unsure about using a particular material, ask your County F.A. For fear of serious accidents, the F.A.'s guidance is that 'home-made' goalposts should never be used. If you want your own goal-posts made, it is a job for professionals who should make them according to F.A. standards. The following information gives you an idea of what is involved.

Remember, when ordering the wood or metal, that you need to add on extra inches (an extra amount the same as the thickness of the wood) to the length of each upright and to each end of the crossbar – this is for the joint at each corner where posts and bar overlap. In addition, if the posts will be slotted into the ground they may need to be about another 18 or so extra inches long (about 460 millimetres). Check this with your pitch agency; if you have your own football ground ensure this is checked by someone who knows what they are doing.

Posts and bars should be the same thickness. The maximum thickness, whether made of metal or wood, is five inches (120 millimetres), but they are often thinner.

Gloss paint should be suitable for the finished posts. White is the regulation colour.

GOALPOST SAFETY

Whether posts slot into the ground, or have spikes, or are weighed down, or are portable, the most important consideration must be safety. The posts must be made such that they can be securely anchored to the pitch. An accident some time ago in which a child was killed by a falling goalpost highlighted the need for safety. The danger is greatest with portable goalposts, which can tip over. They must be anchored somehow.

Where the crossbar is joined to the top of the posts there should be no danger of the crossbar coming loose from the posts by accident. (A typical joint is made by cutting corresponding blocks out of each post and out of the crossbar so that the posts slot under the crossbar and support its weight. Very large nuts and bolts, checked before each match, are in order.)

If you use portable goals, they must be of lightweight material for safety. After use they should not be left standing. The best thing to do is to dismantle them, take them away, tie them together and chain them to a fence or something similar, padlocked.

For safety's sake, hooks used for fixing nets to goals should be made of plastic, not metal. Alternatively, nets can be taped to goals.

Children or adults should never be allowed to swing on the goalposts or play with any part of them. This goes for all goals, fixed and portable.

METAL GOALPOSTS

Metal posts should be round not square. Contact your pitch agency to check their regulations for erecting the posts at their pitch. At some pitches, spikes in the feet of the posts are banned. One club had their posts made with spikes at the bottom, but then were told to adapt their posts to be held down by weights. When they brought their expensive new posts to their ground for the first time, they found there were slots for thick posts built into the ground – and they had to improvise to position their portable goals above these. They couldn't make their goals stand up straight for a whole game – dangerous stuff.

WOODEN GOALPOSTS

These may be square or round, square being less expensive. To stand up to a fair beating, the wood should not have weaknesses, such as knots. Unfortunately, wood without knots does not come cheap. I have heard of teams hiding knots with thick paint – silly, since safety matters most.

FOUR CORNER-FLAGS

Corner-flags ought to have five feet (1.5 metres) showing above ground in addition to several inches in the ground to secure them, and the tops should not be pointed. The reason for the height is the danger of a player losing their eyesight by falling head-first into a corner-flag. Ideally, corner flags should be made of a flexible material that bends easily.

To save money you may decide to make your own corner-flags. I am told insulation tubing is good for the job, and it bends if you collide with it: the top should still be rounded for safety. It should stand upright unsupported. The flags should be clearly visible from a distance. This tubing is quite cheap and can be bought from DIY shops.

You will sometimes see two extra flags to mark the half-way line, but this is not compulsory. The regulations are set out in Law 1 of the Laws of the Game.

FIRST-AID KIT

It is normally compulsory for each team to have a first-aid kit. You can buy simple first-aid kits from high street chemists, and not too expensively. Replacing the contents of the kits as you use them up costs more in the long run.

A first-aid kit **need not** include the following two things:

■ a magic spray for treating muscles – these sprays encourage amateur players to play on with injured muscles and aggravate the damage to their body;

■ a single sponge and bucket of water – using the same sponge and water on more than one player risks cross-infection. If you watch a professional physio you will see that whenever he uses the sponge and water he immediately leaves the pitch to go and get a clean sponge and clean water. This is to avoid any risk of spreading infections.

As for what a first-aid kit **should** contain, start from this list and you should be fine:

■ A guidance leaflet explaining how to use the first-aid kit.

■ Pairs of surgical gloves.

■ Sterile triangular bandages.

■ Safety pins (for the bandages) – these are of course for players who are taken off the field; the referee might not let them play wearing safety pins!

■ Sterile eye pads, with the attachment to hold them on.

■ Dressings: sterile adhesive dressings (commonly called sticking plasters) – get ones that come individually wrapped; a small box may contain a few dozen; plus unmedicated dressings, in medium, large and extra-large sizes.

■ A bottle of sterile water (because tap water may not be available at the ground). For sterile water, it may be better to use tap water that has been through a filter. You can get a water-filter from many high street chemists.

■ A note-book and pencil for noting the circumstances of any serious injuries.

You will find notes on the first-aider's job in chapters 4 and 16, and in Appendix I.

TRANSPORT

Your home pitch might be nearby (or not), but at any rate how are all your players going to get to your away matches? If you travel together, and no-one has access to a minibus (and most don't) do you have enough car-owners in your team? Will you need four cars to travel to your away fixtures? If you don't have enough transport, will public transport do?

If you are not sure that you have enough transport, ask other club secretaries what solutions they may have found for travelling to games in your area. Don't

top tip

You'll probably need an A–Z map book of your district, to find some of the more obscure away grounds. Write your name on the cover of your A–Z. I've lost count of how many A–Z books I've bought. What usually happened was this: when the team set off in the cars for an away match, I would lend it to any car full of players who didn't know the route. But in the rush to get home, I didn't always manage to get it back.

leave this to the last minute. Ask your club these questions in a team meeting.

THINGS YOU WANT TO HAVE IN THE KIT-BAG

There follows a list of extras that are not compulsory – but which you may consider getting for your kit-bag.

- A roll of gaffer tape. This has many uses. I have seen gaffer tape used for instant repairs to torn nets, for tying nets to goals when the roll of string goes missing, for on-the-spot repairs to tears in football boots, and for holding up shin-pads. If you tie nets to the goal with tape, you will probably need scissors or a penknife to get it off again after the game.
- A stud-key. Running in boots with missing studs can be painful. A stud-key for tightening loose boot-studs may come with a box of new boots. Since many players don't think to bring their stud-key to a match, you should.
- A spare set of shin-pads. Since it is compulsory for players to wear shin-pads, it is best to buy an extra pair to keep in the kit-bag. They will be ready to lend to any player who turns up without his own.
- A referee's whistle. You may need this because you may one day have a stand-in referee, as explained in Chapter 17: 'Referees and the laws of the game'.
- A mallet or hammer. If you encounter bone-hard pitches in August, you may need something to drive pegs into the ground (to secure the nets).

ITEMS YOUR PLAYERS SHOULD OWN

In addition to the goalkeeper's gloves and cap there are other items individual players need to buy for themselves.

SHIN-PADS

Remind players that they cannot play without shin-pads. A referee can refuse permission for a player not wearing them to enter the pitch.

FOOTBALL BOOTS

For all the people who tell you that a footballer is as good as his feet, not his boots, there is another side to the coin. And that is this: the boots a player chooses will affect his performance for better or worse – because the margins between success and failure can be very fine indeed.

Only in the last few years have manufacturers begun to treat the boot as more than a tough protection for the foot. That's one of the reasons why we all know players who look skilful in their training shoes and yet are only journeymen players five minutes later when they've changed into their football boots.

The fact is, a brand name is no guarantee that the boot is right for the player. I'd tell my players to try a variety of pairs in the shops, because boots, like feet, come in many shapes and sizes. There's no point blaming the boot if you lack skill, but somewhere there should be a football boot that fits your foot better – it just takes patience to find it. But the boot that helps you to play to your best may not be an expensive famous brand.

It is permitted for football boots to have studs, but not spikes. Screw-in studs and moulded studs are normally fine.

true stories

An expensive mistake

Of course, simply changing into a modern pair of boots isn't going to help if they are not right for you. A key player in one team paid a lot of money for boots with moulded ribs. A few weeks later I noticed he had put an old pair of boots back on, so I asked him why. He said, 'The new boots do make the ball curve more, they say 20 per cent extra. But if you already curve the ball to place it, you forget it's going to curve an extra 20 per cent and miss where you placed it.' With games coming up, he didn't have time to get used to the difference. He asked me if he knew anyone who wanted a pair of fancy new boots, since he wanted to sell them and get some of his money back.

So the answer isn't simply modern boots. It is the right boots for you.

MAINTAINING YOUR OWN FOOTBALL GROUND

If you have to maintain your own football ground, it goes without saying that you will need a range of equipment for maintenance of the turf. The Football Foundation can advise on this. In some leagues, clubs with their own grounds are asked to use rope to cordon off their pitch. Ask your league secretary if this is necessary.

CHECKLIST

The first part of this list includes things your club should normally own or have access to. To be ready to start the season, a tick against everything on this part of the list is a good sign.

The second part of the list includes helpful extras to consider having in the kit-bag. A stitch in time, and all that.

Chapter 15: 'Match day – all packed up' details more items you will need on match-days, but at this stage this should give you the idea for stuff to buy or borrow. The next chapter gives you another important checklist for pre-season. It's time to see if your behind-the-scenes work for the season is sorted, and time to nail down any unfinished business

tick	THINGS TO HAVE TO BEGIN THE SEASON
	a home pitch (see Chapter 7)
	a pair of goalposts
	a pair of nets (or access to a pair of nets for home games)
	ties/string
	scissors/penknife
	tent pegs
	4 regulation-size corner-flags (or access to flags for home games)
	complete home strip (numbered shirts, shorts, socks)
	complete change strip (or access to one whenever you need it)
	two match-quality footballs
	football pump and adaptor
	first-aid kit
	a kit-bag – big enough to carry a crumpled muddy kit and other bits and bobs
	a means of transport to and from grounds
tick	OPTIONAL – THINGS YOU SHOULD CONSIDER HAVING
	a roll of gaffer tape
	hammer for tent-pegs
	stud-key
	spare pair of shin-pads
	referee's whistle
	an A–Z map (or book) of your district
	a spare pair of goalkeeper's gloves

chapter 9
PRE-SEASON CHECKLIST

Now that you have done so much towards setting up your club behind the scenes, at last it's nearly time to think about football. Let's go through a checklist. Feel free to copy the checklist (for your own club's use only). You will have to do almost everything listed every year before a new season starts. A fresh copy to tick every year may be handy.

The number of boxes you can tick now will give you an idea of how far you have got, and how much work there is left to do. Anything you can't tick as 'done' needs attention before the season starts.

Although the checklist sums up what we've dealt with so far, you'll also notice a few things in this checklist not covered yet, such as training and how to get messages around your squad. For ideas on how you can keep your team in touch with you, turn to the next chapter, 'Keeping Your Squad in Touch'. For ideas on training and friendlies, see Chapter 11: 'Pre-season training and friendlies'. For information on the Children Act, see Appendix I at the back of this book.

(N.B. The sort of things you shouldn't need to do every year are setting up the bank account, registering the same players with the league, setting up a system for keeping in touch with your squad, and – hopefully – appointing a manager. But it is safe to assume that a good deal of paperwork is repeated annually.)

tick		
	Typical deadline	'Have you done this yet?' See the list below
		RESOURCES
	August	See the checklist at the end of chapter 8
		PAPERWORK
	Immediate	Any conditions of the Children Act complied with
	June	Home football pitch booked
	June	Home football pitch fee paid (see Local Arrangements)
	June	Club bank account set up
	June	County F.A. affiliation form completed and sent off
	June	County F.A. affiliation fee paid
	June	Any County Cup registration completed and sent off
	June	Any County Cup registration fee paid
	June	County F.A. public liability insurance deal agreed
	June	County F.A. public liability insurance deal paid
	June	Any personal accident insurance deal bought
	June	League registration form completed and sent off
	June	League registration fee paid to your League
	June	Any League Cup registration completed and sent off
	June	Any League Cup registration fee paid
	June	A copy of your League's constitution signed and returned to your League Secretary (keep a copy)
	July/August	League fixture list received from your League Secretary
	August	Copies of the fixture list given to your players
	August	Ground staff/pitch agency given dates of home games
	August	Every player registration form sent to the League

tick		
		MEETINGS TO BE ATTENDED/SET UP
	May/June	Your Club's Annual General Meeting
	June	Your League's Annual General Meeting
	every month	Monthly League Council meetings
	every month	Monthly Club General Committee meetings
		PEOPLE APPOINTED AT YOUR CLUB
	May/June	Club Officers (see Chapter 4)
	July	First aider
	July	Training coach
	August	Team manager
		SQUAD PREPARATION
	July	Dates set for training sessions
	July	System for getting messages around your squad set up
	July	Friendly fixtures with other clubs arranged

chapter 10

KEEPING YOUR SQUAD IN TOUCH

Before the season starts, ask your team members the best way to get messages to them all – especially urgent messages. (In Chapter 4, this was on the suggested agenda for your club AGM.) When something goes wrong for teams, outside of actually playing football of course, the reason is frequently that a message has not got around. You can ultimately account for nobody but yourself, but do what you can to ensure your plans don't founder due to a communications breakdown. Typical messages could be: whether the next game is home or away, whether certain players will be needed, where they should meet, what time you need them there, or if the game has been called off.

You will want to avoid the situation where your club secretary spends a whole night trying to phone round 20 players all by himself. I and several of my friends who have run clubs have had our Friday nights devastated this way. The cause has often been unforeseen circumstances – such as being notified on a Friday night by the authorities that all pitches would be closed due to bad weather.

Nevertheless, such a nightmare on the phone could have been avoided pretty simply if we had planned ahead. Here are some of the best ways to get messages around.

TELEPHONE CHAINS

You might consider forming a 'telephone chain' for messages. A chain saves the club secretary having to make 20 phone calls all by himself every time there is an urgent message to spread around. Here are two kinds of telephone chain.

DELEGATED LIST

Write the names and telephone numbers of all club members on a sheet of paper. Split the names into, say, four groups and give a copy of this list to four reliable members chosen to ring the four groups on the list. Make sure each of your four reliable members knows which is his group to ring.

When there is a message to pass on the club secretary rings up each of the four chosen members with the message. Each of these members makes sure everyone in his group gets the message.

SIMPLE CHAIN

Write the club secretary's name at the top of a sheet of paper. Underneath it write the names and telephone numbers of all your members and give every single club member a copy of this list. When there is a message to pass on, the secretary rings up the name under his own name on the list and gives his message; the member who receives the message passes it on by ringing up the next name on the list, who rings up the next name and passes on the message, and so on…

WARNINGS

1. This depends on everyone in the team being happy for their phone numbers to be known by others. It may not be advisable to publish all of your squad's telephone numbers without their permission – for privacy's sake.

2. Telephone chains depend on people passing on the message correctly – we all know about Chinese whispers.

3. Don't forget that messages should also be passed to anyone who cannot be contacted by phone – this is where help from your members can be especially useful.

4. The chain can break down if someone is unable to call the next person on the list. In this case, the best thing to do is ring the person after the missed member. This at least keeps the message going round. However, attempts to contact the missed member should be continued by the same person whose job it was in the first place. If attempts to contact the missing member fail, the club secretary should be informed, so that he can follow this up.

5. Land-line phone numbers are usually more reliable than mobile numbers, but there will probably be some club members who can only ever be reached on their mobile phones.

ANSWER-PHONE MESSAGES

If you have a telephone voicemail service or answer-machine at home, or a voice-mail service on your mobile phone, you can change the message on it every week, and record a new message to tell your players where and when to meet for their next match. Players get the message just by ringing you up and listening to your message. This is handy if you can't be in to take calls yourself. But it only works if your players remember to ring your number. I know lazy players who would never dream of picking up the phone to make the call – they expect someone else to pass the message to them.

E-MAIL AND TEXT-MESSAGING

If you and many of your members can be contacted by e-mail, this will of course save you a lot of time. Text-messaging is another possibility, of course.

NOTICE BOARDS

If your team is a pub team or sports-club team, you may get permission to use a notice board to pass on messages. However, notice boards are not foolproof. Some members will never think to look at a notice board, even if you remind them. So even if you use one, you should have another way of getting messages around the team too.

WORK- OR PUB-BASED TEAMS

Passing on messages may be easier if your team-mates are also your work-mates and you see them every day, or if you all drink in the same pub – so long as people can remember the message the next morning.

TEAM MEETINGS

It is a good idea to have special meetings for the whole team from time to time when everyone has a chance to discuss whether things are working well. But, for spreading urgent messages, this may not be good enough. The easiest way to get messages around is when you see all the team together. Give your message once in a meeting and all team members hear you.

TRAINING SESSIONS

During the season, regular weekly training sessions may be a good time and place to pass on messages. When I was first a club secretary our team trained on Thursdays, and I spent much of each training session, pen and paper in hand, going from player to player asking who would be available for the next match on the Saturday, or who had other commitments, or who was just not sure if they could play. It took a while some days to find eleven available players! I phoned the manager on the Friday night to give him some idea who should be in his squad on the Saturday.

If you don't have formal training sessions, match-days are a good time to pass on any messages that are not urgent – when all the players are in the changing room. For urgent messages you are probably back to using the telephone.

FIXTURE LIST

As club secretary, you should have received (probably by July) from your league secretary a copy of your league's new fixture list for the coming season. Your players will appreciate it if you give each of them a copy. With the fixture list, they can see when they have games, when they have a free weekend – this means they can make plans, which is so important to players with families, and those with weekend jobs.

So make copies of the fixture list. Do remind your players that fixtures will change from the published list – because of postponed games and cup draws.

WRITING AN OPEN LETTER TO YOUR TEAM

To help you keep your team in the picture it is a good idea to write to each member. Here is an example of a letter that can be adapted for your own circumstances. It includes details of key club personnel. All your squad should know these names. But, again, ask the people concerned whether they want their phone numbers printed for all the squad to see.

'WOULDBE F.C.'

Twelfth of Whenever

OPEN LETTER TO THE TEAM

This will be our first season in the .... Football League. This letter is to put you in the picture about everything that's going on at our club.

Who's doing what in our club?

- Manager: ....
- Chairman: ....
- Secretary: ....   Secretary's telephone number: ....
- Treasurer: ....
- Players' representative on the General Committee: ....
- Resources officer (responsible for the club's nets, kit, etc.): ....
- Team captain: ....
- First-aiders: ....

It is important that as many people as possible are willing to share small responsibilities. This way we will avoid a big weight on one person's shoulders. Anyone who would like to contribute some time or effort can ring me on ....

Players

Everyone wishing to play for 'Wouldbe F.C.' will have to complete a Player Registration Form. I will have forms at training/our meetings.

Training

Pre-season training takes place on: ....(DAY) ....(TIME) at: ....(GROUND)
We charge £1 per training session as a fund-raiser.
Please be there on time. This is where we can get the whole squad involved and get everyone up to a certain level before matches start. Turn up regardless of weather. Bring with you as many footballs as you can. If you want water to drink, bring your own bottle.

Attitude

Our aim is to develop a cohesive team. Players are encouraged to think for themselves, to train and play as a team, to bring enthusiasm and self-discipline. Players are free to express their views, but the manager's word on tactics and team-selection is final. Players waiting to be picked should be patient, reasonable and take their chance when it comes. We hope you will find us honest and fair.

Likely dates of pre-season friendlies

We are arranging a few pre-season friendlies in August. These will probably be on these dates:

1. August ....
2. August....................
3. August....................
4. August....................

At training we will announce up-to-date details of the friendlies.

Info about our games

Games are played on ....(DAY)
The time for kick off is normally ....
The date of our opening league game is: ....
We will also compete in the .... Cup.
Games are officiated by County F.A. referees.
Our home ground will be at: ....
We will/will not have the use of changing/showering facilities there.
Our home colours are: ....
Our away colours are: ....

Money

As for where the money goes, here are some of the costs to our club:

F.A. registration £...............
League and cup registration £...............
Pitch hire £...............

There will be extras to pay for (e.g. match balls, referees' fees).

Subscriptions
Each time you play a full match for the team, you pay £......
For part of a match you pay £......
From this, fees to the referee and the league are paid, and money is raised.
If anyone has not paid their Annual Subscription yet, please see the Treasurer.
Any cheques should be crossed and made out to .... (GIVE
THEM THE EXACT NAME OF YOUR CLUB'S BANK ACCOUNT)

Ideas for raising cash are not just welcomed, they are NEEDED, now and for
the future. Please pass ideas on to the Treasurer.

OUR WEEKLY PLAN FOR WHEN THE SEASON STARTS
During the week between matches:
1. You need to know where to be for your next game. So...
- Pin up your own copy of our fixture list where you will see it
- Update that fixture list any time you find out about a cup game or a post-
  ponement
- Every week check where and when to meet – find out at training or ring the
  club secretary
- It is your own responsibility to know whether a game has been scheduled
  (there are always some rearranged games to catch you out). It is NOT the
  secretary's job to ring round twenty people. If you don't find out you can
  lose your place.

2. When you CANNOT play the next game tell the club secretary before the
weekend. He's not a mind-reader. This way we make sure we have eleven players available.

3. Training during the season will be at ....(GROUND) ..... (DAY)
.....(TIME)

Before matches
4. Always bring £... on Saturday morning – that's what you pay as your sub

scription if you play the whole match. The Treasurer is keeping records of who has paid.

5. If the game is away and you can bring a car, please bring it to carry others.

6. Always be on time. Why make the others wait? The times to meet will be announced, and you can check with the club secretary.

7. Remember to bring your BOOTS and SHIN-PADS – always compulsory.

8. Bring your own bottle if you will want water to drink at the match.

Team discipline
9. Act in accordance with very high standards of conduct, and encourage everyone else connected with our club to do the same.

After matches
10. Always hand ALL the club kit back after the game: shirt, shorts, socks. NEVER walk away in ANY of it 'to save time'. Stuff ends up missing.

11. Your turn to wash the whole kit will come.

12. Don't leave without letting the Treasurer collect your subscription money (£..../£....).

Kind regards,

(Club Secretary)

If you feel unsure of any of the details I've suggested in this letter, you need to give attention to them before the season starts. Clear messages make for a happier club, and the players will be able to concentrate better on their game.

Of course, you may not want to write long letters like this to your team, but there is probably some information that is best given to everyone in writing, such as their own copy of the fixture list.

NEWSLETTERS

I leave this to last for two reasons: you may not have time to do a newsletter, and it is not useful for passing on urgent messages. But if someone can prepare a newsletter, here are reasons for one:

- you can remind everyone of the correct time to turn up for games
- you can publish dates of rearranged games – for players to update their fixture lists
- you can print other results and your league tables
- players offering a lift to your matches may advertise here.

The club secretary will probably have enough to do without having to prepare a newsletter, so why not ask your team if anyone would like to have a go at it?

A LAST WORD ABOUT KEEPING YOUR SQUAD

This chapter has been all about keeping your squad together. This is not always easy. There will be unhappy members. No matter how big your squad, only eleven members will think the manager has picked the right team. Part of running a club is keeping everyone involved. A good system for getting messages around is part of that. Clubs can lose players simply because they feel out of touch – or messages don't reach them. Training sessions are also helpful in keeping your squad united. That's what the next chapter is about.

CHECKLIST

- decide on the best ways to get messages around your squad
- give every club member a copy of your fixtures
- give your members other useful information about your club.

chapter 11

PRE-SEASON TRAINING AND FRIENDLIES

The park football coach faces the same kind of problems as a professional, at a different level. How will he get his players fit? How can he develop their skills? And most of all, how does he turn this bunch of individuals into a team? This comes down to four areas: fitness, players' technique, team tactics and the players' mental attitude.

You can learn these things. This chapter is a basic guide to producing a better team. The end result should also be a happy team – the key to getting players to turn up for cold, wet morning kick-offs.

There are many books and videos on football training. I do not claim to have the authority of a qualified coach, and offer suggestions for basic coaching only. This chapter takes a realistic attitude to training in amateur football. Other coaching manuals take it for granted that you have one football for each player, and enough staff to coach players in different groups all at once. But the truth is, many park teams make do with less than half-a-dozen footballs, with only one person to do all the coaching. This chapter suggests how that coach can get the best out of sparse facilities.

It includes road-tested training techniques, many gleaned from the routines of Premier League clubs. Used sensibly, they should improve your players' skills, balance, fitness and understanding of team-play.

YOUNG CHILDREN

The training plan in this chapter is demanding and not intended for younger children, who would be bored to tears by it. For advice on training for children, including mini-soccer, contact the English Schools F.A. or read specialist books. The choice of coach may be influenced by considerations about the Children Act. (For more on this, see Appendix I at the back of this book.) Your County F.A. could advise on courses for coaching children. They are not compulsory.

CHOOSING YOUR COACH

A question for any club is: who is the right person to be in charge of training? You will probably make your General Committee responsible for that decision. You'll look for someone who has seen and played some football (at any level, not necessarily professionally!). In addition, some people have a knack for seeing the potential in a player, how well he will fit in with team-mates, and how consistent his performances will be. Others don't have that insight. Most of us only guess. What any coach can do is encourage and cajole players, to bring the best out of them. A calm and encouraging word can achieve more than throwing cups of tea at the wall of the dressing room. Only now and then is a rollicking really effective – and at amateur level you need to think twice before dishing out a rollicking to unpaid players who are there for the enjoyment of playing.

A coach will do things according to his or her own personality. Picking the coach or a manager means picking the right personality for your club. Of course, at many clubs the coach is also the manager. If you haven't appointed a coach or a manager yet, the next few pages should help you to get training started yourself.

top tip

Training should be fun for players of any age. Fun in training helps with team spirit. It may be a sign that something is wrong if players arrive at training looking unhappy, or leave unhappy. So keep training varied and fun, letting the players have enough leeway to enjoy it. You need discipline, too, of course, but not such as would impress in National Service!

A CLUB POLICY: WHO PLAYS IN MATCHES?

Here is a problem: whatever time you decide to train, there are always players too busy to turn up at that time. That calls for a club policy about who gets into the team – so that players know where they stand. Your club can make its own policy. Here are questions that might be asked:

- If someone always misses training, will you let him play in matches?

- Should people who turn up for training be first on the team-sheet for matches?
- Do you need all your players to train together?
- Should you have more than one session, for different people at different times?

If your best player doesn't train regularly, someone has to decide if he deserves to play or not. This happens just the same at professional clubs as in park football teams. It shows up because there's always a voice crying, 'It's not fair if he plays instead of me. I know he's a good player, but I turn up for training and he doesn't.' The 'who plays?' policy could be made by any of:

- the manager (it usually is the manager who decides)
- the General Committee
- a vote of the whole club at a meeting.

Ask members at a club meeting who should dictate the policy. Then make the policy, and announce it.

true stories

The story kept changing

Once you have a club policy, you have to stick by it. If you don't, players won't know if they are coming or going.

A friend of mine signed for a club where he was told it would be the players who trained every week who would be picked for the team. The manager said this and it was his decision to make.

My friend trained all summer with them. The week before the season started a new player was signed, and my friend was dropped. Players who hadn't trained regularly were also picked to play.

The manager had decided a better policy would be to select what he thought was a stronger team. But he did not announce any change in policy. Because what he saw wasn't in line with what he had been told, my friend left. He felt the manager had scrapped his principles.

Unlike many coaching handbooks, let's start with practical questions for park teams. When and where will you train?

WHEN TO TRAIN

You should ask your players at a team meeting when they can all train together. Four to six weeks should be long enough for pre-season training together. Much longer and players get bored; much less and they haven't really come together as a cohesive team. So you may wish to start training by the middle of July at the latest.

Ask players whether they can train together more than once a week. If only one session is possible, decide whether to train more with the ball or to do fitness work.

To keep fit, players should be able to train two or three times a week, but remember they can go jogging or go the gym on their own. It saves time if, before the team meets for pre-season training, players have been building up fitness in short runs for a few weeks. If players are not used to exercise, especially older players, it's a good idea for them to visit their G.P. for a check-up first. Fitness work should not normally be done every day – that can cause fatigue.

WHERE TO TRAIN

The training programme on the following pages is most suited to outdoors. Here are pros and cons when choosing where to train.

OUTDOOR TRAINING (A PUBLIC PARK)

PROS:

- you don't need permission to train on a public park
- you don't have to pay to use a park, so sessions of two or three hours are possible
- the park is always open – choose any time and day that suits you
- there is space for players to do different exercises at the same time.

CONS:

- you can't stop other people using the same part of the park at the same time
- you may not have portable goals with nets
- bad weather might interfere with training
- in winter, you can't train in the dark evenings.

INDOOR TRAINING (SPORT CENTRES)

PROS:

- you can have the place to yourself

- it doesn't rain indoors
- five-a-side goals are provided if you ask
- you can train on dark winter evenings.

CONS:

- paying by the hour means fuller training sessions are unlikely
- there is less space than in a park
- when indoors, lads only want matches, not training drills
- you can choose times only when the sports hall is not booked
- the hard floor and the hard walls can cause difficulties.

As for artificial pitches, my own opinion is that some outdoor synthetic pitches have more of the disadvantages (especially where slippery when wet) and fewer of the advantages over natural pitches.

The suggested length of sessions is two to three hours. This is subject to the age and fitness of those taking part, and you should apply your own common sense.

LET'S START TRAINING

Let's assume it's early July now... let's get the footballs out, and go through some suggestions for training. Writing in the real world, we're working on this basis:

- you've only got one training session per week
- the players have agreed to train for two hours
- you are training on a public park
- you've got about 20 players
- but your club only has four footballs
- you're in charge.

Beforehand, tell your players to bring:

- their football kit
- their football boots and training shoes
- their own football if they have one.

In addition, you as coach should take:

- a whistle
- a pen or pencil, and paper
- a first-aid kit and water
- as many footballs as you can.

As coach, try to be first to get there. Players don't like bosses to be later than them.

FIRST TRAINING SESSION

You don't have to be a qualified coach (and I am not) to understand my first suggestions: check that the field is clear of dog-dirt and broken glass; and write down the names of all the players who turn up.

If the ground will take a football boot stud, suggest to your players that they change into their boots before starting. Where possible, practise in the footwear you will play games in, to get used to how it feels when striking the ball. Some players train in so-called training shoes, and then change into football boots for matches – and wonder why the contact their foot has with the ball isn't the same.

For the first session, I suggest only a warm-up, and then – so long as the players are younger (and not too unfit) – let them play a short practice match. This will make the first session more fun.

A WARM-UP ROUTINE

This chapter includes only suggestions generally recommended by qualified coaches. One of the most important things for players to know is how to warm-up properly. Coaches must not push players' bodies too hard with unfamiliar tasks – too much physical stress can cause injuries, even in a warm-up.

JOGGING

A gentle jog to warm up is a good idea before stretching exercises.

STRETCHING

Stretching is very important and should not be hurried. I know players who will not spend long stretching when they have a short time to play, but they should learn to do so. As players arrive, don't let them go kicking footballs off to the horizon. Keep the players together, and get them warming-up at once.

You may wish to talk players through the stretching exercises, with instructions as below. Tell them to go at their own pace – it's not a race. Stretching should be gentle, starting light and slowly stretching the muscles more. Tell them not to do anything too quickly – and if anything starts to hurt, to stop doing it. (They can save tough guy stuff for matches.) The suggested routine starts like this:

Stretches for the top half of the body
- Breathe deeply.
- Loosen your neck by turning your head slowly.
- Turn your shoulders from side to side.

- Lean to the side, bending at the waist – then to the other side.
- Raise your arms and windmill them around.
- Gently roll your hips.

Stretches for the legs

- Take up a position like a sprinter on the starting blocks. Push your back foot further back, straightening that leg slowly. Bring your chest down towards your front leg. Stop, and do the same again with the other foot forward.
- Lie on your back. Keep one leg straight on the ground. Gently bend your other leg at the knee and gently pull that knee towards your chin. You can use your hands to pull your leg – gently – until your thigh is approaching your chest. Do the same with the other leg.
- Still lying on your back, keep both legs straight on the ground. Lift one leg off the ground. Keeping the leg straight and off the ground, put your hands behind the thigh. Gently lift that leg towards an upright position. Only lift your leg as far as is comfortable. After a few weeks you will be better at this.
- Stand on one leg with your raised foot behind you. Grab that free foot behind you. Keep both knees together, and gently with your hand pull that foot towards your backside. Do the same with the other leg.
- You should start to feel loosened up. Repeat these exercises if you want.
- Standing up, put one foot several inches in front of the other. Keep your back straight, and bend both your knees a little. Very slowly, bend the knees more. Keep your weight on the back foot and your feet flat on the floor. Stop if this is uncomfortable. Do the same with the other foot back. These exercises are for building up slowly over a few weeks.
- Stand up, both feet on the ground. Raise the heel of just one foot, taking the weight with your toes. Roll that foot gently around. Do the same with the other foot.

Take the players for another gentle jog for a few minutes. Tell them it's not a race, but they should try to keep up with each other – at the pace of the slower runners. For the jog, you could also give them extra instructions, such as:

- when you shout 'One!' they are all to jump together to head an invisible football;
- when you shout 'Two!' they are all to bend and touch the ground with their fingers;
- when you shout 'Three!' they are all to turn a full circle on the spot, and continue running gently.

As I said, it's not a race. It's all about suppleness. It's also about getting them all doing the same things. They are going to start feeling like a team soon.

After the run, give them all a couple of minutes to do some stretching. Ask them to check if any muscles need to loosen up, and to work on them. It's worth taking time to repeat any of the above exercises. After all, athletes might warm-up for an hour. Some footballers don't even manage five minutes.

THE PRACTICE MATCH

As for the practice match, this does two things:

- it creates a good feeling – it makes them like you for letting them play... before you force them to do unpopular training drills;
- it gives you a chance to see how much work it will take to get the team in shape.

I must repeat that if players are too unfit, you should skip a practice match and go on to easy fitness work, perhaps with the ball (see later in this chapter). Some professional clubs will not let players kick a ball in anger until they have spent weeks building up their muscles – because a pulled muscle sets a player back for weeks.

HOW TO PICK TEAMS FOR A PRACTICE MATCH

Whatever number of players you have, you can split them into two teams. During school days most teams were picked by choosing two captains and letting them pick sides. This is what some of your squad will want to do – because they like to be top dog, or because they want their best friend to be top dog. Do not let them do this. This is a terrible practice, because players first pick their best friends – no good for team spirit. It's hardest on players who are last to be picked – they feel unwanted and their confidence is damaged. Any team that damages confidence in its own players will suffer. When you need those players without confidence in themselves, they will not perform to their best.

Instead, look at the colours of the shirts all your players turn up wearing. Work out how to use these colours to make even sides. For example, it could be white shirts versus all the coloured shirts, or whites and yellows versus the rest.

Some of your players will hate this – because it will split up friends into different teams – and I'm talking about adults here, not children. Don't listen to them. You are building a whole team, not keeping little cliques happy. Do not let people swap sides. One team may be better than the other. Tough. Let's see what they are made of. Tell them that.

Once teams are picked, let each team select its own captain for the day. Give them a few minutes to organise themselves into positions in defence, midfield and attack with the players they have. Then start the game.

If a game is hopelessly one-sided, and rolling up sleeves won't make a difference, you can always stop the game after half-an-hour and pick new teams by different colour shirts. But don't give players advance warning of this. They've got to learn to get on with it, especially the losing team. I don't listen to teams who whinge when they lose practice games. They've got to toughen up, and learn how to dig in, harrying, positioning themselves to hinder the other team's attacks, tackling.

THE 'PITCH'

It doesn't matter in your first practice match if the teams are seven-a-side or seventeen-a-side. But it does mean you need to think about how big the 'pitch' needs to be. Public parks don't normally have football pitches marked out in the summer. Use common sense to decide if the ball is far enough away to be 'out of play' for a throw-in or a corner. Bags do for goalposts. Put the goals as far apart as you think makes sense for the number of players. If in doubt, make the pitch bigger for this first game. Let them have room to play.

You could just watch players to see which ones:

- do a lot of purposeful running
- run round like headless chickens
- take up useful positions
- just stand around waiting for the game to come to them
- can control the ball with their first touch
- pass instructions to each other, or remain silent.

You may wish to make notes. This will give you an idea of what training needs to achieve. Most players will be rusty after a long break, but don't worry at this stage. They will get better and better.

By the way, one kind of problem player to watch out for early on is the one who makes a show of drawing attention to team-mates' mistakes – of course he doesn't like anyone to point out his own mistakes. There is a place for honest discussion of mistakes, but this kind thinks he's the manager, and the coach and the referee, as well as a player. Deal with him honestly and firmly by telling him he can pass his opinions on to you after the match, but he can keep them to himself the rest of the time. His complaints may be made in the heat of the moment, or be a bad habit, but you can't let fault-finders ruin the team spirit. Team spirit depends on players backing each other up, not pulling each other down. Encourage your players; give them confidence. They can improve.

REFEREEING THE PRACTICE MATCH

This is what the whistle is for today. If you don't really know the rules of the game, ask someone else to referee. (To learn the rules of the game thoroughly, read the F.A.'s 'Laws of the Game'. You can find out in Appendix III how to get a copy.) Tell your players whether or not you will use the offside rule today. It will make life easier to do without it – you want to concentrate on watching what your players do, not watching for infringement of offside rules. Your players will probably want a practice match at training regularly.

THE WARM-DOWN

The warm-down after training sessions surprises some people who have never heard of it. This exercise is understood to get poisons out of your system, and to protect the heart. My suggestion is that a jog round the field once may do. Keep the players together – it is not a race, and sprinting defeats the good that the exercise is meant for. Players may slow down, and speed up, but not sprint. The really sensible players finish by repeating their stretching exercises too.

TRAINING DRILLS FOR THE NEXT SESSION

First, if the ground is suitable, suggest that players wear their football boots, as last time. Do the warm-up routines for as long as they need, as above.

Now for ball work. A lot of exercises done at successful clubs are surprisingly simple. To begin with, here are exercises that reinforce the old adage, 'Football is all about giving and receiving passes.' The simplest is the 'Clock'.

THE CLOCK

This is a good exercise for early in the session – it doesn't use up a lot of energy. No-one should pull a muscle here – the only thing to concentrate on is the players' control of the ball. One skill of the coach is how to get the whole team into a passing exercise with so few footballs.

All the players stand in a circle, except one player (Player Y), who stands in the centre of it. He stays in the centre. Keeping the ball low on the grass, he passes the ball to a player on the edge of the circle (Player 1 in Figure 1). Player 1 passes the ball straight back to Player Y in the centre. Player Y then turns and passes to Player 2 on the edge; and Player 2 returns it. When the ball has done the whole circle like this, someone else takes a turn to stand in the centre.

With everyone watching, this exposes who has a good touch and who needs to practise more. Tell the players they should need only two touches of the ball – one to stop it and one to pass it – but if they need to take an extra touch they should do so. The important thing is to have the ball under control.

If you have more footballs, split the players into groups of five or six and send them off to do this same drill in their smaller groups. Having fewer players in the circle gives them all more touches of the ball.

There are endless variations of the Clock exercise:

- tell everyone to take just one touch of the ball;
- or tell all the players to use only their weaker foot for a while;
- or you can make the players round the edge step backwards to make a bigger circle – to practise long-range passing;
- or you can bring the players very close together and make the passing very snappy to practise quicker control;

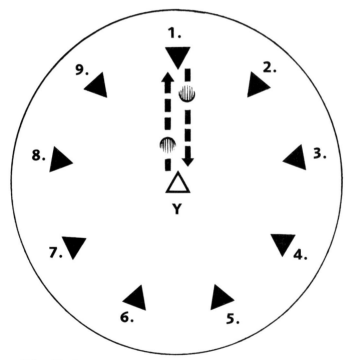

Figure 1: The Clock

- or tell the players to chip the pass into the air – but the ball must land at the other player's feet or chest;
- or tell the players to swerve this short pass with the inside of the foot – again, the ball must land at the other player's feet;
- or put two players and two balls in the centre.

Remember, with everyone watching, and doing this every week, players soon improve their concentration and the accuracy of their kicking. The Clock exercise is slow and soon becomes dull. But professional clubs will do this, or rather more sophisticated variations on it, for lengthy periods.

When people see professionals in a match give and receive a perfect pass every time, they wonder how they do it. It's simple. It's how they practise exercises like the Clock. In training they pass the ball to death like this until they are perfect.

Even doing all the different variations, ten minutes is long enough. Everyone has been standing around for a long time. I'd suggest you take them on another gentle jog. No sprinting yet.

the most basic skills

Here are some very basic questions and answers:

Q. What if the ball always goes up in the air even when I don't want it to?

A. Make sure the ball is next to your standing foot when you kick it. Not behind you, or too far in front of you. Lean slightly over the ball when you kick it, and push the ball with the side of your foot, not your toes.

Q. What if I always miss the other player with my pass?

A. Stop for a moment and look at your standing foot, not your kicking foot. Your standing foot should be pointing in the direction you want the ball to go.

THE POSSESSION GAME

Arrange the players in a circle, not too far apart. Put another two players in the centre of the circle. The players around the edge of the circle have to pass the ball to anyone else round the edge of the circle – but they are not allowed to move from their own spot. All that the two players in the middle have to do is win the ball off them – either with a tackle or by intercepting the ball – and these two can run anywhere inside the circle. (See Figure 2.) Whenever the passing is broken up, the player at fault has to leave the edge and go into the centre, swapping places with a person who has been in the centre.

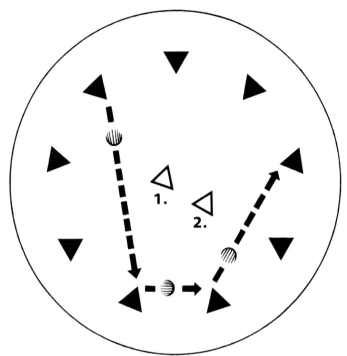

Figure 2: The Possession Game

This will show up who can pass the ball well under pressure. It will also show which players read the game well when they are in the middle – and exposes the headless chickens who run round but never manage to intercept the ball. The ones who know how to wait for a chance to intercept the ball and read the passing well may become good central midfield players or, if they are bigger in build, possibly good central defenders.

After a few minutes the players will be bored. If you have time for another jog, you may wish to do that.

Next, another ball exercise – in early training sessions I like to overdose on these, while players are building up their muscles. The tougher physical work can come a couple of weeks later, as their fitness improves. In the meantime, all these exercises should be improving their balance and their ball skills.

> **Q. What if the ball doesn't stop when it comes to me?**
>
> **A.** To stop the ball, turn the side of one foot to face the ball as it approaches. Lift that foot just very slightly off the ground – only slightly so the ball can't go under your foot. Keep your leg relaxed so it will 'give' when the ball hits your foot. If you keep your leg stiff, the ball will bounce away like hitting a wall. Cushion the ball with a relaxed leg. Most of all keep your eye on the ball, not your foot. And practise.

HITTING A MOVING BALL

Tell all your players to stand in a straight line, with one gap in the middle of the line. That means that you have two lines of players either side of this gap. Tell them all to face the gap. They are now queuing up towards the middle from both sides, and they are going to take turns kicking the one ball backwards and forwards across the gap in the middle, taking only one touch of the ball to do it.

Give the ball to one man at the gap in the middle. He passes to his opposite man in the middle and then turns and runs to the back of the line – leaving the man who was behind him in position to receive the ball back from his opposite number, pass the ball to the next man at the front of the opposite line, then turn and run to the back of his own line, and so on. (See Figure 3.) Tell the players to keep the gap fairly small. The ball is pinging backwards and forwards over this small distance in the middle.

Remind everyone to hit the ball gently back with their first touch, and then run to the back. Passing the ball back with their first touch means they are practising hitting a moving ball – an essential skill. Over the weeks they will get better at this. Don't be surprised how difficult some of them will find it at first.

Figure 3: Hitting a Moving Ball

KEEP UP

It is important for players to learn to control the ball when it is in the air, even if only slightly, because on bobbly and uneven park pitches the ball rarely rolls flat along the ground. Send them into small groups – each group with its own football. Four or five players per group is ideal. Each group has to keep the ball in the air, that's all. They can use any part of the body, except the arms and hands. (See Figure 4.)

This exercise will reveal that some players have developed their skills more than others. As players get better at it, vary it like this:

- tell them the ball must go round the group in the same direction all the time;
- or tell them they must each touch the ball only once;
- or tell them they must each juggle the ball in the air three times before passing it;
- or tell them they can only head the ball to keep it up.

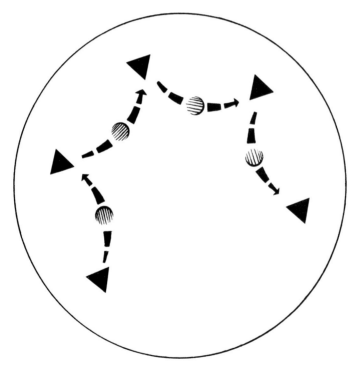

Figure 4: Keep Up

At professional clubs, simple games like this are usually played as little competitions. Anyone who messes up the routine has to drop out. The winner is the last person left in. If your players are beginners and need the practice, it's probably better if no-one drops out – just keep the exercise going for five minutes or so.

DRIBBLING

For dribbling exercises, you need something to dribble round. Coloured cones, are a good investment but you don't have to spend a lot of money on them. If you can afford them, around £40 will buy some 100 plastic cones at a sports shop. Alternatively, you might make use of some of the empty plastic food-tubs some of us throw away, a chance for some recycling.

Arrange obstacles in a line, and get players to dribble a football round them. The important thing is to keep the ball under control, not to race. The best professional dribblers are often not the fastest. They use their close control to create space. So tell the players to concentrate on keeping the ball under control.

TACKLING

Tackling is an under-rated ball-skill. It's more important nowadays – when tackling from behind is illegal – for players to be confident in the tackle rather than to shy away. Other coaching books will explain different kinds of tackles. An exercise that you can easily set up is this: have one defender in front of a small goal (or one defender in front of a goalkeeper and a larger goal). Play one striker against him. For this exercise, the striker must get past the defender with the ball to shoot on goal. All the defender has to do is stop the striker getting his shot in on goal. The defender should practise coming out to the striker and jockeying him to slow down his approach to goal, waiting for the moment when he can time his tackle successfully.

Instead of one striker and one defender, you could have two on two. You can also vary the exercise further by giving the strikers only thirty seconds to achieve their shot, after which they must move back and start again.

HEADING PRACTICE

The most popular heading practice at many professional clubs is 'Head Tennis'. This involves two teams either side of a volleyball net; the difference from volleyball rules is that the ball is headed instead of being hit by the hand.

If you don't have access to a net, here's another practice exercise. If you have four or five balls, give each ball to a player to hold. Line up those four or five players ready to throw the balls. Another player has to move along the line to head each ball that is thrown to his head in turn. He should aim to head each ball back so that the thrower can easily catch it. Your squad can take turns running in front of the line to head each ball.

You can vary this by moving the throwers further away, to make the player head the ball further.

A SHORTER PRACTICE MATCH

As mentioned, you will probably end each training session with a practice match. You should find half an hour enough, unless your training sessions are even longer than two hours. Five minutes will probably be taken up with picking teams.

TWO-TOUCH MATCH

A popular variation for the practice match is a two-touch match. Arrange a full-sided practice match, but tell the players they are allowed to touch the ball only twice during play before another player touches it, no matter what part of their body the ball hits. Once they have touched it twice, they will have to let someone else touch it next.

They need their first touch to control the ball and their second touch to pass it or to shoot at goal. If someone takes more than two touches, a free-kick is given against his team.

Some players hate this game. Tough. This is where good habits start to make a team. As a team, they must learn to think the same way about how to play the game, and they do that better by playing with good habits, such as two-touch, than they would with someone drawing lines on a board with a piece of chalk. Of course some players only want to practise their dribbling instead, but they will have to improve their passing and movement and teamwork too.

GIVE THEM VARIETY

You now have a set of exercises that cover basic ball-control skills, giving and receiving passes, hitting a moving ball with different parts of the body, and moving without the ball. What all good coaches do is mix and match such exercises, inventing new variations to keep their players from getting bored. No-one wants to do same every week, but they have to practise their basic skills to keep them sharp. That should still leave time for a practice match, and a warm-down.

GAMES FOR TRAINING SESSIONS

For further training sessions, carry on with ball exercises. Keep them snappy. You may wish to add tactical games such as the following.

KEEP-BALL GAME

First the playing area: you need a small area to play on, about the size of the 18-yard box (penalty area) or slightly larger – with no goals. If there are no marks on your park, you can use bags to mark four corners of your little pitch, and use common sense to say when the ball is out of play.

Tell your players to get into small teams of about five each side. It's best if they choose along the lines of the colour of their shirts. If you have coloured bibs to use, all the better. You may have enough players for three or four teams.

Six minutes should be enough for each game. Then one team or both can be replaced. Choose the first two teams to go on to the little pitch. The other teams can watch. The object of the game is for a team to keep the ball as long as possible; that's all. There are no goals in this exercise. In addition, give them this rule: anyone who passes the ball must run at once into a new space. (In this game, standing around after passing the ball is forbidden.)

And that's it. Start the match. Watch carefully. If you see anyone who just passed the ball not making a run into another space, tell him to move. That's the whole point. When he kicks the ball, he must set off into another space.

After a few minutes, you'll see players dripping with sweat. They need to improve their fitness now, and if they do it with the ball, all the better. After six minutes take these teams off and give the other teams a go. This game teaches players about both moving off the ball and closing down the space given to opposing players. It gets very competitive – no bad thing.

KEEP-BALL SCORING GAME

This is the same game, but with a difference. Tell the teams that you will count the passes, which can be long or short. A team gets a point when its players make six consecutive passes without the other team touching the ball. It's up to the other team to get it off them. That makes it competitive. Six minutes is enough, again. The team with most points after six minutes has won. Their prize is to stay on the field. Then bring on the next team to take them on. The winning team always stays on. If they draw, the last team to come on the pitch stays on.

Again, if anyone stands still after playing the ball, tell him to move. At this stage, it doesn't matter if he doesn't know where to run. What matters is that passing and moving becomes a habit. When it comes to matches, passing and moving will be second nature, and he can concentrate on where best to run.

FIVE-A-SIDE GAME

Five-a-side matches are a great way to improve the passing and movement of a team. A favoured routine is for the winning team always to stay on the pitch after a five-minute game. It makes winning worth something – it's horrible trudging off the pitch having been beaten after just five minutes – and is a great incentive to win. This increases the competitiveness – just what you want.

LARGE-SIDED KEEP-BALL GAME

Another practice game is to play a full-sided match with no goalkeepers and no goals. All the two teams do is keep the ball, as before. But they have to make 20 passes to score a point. The passes can be short or long. It's up to the other team to get the ball off them.

If the players are really good at this, you may wish to announce before they start that 30 passes are needed to score one point. On the other hand, if they struggle at this game, you may wish to make it 10 passes. Don't forget to count the passes, or they will get annoyed!

MOTIVATING PLAYERS

Games like these are important. Really, you are brainwashing your players until the pass-and-move game becomes natural and instinctive. However, some players will be lazy, and some bored. So let's work a little more on motivating them.

The question a lot of coaches ask themselves is: 'Should I be nice or nasty to my players?' A good coach will be flexible. You must get a reaction from players, either because they like their treatment by their coach – or because they don't like it and they want to prove him wrong. A good coach sees which players respond to encouragement, and which players like or need to be barked at since it helps their motivation.

Do you understand your players, or are their moods a mystery to you? If in doubt, don't criticise them heavily. They may not be motivated by it; they may just decide you are very rude. Encourage them instead of criticising. For instance, instead of saying, 'You don't try hard enough,' say, 'I'm relying on you for that little bit of extra effort.' The great coaches and managers probably know as much about human nature as do psychologists – they just don't have a certificate on the wall to show for it.

FITNESS

Motivation is especially important for fitness work. Only a few really enjoy it. For others it's hard work. Before pre-season training starts players should have been going for short runs. Short runs are better for footballers. But you need stamina too. So, a couple of weeks into training, consider whether a few laps of the field are in order. You may wish to do laps once or twice a week. That's for endurance.

What footballers do mostly is sprint for short distances. You should only do sprint training when players have built up basic fitness and they are well warmed up. The same goes for preparing for matches. When your team is ready, here are a couple of sprinting exercises.

Some players will always be faster than others. That's fine. You need different kinds of players for different positions on the field. Most defenders should have pace. Central midfielders should have endurance. That means they develop their muscles differently. But all players should give their own best at sprint training.

THE DIAMOND

Place four cones in a square about four metres apart, and a fifth cone in the middle of the square. The players do these runs alone, and take turns. They should start anywhere outside the square, then:

- sprint to the centre cone and touch it;
- turn and sprint to the first corner of the square;
- and sprint back to the centre cone;
- then sprint to the second corner;
- sprint to the centre cone;
- then sprint to the third corner;
- sprint to the centre cone;
- then sprint to the last corner;
- sprint to the centre cone;
- sprint out of the square.

The next player does the same, and so on.

This is tough. Players should rest before their next turn. After a tough exercise like this – which gets the heart beating faster – players should go next to a lighter exercise, such as simple ball-work. Later in the session they can consider another high-intensity fitness exercise, such as shuttle runs.

SHUTTLE RUNS

The dreaded shuttle runs come in the good name of fitness. Place five cones in a straight line at, say, four-metre intervals. Call the first in the line 'cone 1', the next one 'cone 2' and so on.

- start at cone 1;
- sprint forward to cone 2;
- turn and sprint back to cone 1;
- sprint forward to cone 3;
- and sprint back to cone 1;
- sprint forward to cone 4;
- and sprint back to cone 1;
- sprint forward to cone 5;
- and finally back to cone 1, still sprinting.

You may wish to make it harder gradually, putting cones further apart. Be warned: it's tough at first. Players will struggle to finish with a sprint unless fit.

Once you start these exercises, it may be appropriate to keep them up every week, but remember that players should not begin them until warmed up, and not do them if injured. It would be better for them to wait until they are coming back from injury. Some professional clubs use shuttle runs to bring players back to fitness after injuries – cruel.

You are going to struggle to fit everything into two hours of training. Once you have started the tougher fitness training, consider keeping it in the routine long enough to ensure fitness levels are maintained. This is to be fair on the players who have put in so much effort. If you need to save time, drop some of the ball-work from training.

GOALKEEPERS' TRAINING

Good goalkeepers should be easy to spot in any squad, but many coaches seem confused about what makes the best goalkeeper. The main qualities of a goal-keeper are: the ability to catch the ball, good positioning, good reflexes, agility and courage. But by far the most important skill is the ability to catch the ball. Goalkeepers should practise catching the ball cleanly as much as they do shot-stopping or goal-kicking.

Some coaches seem more interested in very tall keepers, or keepers with a powerful goal-kick, but these are far less important than any of the above abilities.

For catching the ball, keepers should practise: keeping their eyes on the ball, keeping both thumbs squarely behind the ball and spreading their fingers, and good body posture – which means staying on their toes, legs slightly bent, leaning slightly forward, head nice and steady, hands not too far apart.

TRAINING TO SCORE GOALS

Since it's the object of the game, this deserves more thought than some guides give it. When you have a kids' team, most kids see themselves as strikers. In their twenties more players think they are midfielders. It's up to the coach and manager to spot the strikers in your team. It may be obvious – you may have one player who keeps scoring goals. Most teams are not so lucky. So here are three things to look out for in training:

- a striker can control the ball with his first touch
- a striker can beat his man to get a sight of goal
- a striker can hit the target.

Defenders deny strikers space. So getting into position to shoot depends on having the ball under control in tight spaces. That means that with his first touch of the ball a striker can bring it under his control.

A striker needs a sight of goal to shoot at – which means getting past the defender who would shield the goal from him. Here are the three ways to beat a man: using superior physique, using ball-trickery, and finding space. Most strikers only have one or two of those three attributes – any one is enough. But that is where the best striking partnerships come in. Most partnerships combine two or three of these attributes.

A famous England striking partnership matched Peter Beardsley's ball-trickery with Gary Lineker's pace and ability to find space, giving England all three beating-a-man qualities in attack. Here's what this means:

- **Physique:** can mean pace, strength or height. A player with such physical attributes should learn to use them to get a clear attempt on goal.
- **Ball-trickery:** you can improve dribbling skills in training, but players with especially good balance will do best.
- **Finding space:** this means moving round the box, not looking for the ball, but for space, losing your marker. Teach strikers to gamble on a space, such as attacking empty spaces in front of the goalposts – again and again – each time gambling it will be the moment when the ball goes there. Patience and hard work has its rewards. (With the most natural player, the ball seems to come to him; he seems to appear out of nowhere. This is an instinct – virtually impossible to teach.)

When shooting, the more important thing than picking your spot is simply being on target. Strikers can practise this. Strikers should practise:

- shooting at a target (big or small) with or without a goalkeeper;
- shooting from all angles and from all distances;
- shooting with a moving ball and with a stationary ball;
- kicking the ball on the ground and kicking it in the air;
- shooting on the run and standing still;
- hitting the ball first time, and also controlling it first before shooting;
- bending shots and hitting the ball straight;
- shooting with power and just placing the ball.

You can't afford time in training for all players to do so much shooting practice, but everyone should do some. In an ideal world your strikers should put in regular hours either on their own or in ones and twos to do this.

TACTICS

You can use training to practise tactics. The training routine in this chapter is for a pass-and-move style. Other kinds of match tactics, such as the long-ball game, playing on the break, or set-pieces, such as corners and free-kicks, can be researched in other books – see Appendix III for some ideas.

TEAM FORMATIONS

How you create attacks or defend depends on the team's tactical formation. Sooner or later, players will ask what formation the team will play in. There are many formations and many subtle differences between them. You can pick up ideas from playing and watching football and from books and videos. There is no end to finding the formation that brings the best out of your players. For the uninitiated, here is a brief description of the most common formation: 4-4-2.

In this system, four defenders play in front of their goalkeeper. Two of these defenders work together as central defenders. These two are usually taller and stronger, and inevitably have to head the ball away from their goal a lot. The other two play nearer the left and right edges of the pitch as full-backs. These are a left back to the left of the goal, and a right back to the right of the goal. They are expected to join in attacks more than the central defenders, typically from positions near the edge of the pitch.

Further up the pitch are four midfielders. Again, two work together in the centre. Usually one is assigned to more defensive work and the other to more attacking work. The other two midfielders play nearer the edge of the pitch, one for the left edge, one for the right. They are often called wingers, and these are often the team's more skilful players. They are expected to assist the defenders behind them, and the forwards in front of them. They typically join in attacks from positions nearer the edge of the pitch, where there is more room to play in.

There are two forwards, also known as attackers or strikers. Ideally they should have differing styles of play, as explained in the section on strikers above. They should also be willing to assist the midfield players.

This formation is popular because it is easy for players to understand. When players work hard in this formation, they usually find that team-mates are close by wherever they are on the pitch. Typically, left-footed players fill the positions nearer the left side of the pitch, and right-footed players take the right side.

DEVELOPING THE TEAM

This pre-season training plan should get you started. But it is just a foundation. A new team takes a couple of seasons to find itself. So the team must work extra hard until it really begins to play as a unit. A good team spirit, and good organisation on the pitch, in whatever system, are the most important things. You must go on learning and developing your own team. You will spot your team's strengths and weaknesses. You will work out ways of playing to your team's strengths. Your players' thoughts and ideas will probably be useful.

Playing and watching matches live, including amateur matches, teaches you the game. Watching football on TV cannot help much. Some books on tactics and techniques are listed in Appendix III. These include training methods of professional clubs. If you study for an F.A. coaching badge, you could coach your team so much further.

LOOKING AFTER NEW PLAYERS

If a new player is at training, a simple thing you can do to make him feel part of the club is this: before training, ask a team-mate to be the new player's 'buddy' for the day. This can stop potential players feeling unwanted and drifting away.

IF ONLY A FEW PLAYERS TURN UP FOR TRAINING...

If low numbers remains a problem after following all the steps in this chapter, ask players for suggestions for what would encourage more of them to train together. It could be, for example, that training indoors, or in a different location, or at a different time will help.

However, if you still lack players at training, it may simply be that you have players who only want to meet on match days, something you may just have to accept.

On the other hand, low numbers at training may be a sign of problems ahead, and your General Committee may have to discuss the idea of advertising for new players. If the squad is simply unhappy, there could be many factors contributing to this. Good leadership is important. The coach and club officials have a part to play in making players feel valued. Chapter 5 has some suggestions on this matter.

BUILDING UP TEAM SPIRIT IN TRAINING

Have you thought of splitting your squad into groups? Having groups – let's call them A, B and C (although you may prefer more colourful names!) – is a way of getting players to talk to each other, including players who wouldn't normally chat. But don't let any cliques stay together. (However, with young children, you may want to let them stay with their friends to help their confidence.)

A, B and C groups could take turns to put the goal-nets up before matches, to take the nets down, and so on. This stops the lazy ones leaving all the work to the same few every week. You could also ask your groups to think of ideas for raising money for the club, producing more ideas.

TEAM TRAINING DURING THE SEASON

This chapter has described pre-season training. During the season, matches dominate everyone's thinking. If you can keep up a mid-week training session, you should. It will help to keep up the level of fitness. Choose some training routines such as ideas from this chapter. Always start with a warm-up. Never do any hard running before a warm-up.

On dark winter nights, you will probably want a sports hall or floodlit plastic pitch. In that case, playing five-a-side helps to keep the good habits built up in pre-season.

FRIENDLIES

Pre-season training should include friendly matches. It is up to you how many friendlies to arrange. If you play only one or two, the players will not be fully match-fit when it matters. Match-fitness means being mentally sharp as well as physically fit. This comes with playing games.

Friendly games are an opportunity, in a less pressurised situation, to experiment with your team. To know how to prepare for matches, see Chapters 15 and 16. Things you would like to take for granted during the season, such as having a pitch and a referee, can be as rare as gold dust in pre-season. So you need to plan ahead and be resourceful.

FRIENDLIES: PLANNING AHEAD

Most clubs arrange friendlies with teams from within their own league, because they have few other contacts. When it comes to finding teams to play in friendlies, it's first come first served. Some teams arrange dates for friendlies several weeks in advance. If you leave it till the last minute, you may find other teams are already booked up.

FRIENDLIES: THE PITCHES

Be warned that bone-dry summer pitches are a common cause of injuries. What's more, you may find you are not allowed to play pre-season friendlies on your home ground if it is owned, for example, by the local council. Ask them by all means, but if they say no, you need a plan B. Plan B includes these options:

- ring other club secretaries and ask if their grounds are available. If yes, offer to visit them and play a friendly. The availability of a ground tends to dictate things;
- hire a plastic pitch for a full-size match;
- play an informal friendly on a park with bags for goalposts;
- ask the head of a school or university for permission to use their sports grounds.

FRIENDLIES: THE REFEREES

Qualified referees often refuse to officiate at informal games since their insurance may not cover them in case of accidents. Club officials often end up refereeing these games. If that includes you, don't be fooled by the word 'friendly'. Players have been known to fight in friendlies. Part of pre-season is getting used to discipline again.

If you know the game well enough to referee friendly matches, it is up to the two clubs to agree that you can. Otherwise, ask both teams if they know anyone who can be trusted to handle a game. I know unqualified referees who have done a better job than some qualified referees, although this is rare. For more on being a stand-in referee, see Chapter 17.

FRIENDLIES: THE CHANGING ROOMS

You won't be surprised to know that you won't always have access to changing rooms for friendlies. That's why players have had to change in cars, behind fences, and in freezing conditions. You have been warned.

FRIENDLIES: THE KIT-BAG

Chapter 15: 'Match-day – all packed up' explains what should be in the kit-bag for a game, including such things as a first-aid kit. You will need much the same kit and equipment for a friendly. People tend to cut corners in pre-season games. Use friendlies as a chance to practise organising matches off the field as well as on it. Do take extra bottles of water to summer games, as there is a risk of dehydration for players when it is very hot.

FOOTBALLING HOLIDAYS

An alternative for pre-season friendlies is the football package holiday, for individuals and teams. For a few hundred pounds each, you could have a week or two abroad playing teams of various nationalities. Your County F.A. should have details of tour operators who sell this kind of holiday. Before playing foreign teams at home or abroad, ask your County F.A. to arrange for the various national F.A.s to give their approval – they normally need a few weeks' notice for this.

MORE ABOUT COACHING

For more on the F.A.'s local coaching courses, ring your County F.A. or the F.A. on 01707 671800. Organisations such as the F.A. Torch Trophy Trust offer some funding to coaches. The Football Foundation may also decide to put resources into grass roots coaching. Contact details are in Appendix IV. For children, there are Football Academies, run by professional and some semi-professional clubs. For more on this, phone your nearest professional club.

CHECKLIST

- ask your team members when and where they can train, and how often;
- decide who is going to coach the team;
- ask your club to decide whether players must train in order to play in matches;
- arrange training sessions and friendly matches.

part two
THE SEASON

chapter 12

COMMUNICATING WITH YOUR LEAGUE

Inside a club, a communications breakdown can have severe effects – Chapter 10 dealt with that. This chapter is about other crucial communications: a couple of phone calls that you, as club secretary, can expect to make regularly. It's at the heart of your job.

TWO IMPORTANT NOTICES

Two crucial messages concern match confirmations and team colours. These come under rules that are decided locally. Some competitions insist on the messages being sent in writing. Most leagues allow a phone call instead. Putting a message in writing (e-mail might do) helps to avoid misunderstandings. Ask your league secretary what is required. This chapter is based on the likelihood that you will make phone calls.

Some competitions insist that when there is a clash of colours, the home team should wear a change strip. In most competitions the away team changes its strip. If in doubt, ask the competition's secretary. You will see where all this fits in shortly.

These calls are effectively courtesy calls to ensure there are no misunderstandings. Normally these calls need to be made ahead of every match, all season long.

- **You ring the referee when you are the home team** – a few days before you play a match, the secretary of the home team rings the appointed match referee to confirm the date of the match, the time of kick-off and where the match is to be played.
- **You ring the secretary of the other team** – a few days before the match the secretary of the home team rings the secretary of the away team to confirm what he should already know about the coming match: the date of the match, the time of kick-off, where the match is to be played, and what colours the home team is wearing. (That includes shirts, shorts and socks. Remember to

check and report the colour of your goalkeeper's shirts too, in case they clash with the opponent's kit.)

If your league requires this message to be in writing, then it probably requires the away team to confirm receipt of the message.

WHEN SHOULD THESE CALLS BE MADE?

As club secretary, you need to confirm with your league secretary the deadline for making these calls. Some leagues say that the calls must be made at least four clear days before a match. Others have a different deadline. Of course, you can make the calls early – no need to wait till a deadline. In some leagues, teams may be fined for forgetting to make one of these calls.

THE TELEPHONE NUMBERS

Before the season kicked off your league secretary should have given you the phone numbers of the other clubs, as well as those of the referees. He should let you know if anyone changes their phone number. If you don't have the numbers make sure you ask your league secretary for them.

In some leagues, e-mail is becoming very popular for getting news and messages around in a cheap and quick way. Many leagues prefer their club secretaries to speak to each other. One risk with e-mail is that if you don't get a reply, you don't know that the message has been received – so you end up picking up the phone anyway.

WHAT CAN POSSIBLY GO WRONG?

By now you're probably wondering what can go so wrong as to be worth all this fuss. As a club secretary, you have in your hands the power unknowingly to destroy league officials' weekends. Where there are misunderstandings, they are usually about:

- whether the match is on or off
- at what time is the kick-off
- at which ground the match is being played
- what facilities are available at the ground for getting changed
- football strip colours.

But when you are focused on other things, such as trying to find eleven fit players for your next game, it's easy to overlook these two calls. That's when chaos can strike.

Friday night's all right for bedlam

A game had been postponed in one league. Let's call the home team Homer and the away team Traveller. A new Saturday date was set for it, some weeks later. On the Friday night before the rearranged match, it all went wrong. About 6pm the league secretary took a call from Traveller, worried at not having had the courtesy call from Homer to confirm where to turn up for the game. Traveller wondered if the game had been postponed again without anyone telling them. They'd tried to call Homer themselves the day before – but no-one answered. They worried that it was going to come down to their having to phone all their own players that Friday night if, after all, the game was off.

We reassured them the game was on, and promised we would phone Homer to tell them they'd forgotten to make the call to Traveller. We guessed at what was going on – we already knew that the new Homer club secretary was struggling with the administration work. So we wasted no time in ringing him. No-one home. We tried ringing the man who had been Homer club secretary before him. No reply. We began ringing round all the Homer players till we got through to one of them. We asked him if they were ready for the match in the morning. 'What match?' he said.

After ringing another Homer official it seemed they had not made the courtesy call to their referee either. And we know from experience that when referees don't get a call they think twice about turning up.

We explained to Homer that the fixture had to be played. It wouldn't be fair on Traveller to make them ring round all their players on a busy Friday night to cancel the game. Instead we wanted Homer to ring their players to get eleven together for the morning. The mix-up was down to the sloppy work of their club – so they had to fix the mistake. All this had taken two hours, but we couldn't honestly know for sure how things would turn out the next day.

On the Saturday afternoon I spoke to Traveller on the phone. All had not gone well. Both teams arrived at the ground. So did the referee. The only problem was Homer's groundsman didn't. No goalposts. So both teams had driven to a privately owned ground where they were kindly allowed to play their game. But now the referee had no intention of leaving late. So he told both teams they would play only 35 minutes in each half, making the game twenty minutes short. Given the circumstances, both teams agreed.

Homer won. We accepted the result as valid because both teams had agreed to a shorter game beforehand. Just don't tell Traveller all's well that ends well.

true stories

Who didn't read the fixture list?

Here are two teams; again, let's call them Homer (for the home team), and Traveller (for away), and they need a referee. On the Friday before a Saturday match, Homer phoned me saying they were the away team (I'm not kidding), and had been told by Traveller that there was no referee allocated for their game. They asked what we could do about it.

Under the impression that all the games had referees I immediately checked my match list. The mystery was solved in a flash. I told Homer, 'On the fixture list, you're not the away team, you're the home team, and you were supposed to call the referee yourself.' But Homer's secretary told me that they'd actually had the courtesy call from Traveller who had thought they were the home team. I told him to look at his fixture list. 'Oh yeah, you're right,' he said. 'It says here we are the home team.'

After phone calls to the parties concerned, I repeated to Homer that a referee had been appointed for their home ground, so they should play at home. They'd have to make a late courtesy call to their appointed referee, and tell their players to play at home instead of travelling away.

Homer agreed, but they were unable to speak to their appointed referee that Friday night. They did leave a message for him. Next (unbeknownst to us) the clubs made their own plans. Both teams were happy to play at Traveller's ground – and Traveller booked another referee.

On Saturday morning, with Traveller's referee at Traveller's ground, they played. Meanwhile, Homer's appointed referee – the one who was not by his phone the night before – went to Homer's ground, only to find himself the only person there. He complained to our league secretary who had to apologise and pay his fee for his wasted time.

Worried about losing referees to other leagues, we were not best pleased by the waste. The moral is not only to make the courtesy calls to the other club and the referee on time – but to check your information is right in the first place, and that you understand it.

You can appreciate the importance of courtesy phone calls. Some leagues say that if the home team hasn't made the courtesy call by the Tuesday night, the away team is to phone the league secretary by the Wednesday to complain – to give the league secretary sufficient time to solve the problem.

HOW YOUR REFEREE IS APPOINTED

Typically, you have your league secretary to thank for arranging for a referee to cover all your games. Sometimes a league might appoint a referees officer to take this work off the league secretary's shoulders. This is how it works

1. There is a Referees Association, which should have a Referees Society for your district. They will be responsible for notifying official referees in your area of the refereeing needs of different leagues. They will do so before the season starts.

2. A panel (a number of referees) may then be drawn up to cover your league.

3. Your league secretary (or referees officer) will contact this panel of referees. He will send them copies of your league's fixture list before the season starts. The panel will agree who can cover which games, perhaps making a plan to cover the first months of the season, and another plan later to cover the remaining months. Some leagues are more ambitious and try to cover the whole season with one major bit of organising. A few leagues have a week-to-week existence when it comes to finding referees to cover games. The more senior your league, the better the situation should be.

4. Before the first game of the season, your league secretary should normally send your club secretary a list of the referees for your home games and their phone numbers – enabling you to make those all-important courtesy calls. Your league secretary should also tell you what the match fee for your referees is, perhaps also that for any official assistant referees. If you lack this information with the season approaching, ask your league secretary for it.

CONTINGENCY PLANS FOR APPOINTING REFEREES

If only it could possibly all go as smoothly as that. But it's not a perfect world. That's why leagues also have contingency plans. A referee could become ill, cancelling his appearance at short notice. There is also a shortage of referees for grass-roots football, so some leagues do not have a panel of referees big enough to cover all their games every week.

For such reasons, there are – in some regions – emergency contacts for finding spare referees. If you lose your scheduled referee, your league secretary may be working on the telephone to find a referee to cover your game. This calls for patience on everyone's part. It will be very important for you to be able to receive any phone message from the league secretary.

If your league fails to provide a referee, there may still be a few options. These are outlined in Chapter 17.

DIFFERENT SYSTEMS

In a small number of leagues, the business of appointing referees to matches is done differently. One way is for each club to appoint referees to its own home games from a list of referees. However, this practice can lead to accusations that certain referees are 'homers' and is rarely encouraged. Another problem is that all the clubs may be ringing up the same few referees one after another – a waste of time and resources. Pity the referee at home getting call after call asking him to cover a bunch of games that all kick off at the same time – he is likely to feel that this is harassment.

WHO WILL YOUR REFEREES BE?

Referees are usually organised regionally, so all your home games, for instance, probably will be covered by quite a small group of local referees. As for what kind of referee you may get, referees are classed according to their ability and experience. Normally, the more senior your league, the more senior your referee.

You will find that some new referees are very good indeed, as good as some of their higher-ranked colleagues. Others may show their inexperience. How well they are treated by clubs may determine whether they stay in the game or quit before they've had a chance to pick up vital experience.

ASSISTANT REFEREES (LINESMEN)

Most amateur leagues do not have official assistant referees (linesmen) appointed. The clubs provide their own assistant referees. Some competitions insist that each club provides an assistant referee, and then fine clubs that fail to do so. In local park football, it is normal to see one person from each club with a flag, be it club officials or team substitutes, 'running the line' – taking the responsibility of assistant referees.

To prepare for this, your club may wish annually to appoint one or two members as its assistant referees (see Chapter 4). Of course, you need someone who knows how to apply the Laws of the Game – some players don't. Some competitions don't even allow substitutes to run the line. There is more on this subject in Chapter 17.

The most senior amateur leagues do have properly qualified and officially appointed assistant referees, and in that case, the business of making courtesy calls to them may apply (as well as paying fees to them). Check your local arrangements.

SUMMING UP

There has been one main message in this chapter: the home team's courtesy calls are the best barrier between your plans and chaos. They may save confusion and heartache for your club. On more than one occasion, a team has failed to turn up on match-day due to a mix-up over fixture dates, and had to concede the three points to the team who did turn up. Painful.

The safest thing to assume is anything that can go wrong will one day go wrong! Your league secretary will also be very keen for you to make the courtesy calls. You have the power to make or break his weekend. So often when others are out for their Friday evening, league secretaries are trying to make sure that all the matches go ahead as planned. In the next chapter we will look at how the courtesy phone calls fit with other jobs into a weekly routine for your Club Secretary.

top tip

Many league officials would agree: it's apparent from experience that teams that are most successful on the park are almost always the same teams that are best organised behind the scenes too.

It seems a club needs to be well organised for its team to play at its best. I can't really explain it, but we've seen it to be true time and again.

CHECKLIST

- for your home games make sure your league secretary gives you a list of referees and their phone numbers;
- ensure you have phone numbers for the other clubs;
- always check the fixture list to see if you are home or away;
- make the courtesy call to the referee (when you are the home team);
- make the courtesy call to the away team (when you are the home team);
- find out what is going on if you don't receive a courtesy phone call (when you are the away team).

chapter 13
A CLUB SECRETARY'S WEEKLY ROUTINE

As a club secretary your routine during the season is different from any other time of the year. The pattern of your day-to-day life will change to fit it. How you arrange that is up to you. In this chapter are suggestions you may find helpful.

The first half of this book was all about building your club. Now we're getting ready for matches. A routine will help you to:

- remember what you have to do
- stay on top of your work
- spread a variety of jobs over the week
- get through an eight-month season.

The sooner you have worked out a weekly routine that you can live with, the more you will benefit. This is not only good news for you, but for your team, officers of your league and other clubs that are dealing with you.

Of course, from league to league the timing for the day-to-day business will vary, not least because matches are played on different days, and deadlines can vary. My plan in this chapter is based on playing on Saturdays. If you play on a Sunday make the necessary adjustments to your timetable, but above all talk to your league secretary to find out what deadlines your league expects you to meet.

MONTHLY ROUTINES

Your routine may include things that happen once a month, in addition to weekly duties. For example, make time for going to a monthly League Council Meeting, or your own club General Committee Meeting (if you have them). You'll probably have a meeting of one kind or another to put into your diary almost every month.

AVOIDING BACKLOGS

Not every week, but now and then, you may have to sort out some extra paper-work from your County F.A. and your league secretary, such as to pay a fine or to register a player. Aim to do your paperwork as soon as you can. It's not rocket science – you just need to stay on top of it. (Remember gremlins breed in backlogs.)

AN IMAGINARY CLUB SECRETARY'S WEEKLY ROUTINE

For club secretaries, here's a typical weekly routine for the playing season. This could be any week. Even the first and last weeks of the season may be much like any other.

Monday: a day for getting messages round our club
If we have a game on the coming weekend, I make sure our players know where and when to meet. Need to get such messages round our club, and want to sort it out sooner rather than later. This should take some pressure off me later in the week.

Tuesday: courtesy calls – part 1
A match coming up this week means a deadline day for all those courtesy calls. For us that means today. So:

- if we are the HOME TEAM this week, ring the away team and the referee too. Don't give up even if no-one answers. These calls have to be made. Try, try, try again. And even if you have a left a message, try again to speak to the other person later.
- if we are the AWAY TEAM this week, I must be able to receive the courtesy phone message from the home team. If I have to go out, I must leave the answer-phone machine on to take the message from the home team.

Wednesday: courtesy calls – part 2
Don't forget, if the courtesy calls have not been made successfully, they are a priority. So:

- if we're the HOME TEAM, I should be trying again to ring the away team and the referee.
- if we are the AWAY TEAM and have still not had the phone call, I must get on the case – ring the other team or the league secretary to find out what's going on.

TRAINING: Our team has a training session mid-week. Wednesday is our training day, and I must spend part of the training session going from player to player, pen and paper in hand, writing down who will be available for the next match on the Saturday. This is also a chance to check on injuries, to see who is not fit, or who may recover in time for the next match.

Thursday: courtesy calls – part 3

If the home team still has not made its courtesy calls to the away team and the referee, this is now an urgent priority. Arrangements for the match at the weekend are in danger of falling apart over these two calls. Must ring the league secretary to ask his help to make sure it does get sorted out.

MAKING SURE WE CAN PUT A TEAM OUT – part 1: By now we have established which players are available for the game at the weekend. To give the manager a choice, try to make sure we have not only eleven players but hopefully a few more for substitutes. And if it looks like we may be short of players, it's time to act quickly to find our other players, ringing them up.

Friday: checking the kit-bag

Must check the kit-bag to make sure nothing is missing, from pegs for the nets to the players' socks. If anything is missing, now is the chance to find it before the match on Saturday.

MAKING SURE WE CAN PUT A TEAM OUT – part 2: If worried that this or that player might not turn up for the match, this is probably the last chance to give them a call. I must also phone the manager on the Friday night and use my notes to give him some idea who would be in his squad on the Saturday. Tell him any news of players missing through injury or whatever. (A club secretary often knows these things before the manager, through being in touch with people in the squad.)

Saturday: keeping the show together

Match day. Must be on hand to ensure everything runs as smoothly as possible. (Chapters 15 and 16 will tell you about what needs to be done on match day.)

TEAM SHEETS AND OTHER STUFF: After the match, have to send a team sheet off to the league secretary. If we are the home team, also have to telephone the match result to the league secretary. (See Chapter 19 for details on normal duties such as these after matches.)

Sunday

A day off in our League – unless it's my turn to wash the kit. (Of course, much park football takes place on Sunday rather than Saturday.)

what to do now

You need pen and paper and thinking time. Write a plan for your own personal weekly routine. You could copy the routine I've shown you if it fits with your team and the competitions you will play in. Of course that was just a sample routine. Your routine is bound to be a little different. As you get used to the job during the season, you can fine-tune your own routine.

A SECRETARY'S TYPICAL WEEK: Q&A

The other thing about a typical week is that something untypical happens. Here is where to find help on the sort of questions that might crop up during the season:

Q. **What if my manager wants to sign new players before our next match?**

A. Your league may have special rules to allow this. (See Chapter 5.)

Q. **What if the home team never phones me to confirm details of the game?**

A. Assume the game is still on, and turn up for the game. (See Chapters 12 and 20.)

Q. **Who can I ask if I have a query about the league's rules?**

A. Normally you should phone your league secretary, unless your league tells you any differently.

Q. **One of our players has been given a red card but wants to appeal against the decision. What can we do?**

A. See chapter 18.

Q. **We cannot raise a team for our next match because too many players are missing. What can we do?**

A. To find out about signing extra players, see Chapter 5. To find out about rules for getting games called off, see Chapter 20. But you will probably have to put some kind of team out.

Q. The other team wants the game called off. Should we agree to that?

A. See Chapter 20.

Q. The club is running out of money. What can we do?

A. See Chapter 6 for ideas.

Q. Some players with family commitments want to be told whether or not the manager will pick them to play this weekend. What should I tell them?

A. Discuss this with your manager and perhaps your club's General Committee if you need to – your club may decide to have its own policy about whether it can afford to tell players in advance whether or not they have a place in the first eleven. You don't want to find yourself short of players on match day when you've told players not to turn up! On the other hand, you may need to show consideration to people with other commitments.

Later chapters spell out the practical detail of your weekly routine as club secretary. But next is a dreaded subject: fines. Most leagues use fines to make sure clubs keep their act together. You are better off having an idea of what to avoid.

CHECKLIST

- plan your weekly routine as club secretary
- pin up your planned weekly routine next to your telephone – as a reminder to you of what needs doing.

chapter 14
HOW TO AVOID FINES

I'd be rich if I got a pound every time club secretaries have told me, 'We don't want it to get serious,' after their clubs have been fined. I understand their point. Amateur football is a pastime, a hobby, a recreation. Clubs are well aware that they are not professional standard, and they want to enjoy themselves. It's a 'gentlemen's game'. They'd tell you getting fined for not turning up for a meeting is galling. They don't want it to get serious.

Funny thing is, though, when they suffer because another club messes them about – such as failing to ensure the match referee turns up – often the same club secretaries expect league officials to take action to sort it out – and that could mean two or three hours on the phone trying to save a club's match. What is not serious for one club is serious for someone else.

The league secretary is usually there to help, but not to do the club secretary's job. Those league secretaries who get hassled generally prefer to fine clubs for not doing things properly, rather than let things slip to the point where they are spending two hours on the phone to make sure a match goes ahead. That's the rationale for fines.

WHO CAN FINE US

Your league and your County F.A. have the power to fine your club and individuals. County F.A. fines are dealt with in Chapter 18; so in this chapter I will concentrate on league fines.

FINES FOR WHAT?

The vast majority of fines are issued because of teams slipping up in their admin-istration, missing meetings, letting other clubs down by failing to make essential phone calls. Deadlines usually carry fines in tow. If you ever are late paying fees, doing paperwork, or making phone calls, don't be too shocked if a fine drops through your letter box.

HOW DO WE AVOID FINES?

Set aside time to read your league's rules. It may seem dull, but they should tell you most of the do's and don'ts. They won't tell you much about what fines or other punishments you get for breaking the rules, since these are usually set by the League Management Committee. But knowing what the rules are is a start.

Keep a pen or pencil to hand when you read your copy of the constitution so you can scribble notes in the margins about what the rules mean to your club. Your own notes will prove handy when you come back to it.

MAKE SURE EVERYONE AT YOUR CLUB KNOWS THEIR JOB

At a club meeting remind anyone with a job to do that your club could get fined if they let things slip. Explain that all the clubs are under the same rules. Ask your members to ring you if ever they need someone to take over their club duties. This gives you the chance to ask someone else to stand in for them, to get their work done.

AND IF YOU DON'T LIKE A FINE...

If you object to a fine, contact the league secretary at once. Tell him you want to appeal against the decision. Your league rules should explain what to do next. There should be a rule about how to make a complaint relating to your league. Typical rules are that you must appeal in writing within so many days, perhaps five. You will probably need to deposit some of the club's money with the league until the complaint is resolved. If you are not sure, ask your league secretary.

The main thing to remember is that you probably only have a few days to appeal. Speak to your own club's General Committee as soon as possible to give them a chance to discuss whether to appeal against the fine. If you don't appeal, don't delay – pay the club's fine before any deadline.

IF WE APPEAL, WHAT HAPPENS NEXT?

Many leagues have a sub-committee to hear appeals. Otherwise your League Management Committee or League Council will probably discuss your complaint to decide if they were right to fine you. They will let you, as club secretary, know their verdict.

IF THE LEAGUE HAS MADE A MISTAKE...

A question asked by angry clubs is this: if the league can dish out fines for mal-administration to clubs, why can't the clubs fine the league when the league slips up? I have yet to see a League Rulebook with the principle of compensating clubs for errors by league officials. If you feel this is a gross injustice, you could always raise it at your league's Annual General Meeting. That's where someone could propose an amendment to your league rules – and put it to a vote.

If you think a fine by your Management Committee is a mistake and does your club an injustice, you can still appeal against it to the County F.A. (and your League Rules should say just that). Ask your County F.A. to explain to you what you should do to make an appeal. Normally to start things off, what you have to do is send a fee to the County F.A. in advance of the appeal and write a letter to them (with a copy to your league secretary):

- explaining exactly what rule in your League Rulebook (or in the rules of the F.A.) has been misused by the League Management Committee
- saying in what way you think the Management Committee got it wrong
- saying what you want the F.A. to do to put things right.

WHY DO WE PUT UP WITH ALL THIS DISCIPLINE?

The pain of fines is supposed to have a positive effect for the smooth running of the league. Consider the problems Leagues face: on one occasion a club failed to pay its membership fees when all the other clubs had paid; other clubs failed to inform the League of their match results; others fielded ineligible players. There is no reason to assume that you will be at fault like this. However, for a fair game, with everyone competing under the same rules, you need sanctions to apply against anyone who thinks they can go into the season careless of the rules. That's why we put up with this system.

WHERE DOES THE MONEY GO?

The money from a league fine is paid into your league's bank account. That's the pot of money for running your league. Any County F.A. fine, such as for a player being sent off, goes back to the F.A.

THE MISTAKES TO AVOID

Remember first that league fines are different from County F.A. fines. To avoid league fines, it's typically best to watch out for the following mistakes:

Fines for home teams for: failure to make the courtesy call to the away team on time (before a match); failure to make the courtesy call to the referee on time (before a match); failure to tell the league a match result on time; failure to have two match quality footballs. Some leagues may also have fines for home teams for: failure to provide corner flags; failure to provide goal nets; failure to provide two flags for assistant referees. Fines for all teams for: failure to send a team-sheet to the league secretary on time; failure to submit other documents required by the league on time; failure to attend a Council meeting without prior apology; failure to attend the league's Annual General Meeting; failure to keep proper records of the club's money; failure to pay any due monies to the league on time; failure to be ready to kick off a match on time; failure to fulfil a fixture; failure to wear distinctive and matching kit; failure to wear numbers on shirts; fielding an unregistered player; signing a player when he is still signed to another club in your league.

NOTE 1: Each league has the right to set its own list of offences, and to set its own fines. Ask your league secretary for details of your league's system of fines, assuming it has one.

NOTE 2: There is no complete list of what you can be fined for. It is usual for any league to have the power to deal with unforeseen offences as it sees fit. Such power is normally at the discretion of the Management Committee. This rule is usually covered in the League Rules.

NOTE 3: Any League Management Committee normally has a right to seek permission from the County F.A. to suspend a club from all F.A. competitions, as well as from your league. This could be a club guilty of persistent misconduct in matches, for instance, or a club that owes the league a serious debt of money.

NOTE 4: Any fines normally have to be paid by deadlines. Your league should have its own rule about the deadline for paying a fine. Fourteen days is typical. Missing the deadline typically leads to another fine.

A SMOOTH-RUNNING CLUB

A smooth-running club generally will avoid fines. Here's a reminder of things you can do to keep your club ticking over smoothly:

- If ever you cannot do the club secretary's job for a while, arrange for someone to stand in for you, and give his or her details (name, address, phone number) to the league secretary at once. Also inform the County F.A. of this.
- Keep in touch with your league secretary – an occasional chat shouldn't do any harm. Consult him about any guidance your club needs.
- Do have club General Committee meetings regularly, and have meetings for your players to attend.
- Keep your paperwork in one place, such as in a box or a folder.
- Send forms to the league secretary – only send them to someone else if you are told to (such as certain County F.A. papers).
- If you are supposed to send a stamped-addressed envelope with any papers, do so.
- Make sure cheques are made out properly – for instance, when writing out a cheque to the league, write the correct name for your league's bank account.
- Ensure you have delegates for Council meetings who can be relied on to attend.
- If you have paperwork to do, don't let it pile up.
- Do check what deadlines you have for paperwork.
- When you are the home team make your courtesy phone calls on time – and don't give up until you have got your messages through.
- When you are the away team make sure you are able to receive the courtesy phone call from the home team.
- If you are often away from a phone, an answer-machine or someone to take messages would be valuable.
- Make sure your club is ready for matches on time.

ARE MEETINGS TAKEN SO SERIOUSLY?

Normally, going to the monthly League Council meeting is compulsory. Most leagues fine any club absent from such meetings without sending apologies. These monthly meetings are to be attended by representatives of all the clubs. Some clubs value them. Some see them as a waste of time. Ironically, the same clubs who miss Council meetings tend to be the same clubs that have incurred fines for slip-ups too.

Of course, mid-way through a long season, yet another meeting doesn't fill anyone with joy. Still, everyone wants to have the best-run football club in the country. So, as a reminder of what these Council Meetings are for, they are:

■ a chance to influence the direction of the league, such as on discipline
■ a chance to get up-to-date on your bills (take the club cheque book)
■ a chance to pick up useful local tips from other clubs' officials
■ a chance to use the meeting like a doctor's surgery for clubs' problems
■ a chance to ask league officials questions in public about how the league is run
■ a chance to air any grievances.

Sadly, many a club has been lost in mid-season – gone bust for this reason or that, for all their efforts. On occasions, we league officials have felt that if only some of those teams had turned up at league meetings more often we could have worked with them earlier to overcome their problems.

We often ended up in extra meetings, and spent hours on the phone, trying to keep a club going when all was nearly lost. It is in the hope of sparing clubs like yours from trouble, and sparing league officials more unpaid overtime, that I've spelled out how to avoid fines.

CHECKLIST

■ keep your club running smoothly
■ respond to any fine as soon as possible.

chapter 15

MATCH DAY – ALL PACKED UP

You'll recall all that kit and equipment your club bought during pre-season. However, on match-day it's easy to forget to bring a vital item – even the match-balls, the first-aid kit, the goal nets, or the goalkeeper!

true stories

When the away team drove to the rescue

One of our teams thought they were ready for a home game. The players arrived at the ground. But the manager didn't. And neither did the nets for the goal, because the manager had them too. There was doubt about what the manager was doing.

With little time to spare, the away team came to the rescue. It was only a few miles' journey for them to go back home and return with their own nets. So that's what they did, and the match could go ahead.

There were red faces all round. There was a stern inquest after the match about how a communications breakdown like that could have happened. Not the ideal last-minute preparation.

To avoid this kind of embarrassment, let's look at how to plan. On the following pages are checklists, one for the home team, another for when you are the away team. If you ever wanted a fool's guide to preparing for a match, this is it.

The time to use a home or away checklist is before the day of the match. The last minute is the worst time to look for missing items.

To be really certain nothing is forgotten, go through such lists before every game. Make sure you use the correct list, because the home team's checklist is different from the away team's checklist.

Alter these lists to suit your club. For example, rather than spending money on any half-time refreshments, you could ask players to bring their own refreshments. Players have differing tastes: at half-time some prefer to eat slices of orange, others a couple of Jaffa Cakes; some want to drink water, others hot tea.

A HOME TEAM'S CHECKLIST

tick	THINGS FOR HOME GAMES
	Have you made the courtesy call to the away team?
	Have you made the courtesy call to the referee? Is he coming?
	Can you field eleven players? (Seven players is the minimum to start a game)
	Are all the players you might use registered and eligible to play for your club?
	Do all your players and staff know when and where to meet before the game?
	Is your home pitch available? Do you have to tell the groundsman you're coming?
	4 regulation-size corner flags (or access to flags for home games)
	A pair of goalposts (or access to a pair of goalposts for home games)
	A pair of nets (or access to a pair of nets for home games)
	Net-ties/string
	Scissors/pen-knife (for net-ties)
	Tent-pegs (for nets)
	Complete home strip (numbered shirts, shorts, socks)
	Two match-quality footballs
	Football pump and adaptor
	Cash to pay the referee's fee (and any assistant referee's fees)
	First-aid kit (including a bottle of water)
	Transport to and from the home ground if needed for your own team
	Two or three copies of the team sheet for you to fill in

A pen or pencil to fill in the team sheet
An envelope addressed to the League Secretary with a first-class stamp to send your team sheet in after the match
A phone number for the other team in case of emergency
A phone number for the match referee in case of emergency
OPTIONAL – THINGS YOU SHOULD CONSIDER TAKING WITH YOU
A roll of gaffer tape (for emergency repairs)
A hammer for the tent-pegs
A stud-key
Spare pair of size 10 football boots (extra socks can compensate for smaller feet)
Spare pair of shin-pads
Spare pair of goalkeeper's gloves
Referee's whistle
If you have a rota for washing the kit, take it to check whose turn it is
If you have a rota for putting up the nets and goals, take it with you to check whose turn it is
Plastic bags for picking up any dog dirt off the football pitch
Mobile phone
Toilet paper
Refreshments for half-time

Having your own check-list to tick off should reduce worries. As you get accustomed to using these lists, you'll be able to prepare for games blindfolded.

There are a few things in there that I haven't fully explained yet. On the next page is where to find help about the contents of the home and away checklists.

The courtesy telephone calls	Chapter 12
Kit and equipment	Chapter 8
What if we don't have a referee?	Chapter 17
Have your players been informed that there is a game on?	Chapters 11 and 13
All of the team meeting in time	Chapter 16
Making sure your players are eligible	Chapter 5
What if we cannot raise a team?	Chapter 20
What if the other team cannot turn up?	Chapter 20
First-aid	Chapters 4, 8, 16 and Appendix I
A rota for putting up the nets and goals if necessary	Chapter 16
A rota for washing the kit	Chapter 19
Team-sheets	Chapter 19
Transport to matches	Chapter 16
Don't yet have a change strip?	Chapter 8

A REMINDER TO THE HOME TEAM ABOUT MATCH-QUALITY FOOTBALLS

FIFA has a rule on the exact sizes and weights that are permissible for footballs, set out in the Laws of the Game. In adult matches a size 5 football pumped up till its surface is hard will be just fine. Just how hard the ball is pumped up, subject to the FIFA regulations, is a matter for preference. A lot of players, especially goalkeepers, want the ball rock hard so that they can kick it further, whereas some skilful players may prefer a slight give in the surface of the ball to help them 'caress' and manipulate the ball with their foot.

Before kick-off, the referee checks that he is happy with the home team's match-balls. He will choose the one he thinks best. A referee has the right to report the home team to the County F.A. if they do not bring two match-quality footballs.

The referee may also report teams to the F.A. if they turn up for games without other important things, such as:

- properly maintained nets
- corner flags
- numbered shirts
- eleven players
- his fee.

Next is an away team's checklist – a few important things are different. Again, you may wish to go through such a list before the day of every away game. If there is anything you cannot tick off, it's time for action. And again, ensure you make any necessary changes to this list to fit your team's needs.

AN AWAY TEAM'S CHECKLIST

tick	THINGS FOR AWAY GAMES
	Have you received the courtesy call from the home team?
	Can you field eleven players? (Seven players is the minimum to start a game)
	Are all the players you might use registered and eligible to play for you?
	Do all your players and staff know when and where to meet before the game?
	Your usual complete home strip (numbered shirts, shorts, socks)
	A complete change strip in case it is needed (numbered shirts, shorts, socks)
	Footballs for warming up
	First-aid kit (including bottle of water)
	Maps for car drivers to find the ground if necessary (or an A–Z book)
	Transport to and from the ground for all your team who need it
	Two or three copies of the team-sheet for you to fill in
	A pen or pencil to fill in the team-sheet
	An envelope addressed to the League Secretary with a first-class stamp to send your team sheet in after the match
	A phone number for the other team in case of emergency

OPTIONAL – THINGS YOU SHOULD CONSIDER TAKING WITH YOU
A roll of gaffer tape
A stud-key
Spare pair of size 10 football boots (extra socks can compensate for smaller feet)
Spare pair of shin-pads
Spare pair of goalkeeper's gloves
Referee's whistle
If you have a rota for washing the kit, take it to check whose turn it is
Mobile phone
Toilet paper
Refreshments for half-time

WHERE AND WHEN THE AWAY TEAM MEETS

This is crucial. Ensure your players know where and when to meet. You can't afford to wait too long for them. Are they to make their own way to the away ground? Is there somewhere better to meet? Could they meet at a local landmark, your home pitch, or someone's home?

SUPPORTERS

One thing I have not put on the lists is this question: do your supporters know where and when to find the game? They're more than just an item on a list. At amateur level, where there may be just a few supporters, also make a little time to thank them for their valuable support.

CHECKLIST

- before each game, check if your club is the home team or the away team;
- use the home team or the away team checklist.

chapter 16

MATCH DAY – GETTING READY FOR KICK-OFF

This is the second of our two chapters on being ready for your next match. This chapter is about match day itself. If you've followed the plan in the last chapter, then so far you have made the right phone calls and made all the right arrangements, and packed all the right things in your kit-bag.

Surely now, at last, all that's left is to get out there and play football? Well, almost. What's left to do is to ensure that all the arrangements you've made come together on match day and aren't wasted by 'unfortunate circumstances'.

THE STAGE-MANAGER

Planning matches is a bit like putting on a show every week, and the club secretary is usually the stage-manager on match day. This can be difficult for him if he is also a player, because his attention will be divided between the match and the arrangements. This chapter makes it simpler. But if you've heard about how difficult it is to be a player/manager, be advised that being a player/secretary isn't much easier.

I would suggest that these are the main things of concern to him before the match:

- making an early start
- making sure the players have turned up
- making sure all the resources or equipment are ready for use
- ensuring there's enough transport for away games
- making available maps to find the away ground
- being diplomatic when problems arise.

true stories

Only two turnings when you come out of the tunnel...

Some teams don't bother to provide maps to get their players to away grounds. They play the game of 'follow the lead car' instead. You see them on match day, four or five cars snaking through the traffic. I, too, used to think this would do...

We were a park team in Liverpool crossing the River Mersey for an away fixture on the Wirral. We crossed in a snake of cars through the tunnel. At the tunnel exit, the road forks in two directions. You can guess the rest. We didn't see our team's right-back again that day. He drove some way before he realised he was not going to find the other cars again. To make matters worse, we hadn't given him a map in case of something like this happening. He paid his toll and drove back home through the tunnel in frustration.

To make up the eleven, the manager – still registered as a player with the club – put on a shirt himself and reorganised the team's defence.

For all away games after that, I photocopied a map showing the way to the ground, and handed it out to all the car drivers before we hit the road.

GETTING PLAYERS TOGETHER ON TIME

The question of an early start is a vexed one. In any club there can be players with outside responsibilities that mean they have to join your party later than the rest. Others just don't seem willing or able to turn up on time.

This becomes a problem for the manager. I've been in changing rooms when the manager thinks he's decided on his team half an hour before kick-off, based on availability, only to see a few more players wander in minutes later. After a little heart-searching, he decides on what he thinks could be an even better starting eleven. Then, just before kick-off, another late-comer arrives with his boots, putting the manager under pressure to change his mind again.

How can you solve this problem? One idea you might think about is using cut-off times. Here are two such suggestions.

CUT-OFF TIMES FOR MEETING UP

I believe this is a must for away games – when you will probably wait for the team at a meeting place – before travelling to the away ground. Give all your players advance warning that they have only until such and such a time to reach an arranged meeting point, or the team will leave without them.

When one of my old clubs had to travel even just a few miles to away games, for a 10.30 am kick-off, we asked players to meet at 9.15 and agreed a cut-off time of 9.30 am. That's when the cars left our meeting place and hit the road. Anyone arriving after that had to make their own way to the match, or miss out.

This helps to stop the rest of the team being held up by one or two late-comers. Some clubs use the same idea for home matches too.

CUT-OFF TIME FOR ANNOUNCING THE TEAM

A useful idea for home and away games is to tell all your players that the team will be announced 15 minutes before kick-off – with or without them. Warn them that if they arrive after the cut-off time, the best they can hope is to be a substitute.

Then at least everyone knows where they stand. The ones who make the effort to turn up on time aren't galled by a late-comer getting into the team ahead of them. Even some professional clubs use this idea to keep their highly-paid stars in line. It's one way of the right thing being 'seen to be done'.

Some players won't like this policy. I know of a late-comer who arrived minutes before kick-off one day to find himself left out of the team and not even a substitute. He didn't agree with the policy and refused to play for the club again.

ANOTHER TIME-SAVER

To save players waiting to hear what shirt numbers to wear, here's an idea. As soon as you decide your first eleven, write it on a team-sheet, and pin it to the changing room wall. Then your players can see it as soon as they come in to get changed.

ALLOW TIME FOR THE UNEXPECTED

Almost everything takes longer than you think it will. It could simply be time to walk to your pitch, especially where players trek across a dozen or more pitches to reach their own. Players are not robots, and don't necessarily come in for the team-talk when you tell them. It can take five minutes just to get the team all sat down in one room. If you don't leave enough time, the thing that usually gets missed out is a proper warm-up.

THE WARM-UP

Some players warm-up sensibly before a match. As some players don't, you may need to instruct them. You may wish to use the warm-up routine from Chapter 10, finishing it off with one of the ball-work exercises from the same chapter. The colder the weather, the longer players need to warm-up. Try to ensure that all the first eleven, together with the substitutes who may be needed early, warm-up properly, so that no-one starts the game cold. And don't let over-eager players blast the ball fifty yards before they warm-up – tell them to avoid pulling muscles this way.

CONSIDERATIONS FOR THE HOME TEAM

THE REFEREE IN THE BUILD-UP TO THE MATCH

When you are the home team, look out for the referee to arrive. If it's less than half-an-hour to kick-off and the referee is still missing, everyone starts to worry. I'll explain what happens if the referee fails to turn up later (Chapter 17). Bring the referee's phone number with you in case he is late. This used to mean a trek to the nearest public phone box, but nowadays there should be at least one person from the two sides with a mobile phone, a real time-saver.

Make sure there will be cash for the referee to get his fee – in some competitions, payable before the match (perhaps to avoid a confrontation after the match). Some competitions require the referee to collect his fee after the match.

Give the referee the match-balls (to check their quality) long before kick-off. Some competitions then expect that you will leave the match-ball with the referee to bring out ready for the kick-off.

ASSISTANT REFEREES (LINESMEN)

If you have official assistant referees (or one person from each club running a line with a flag) introduce the referee to them a few minutes before kick-off. He will need to let them know how much he expects them to do.

COPIES OF THE TEAM-SHEET

Depending on the rules of the competition you are in, the referee may require a copy of the team-sheet before kick-off, but all he may want to see written on it are names and shirt-numbers. The referee will need to know the names of all the substitutes – if a substitute's name isn't on that list, the referee can refuse to let him play. Some competitions also require that you give the opposition your team-sheet before kick-off. Chapter 19 has more on team-sheets.

PUTTING UP GOAL-NETS

If you have to fix the goals on the nets, you want the nets flush to the posts and the ground all the way round. You don't want glaring gaps for the ball to fly through – this defeats the object of nets. Nor do you want the goalkeeper snagged in them. There follows a four-point fool's guide. You need nets, ties (string), scissors for the string, tent-pegs, and possibly a mallet to hit the pegs. I'm assuming that the goalposts are already upright, and to reach the crossbar you either have a very tall player, or a chair or stepladder, or someone sitting on someone else's shoulders.

1. THE NETS

First, make sure the net is the right way up. (The top of the net to be tied to the crossbar is narrower than the bottom to be pegged to the ground.)

2. THE CROSSBAR

Fix the nets to the crossbar first. If the crossbar has no hooks, use ties, and here's one way to use them (terminology: the 'front' of the posts faces the other goal). Hold the net behind the goal. Pass the top of the net over the crossbar and pull it down the front of the bar. Wrap the net round the bar. To secure it, tie the top of the net to the back of the net under the bar. You don't get more secure than that. Half a dozen ties along the bar should do. If you do it this way, don't blame me for the wear and tear on your net – it's your choice.

If you have a square crossbar, it may help to hook the net round the corners at both ends of the bar. This will make it more secure at the top. Again this adds to wear and tear – your choice.

Now the net is hanging down from the bar. Next to do: fasten it to the upright posts.

3. THE TWO UPRIGHTS

Tying the nets to the post is similar to tying them round the bar. Holding the edge of the net at the side of the goal, pull the net round the outside of a post so that it is wrapped round the post. Use a few ties down each post – instead of tying the net to the post, tie one bit of net to the other behind the post, so that it is really wrapped right round the post. It is important to have a tie near the foot of each post too, stopping the net from flapping and people from tripping over it.

4. THE TENT-PEGS

Tent-pegs secure the net flush to the ground. Do this all the way round, including the side netting and by the foot of each upright. The net doesn't have to be pulled back as tight as a tennis racket – better looser. I've seen the ball hit a taut net and bounce straight out, needing a sharp-eyed referee to say it hit the net and not a player.

Teams seem to run out of pegs every season (losing a couple each week in the mud). Keep an eye on how many pegs are left, stocking up if need be. I've seen teams fix down the back of the net with heavy objects such as bags instead of pegs. Ensure that neither objects nor a loose net present any risk of tripping or injury.

The referee checks the nets before kick-off, and will tell you if he wants them fixed better. In the more senior leagues, he will ask his assistant referees to check the nets for him.

TAKING TURNS TO DO THE NETS

In many teams, every week the same few members do the work of putting up and taking down the nets. It isn't fair in the freezing rain when your fingers go numb doing the ties. What can you do about this? Chapter 11 suggested you form three separate groups in training. You could instruct these groups to take turns to put up the nets at home games. Write down a rota for them and take it to each home game, to remind each group whose turn it is.

There are many little things to be done before kick-off. So next are suggestions for pre-match routines and likely running times, building up to a kick-off at 2.00 pm. This plan should give you an idea of much time you need to allow, for any kick-off time. If in doubt, leave more spare time, within reason. Home and away games need a different length of time to prepare.

TASK SCHEDULE FOR HOME GAMES (2.00 PM KICK OFF)

HOME TEAM: Allow an hour and twenty minutes to get ready for kick-off. Players should be at the ground more than an hour before kick-off. This is asking a lot. But there is a lot to do. You don't want to squeeze out time for the warm-up.

12.40	▪ manager and secretary arrive at home ground and make sure the changing rooms are open and ready for both teams, checking that hot water is running and the toilets have toilet paper
	▪ put the kit into the changing rooms ready for the players
	▪ check with the groundsman which pitch you are on today
	▪ check pitch markings are clear to see (if not, gently ask the groundsman to mark them out again)
	▪ go over the pitch removing any dog dirt, glass or cans, etc.
12.45	▪ the players are due to arrive at the home ground
	▪ final check that all the kit and equipment is ready for use
1.00	▪ players put the nets up on the goals and the corner flags on the pitch
1.15	▪ make sure match balls are fully pumped up
	▪ players are still arriving
	▪ players are getting changed and ready to warm-up
	▪ secretary shows visiting team to their changing rooms
1.30	▪ referee arrives (and any assistant referees)
	▪ half-hour before kick-off is the usual deadline for both teams to be at the ground (the referee may report teams who are late)
	▪ players are still arriving
	▪ players warm-up on the pitch
	▪ manager is deciding on his team selection
1.40	▪ players return to changing rooms
	▪ ask if any player has an injury (an injured player might want to play but it's safer to avoid it, and so any suggestion of responsibility for it)
	▪ if any players are on medication, allow them to administer this to themselves

1.45	■ manager announces his team
	■ players put on the numbered shirts as the manager tells them
	■ club secretary writes the names next to the numbers on team-sheet
	■ referee and opposition given a copy of the team-sheet, if required
	■ referee checks that the two match-balls are of the required standard; if he's unhappy in any way, he'll tell you what he wants you to do
	■ substitutes put track-suits back on over their shirts
	■ players reminded to remove any jewellery that could cause injury
1.50	■ manager gives his team-talk
1.55	■ if the club provides assistant referees, introduce them to the referee and make sure they have flags
	■ referee lets you know if he wants the goal-nets fixed any better
	■ players on pitch to finish warming-up
1.58	■ club captains meet for the toss of the coin on the pitch
2.00 pm	■ kick off

Of course, much of this will take care of itself. Players know what to do; they just need a reminder sometimes to get on with it. Why not copy this task schedule to use as a reminder on match days?

TASK SCHEDULE FOR AWAY GAMES (2.00 PM KICK OFF)

AWAY TEAM: The biggest difference for away games is the time taken transporting a whole team, probably in cars. Allow time for delays in traffic.

12.00 noon	■ manager and secretary arrive at agreed meeting place ■ final check that all the kit and equipment is ready for use
12.15	■ the players are due to arrive at the meeting place ■ check you have enough transport for all the players ■ supporters check they have enough transport too
12.20	■ send a car to check on any players who are missing
12.30	■ if there are enough players, get in the cars ■ give maps to drivers to find the away ground
12.35	■ the cars set off
1.10	■ park cars at/near the away ground
1.15	■ meet other club's officers to show you have arrived
1.20	■ go into the changing rooms ■ players start getting changed and ready to warm up
1.30	■ manager is deciding on his best team on the day ■ players begin their warm-up routines on the pitch ■ half-an-hour before kick-off is the usual deadline for both teams to be at the ground (the referee may report teams who are late)
1.40	■ players return to changing rooms ■ ask if any player has an injury (to cover your club against any later accusation that you forced an injured person to play) ■ if any players are on medication, allow them to administer it to themselves

1.45	■ manager announces his team
	■ players put on the numbered shirts as the manager tells them
	■ club secretary writes the names next to the numbers on team-sheet
	■ give the referee a copy of the team-sheet
	■ substitutes put track-suits back on over their shirts
	■ remind players to remove any jewellery that could cause injury
1.50	■ manager gives his team-talk
1.55	■ if the club provides an assistant referee, introduce him to the referee and make sure both assistants have flags
	■ players on pitch to finish warming-up
1.58	■ your club captain meets for the toss of the coin on the pitch
2.00 pm	■ kick off

You may want to copy this task schedule to use as a reminder on match days.

TEAM-TALKS

How the manager or coach gives his team-talks before the match and at half-time is a matter of individual style. Some managers are able to use a quiet word forcefully to get the best out of players. Others rant and rave, which can have a negative effect.

Team-talks might be given in the changing rooms or on the pitch. Often there is no time to say more than, 'Go out and enjoy yourselves.' (The length of the half-time break is usually set by the rules of the competition you play in.) The most important thing is that each player is told what position in the team he must play. Players should also be put in a positive frame of mind, convinced that they can perform well as a team. They should be reminded to have respect for each other, the opposition and officials.

Team-talks will benefit as the manager gets more familiar with the abilities of his players and of opposing teams, and as his knowledge of tactics grows. You never stop learning, and every game reveals new things. It's normal for players to contribute suggestions for how to overcome the opposition. They should be encouraged to keep comments brief, and leave decisions to the manager. Otherwise confusion spreads among players. Generally, it is not a good idea to make a lot of unexpected changes to tactics, since this is also apt to cause confusion in the team.

Good tactics and team-talks make a difference to team performance. But it is up to the players to fulfil their potential. A good manager recognises when his team has done the best it can, and if they are beaten by a better team it could be that no-one is to blame. The individuals and the team just have to keep improving.

FIRST-AID

You should have a first-aid kit (see Chapter 8). You should also have an appointed first-aider (see Chapter 4). If you have more than one team, that means a first-aider on hand whenever each team plays.

However, this book is not the place to teach first-aid. Your club has a responsibility to see that someone is trained on a first-aid course. Any such course should detail the basics of first-aid for football, covering what to do in the case of cuts and grazes, broken or dislocated limbs, shock, dirt in a player's eye, or a player who is unconscious.

Here are a few guidelines on what to avoid concerning injuries in normal circumstances:

- Don't use dirty water or a dirty sponge – the days of using the same bucket of water all through a match are gone – because infections can be passed through water. A bucket of water, if used at all, should be emptied and refilled each time anyone makes use of it.
- Don't let someone with dirty fingers touch a cut or an open wound. There should be sterile gloves and a padded sterile dressing in your first-aid kit.
- If a player gets something in his eye, don't rub it, and don't use tweezers.
- Don't move a broken or dislocated limb. Leave the player right where he is. The match can wait. Send for an ambulance or a doctor at once.
- If a player may need an operation very soon, don't give him anything to eat or drink.
- If a player is unconscious, don't waste a second, since time saved can mean a life saved. A proper first-aid course will instruct in the different procedures for resuscitation.
- If a player gets a head injury, don't let him play or train again until a doctor

has told him that it is safe to do so.

■ Don't use a 'magic spray' on an injury to enable someone to play on. Players make injuries worse by playing on. The magic spray only takes the pain away – but it leaves the injury there, and it's easy to do more damage. If a player cannot play on without the spray, then he should leave the pitch.

INSURANCE AND LIABILITY

If ever there's a serious injury, write down the circumstances of the injury as soon as possible. If anyone wants to make a claim on your club's Personal Accident Insurance (assuming you have arranged some) then a written account of the incident may be important for the claim. Do not forget to notify the insurers as soon as possible.

If for some reason anyone asks you or your club to admit liability for an accident, don't feel you have to reply straight away, as this could have legal implications. It may be safer to seek advice from your insurers and a solicitor before you say anything. It is safer to let the person give you some contact details and get in touch with them with your answer after you have taken advice, and found out what liability means in the situation.

QUESTIONS AND ANSWERS FOR MATCH DAY

Q. What if the referee doesn't turn up?
A. See Chapter 17.
Q. What if the other team doesn't turn up?
A. Ring a contact number, if you have one, to find out where they are. Your team stays at the ground until the referee abandons the game. The referee's decision is final.
Q. What if we are going to be late to the ground?
A. Try to send a message ahead by phone, and try to get at least seven players (one of them as a goalkeeper) to kick-off the match on time. The referee can abandon the match if you are late.
Q. What if we don't have eleven players?
A. If you have at least seven players – and one of them must wear the goalkeeper's shirt – you have enough to start the game. With fewer than seven, the referee can abandon the game and send a report to the County F.A. See Chapter 20.
Q. What if some of our players turn up after the kick-off?

A. The referee shouldn't let players play unless they are on the team-sheet at the start. If they are named on the team-sheet, late-comers can join in to make up the numbers after kick-off. The referee will signal when they can enter the game.

Q. Does it matter what numbers the players wear?

A. No, but it matters that the numbers they wear are on the team-sheet by their names.

Q. What if the pitch is waterlogged?

A. If the groundsman opens the ground, then it's up to the referee alone to decide if the pitch is playable. He might ask an opinion, but his decision is final.

Q. What if I've forgotten the money to pay the referee?

A. As home team, it is your job to pay him. Borrow if you have to. If there really is no money to hand, ask the referee for an address where you can send his money.

Q. What if my first-aider doesn't turn up?

A. Ask the other team politely if their first-aider would be prepared to help if needed.

CHECKLIST

- remind players when and where to meet before the match
- agree a cut-off time for setting off to away grounds
- agree a cut-off time for late-comers to be included in the team
- make sure someone has been appointed to pick the team and give team-talks
- on match day, make sure your club completes its tasks before kick-off
- make sure you know who your first-aider is.

chapter 17

THE MATCH – REFEREES AND THE LAWS OF THE GAME

This chapter is about how to deal with match officials and the Laws of the Game, and what to do if there is no referee on match day. Details of how referees are normally appointed to matches were set out in Chapter 12.

ASSISTANT REFEREES (LINESMEN)

In local park football it is normal to see one person from each club with a flag, be they club officials or team substitutes 'running the line'. They are taking the responsibility of assistant referees. Chapter 4 mentioned that you may wish to prepare for this by having your club appoint its own assistant referees, ones who know how to apply the Laws of the Game. Of course some players don't, and in any event some competitions don't allow substitutes to run the line anyway.

WHAT THE REFEREE EXPECTS OF ASSISTANT REFEREES

Referees expect less from assistant referees provided by clubs than they would from official assistant referees. A referee can use his discretion to decide how much responsibility he should place upon the assistant referees he is presented with.

It may be that an inexperienced assistant referee will be asked to signal only when the ball goes out of play, and possibly to signal offsides. A copy of the Laws of the Game will show how the flag is to be held for these different signals. Assistant referees should remember that the referee's word is final.

They must also remember to cover up their football kit during the game, to avoid confusion.

MEETING THE REFEREE IN THE MATCH BUILD-UP

When you are the home team keep an eye open for the referee to arrive. When it's less than half-an-hour to kick-off and the referee is still missing, worry spreads as to whether he will make it on time. Have his phone number with you in case he is late.

Greet him when he arrives, make him feel welcome, introduce him to the assistant referees, give him the match-balls, and – if required by the competition – give him a team sheet before kick-off, showing the names of all eleven players plus substitutes. Some competitions require that each club has its own completed team-sheet signed by the referee after the match.

MAKE SURE THE REFEREE GETS HIS FEE

Often it is after the game that the referee receives his fee. Some referees expect payment before the game – either because of local rules, or to avoid a confrontation after the match. Ask your league secretary what you should do. Don't forget to ask the referee to sign a receipt book to say he's received his money. In some leagues, the referee is also paid his travelling expenses by the home club.

THE GAME NEEDS ITS REFEREES

Without a referee there is no game. But many amateur leagues are struggling to keep enough referees. Experienced referees of real quality seem fewer and fewer in lower leagues. As quickly as new referees get their badges, others quit. The problem is that referees are often undervalued and abused. They don't think it worth the hassle.

By encouraging your players to show respect to referees, you do a world of good. Referees are not big game for the great hunter. Of course some players cannot seem to get on with referees. Some people just can't bear anyone telling them they're in the wrong.

CAUSES OF CLASHES WITH MATCH OFFICIALS

If your players show poor discipline towards officials, you need to identify the nature of the problem. Your club has a responsibility for the behaviour of its players. This subject is dealt with more fully in the next chapter. Here are four reasons why players clash with officials.

RESPECT AND DISRESPECT

There is a thin line between saying referees ought to be able to take stick, and saying, 'We ought to give the referee stick.' That is the line between respect and disrespect. Of course some players will argue with referees, but the player who gets himself booked for dissent needs to correct his behaviour.

In effect, the referee is always right – even when he's wrong. A referee is allowed to change his mind, but rarely does. He knows if he lets the players tell him what decision to make he will lose their respect – the game would end before he got that respect back. The game would be out of control and then everyone would lose out.

MISUNDERSTANDINGS – DO PLAYERS UNDERSTAND ALL THE RULES?

Another reason why players clash with referees is disagreement about the rules. Some in the game say that this is even true of many professional players. This is more so nowadays as many new rules have been added, such as the rule about the tackle from behind. Your players probably think they know all the Laws of the Game. But can you be so sure? Test your players' knowledge. Here are a couple of questions you could try on them:

Q. A goalkeeper holds the ball for longer than the rules allow. Is the free-kick direct or indirect?

Q. Directly from a goal-kick, a team-mate in an offside position receives the ball. What should the referee do?

If they are not sure of such rules, that means they are not sure of the consequences of their actions on the field. You won't find the answers to those questions in this book, because, if you're not sure, it's a copy of the Laws of the Game you need. It's a good idea to pass a copy round the whole team to read.

Another cause of conflict: some players seem unwilling to accept that football is a physical contact game. It's frustrating to watch players complaining, especially after minor contact.

REFEREES' DECISIONS

Of course, another reason for clashes with officials is mistakes made by referees and assistant referees, and most of us have let off steam at one time or another because of them. It is the inconsistency of some referees' decisions that raises players' hackles most, because players need to know how far they can go before they'll hear a whistle.

But the game cannot be run by protests. So tell your players to act as if match officials don't make mistakes, because that's how the match officials will treat their decisions. Your players must keep their focus on their performance, no matter to what extent decisions on the day might be a distraction.

GAMESMANSHIP

Gamesmanship, another reason for clashes with officials, is a part of the game we could do without. A small number of players cheat, such as by diving, feigning injury or appealing for non-existent offences. Then there are players who surround any referee who awards a penalty against them – to force the penalty-taker to wait as long as possible before his kick, to make his nerves worse. There are also seemingly silly clashes with officials over cut-and-dried decisions – this is an attempt to push the referee into giving later borderline decisions in their favour so that they will leave him alone. Referees must stick to their principles. No-one has the right to bully referees. If players make their job nigh on impossible, you can hardly complain about his decisions. Discourage gamesmanship by your players if you see any sign of it.

CRIMINAL CHARGES

Criminal charges have been pressed against amateur players who have lost the plot altogether and physically assaulted match officials. The F.A. also apply their heaviest penalties to players who do this. With such assaults going on, it's no wonder that referees have been leaving the amateur game. The next chapter sets out information about where football and the criminal law may run into each other.

WHAT IF WE DON'T HAVE A REFEREE FOR OUR MATCH?

When there are not enough referees to go around, yours may be the match without one. Or sometimes for personal reasons, the referee may be unable to turn up. All is not lost, however.

First thing: don't panic. Some players and officials become pretty agitated about having given up time to play, only to find there's no referee. So you have to keep your head. Let's assume that you have tried to contact the referee by phone – but it looks like you've been left with no official referee and no official assistant referees, and the game is due to kick-off. You and your club officials should get together with the officials of the other club who are now waiting with you at the ground. Together you should discuss the options, of which here are three:

1. Both sides agree to play the fixture for real with a stand-in referee
2. Both sides agree to play a friendly match with a stand-in referee
3. Both sides agree not to play at all, because there is no official referee.

Your league may have a preference or a policy for which option to take in this situation.

First, here is what the three options mean.

1. BOTH SIDES AGREE TO PLAY THE FIXTURE FOR REAL WITH A STAND-IN REFEREE

It is important to note that this is possible only if both clubs agree to it. A stand-in referee, if anyone is willing to do it, could be a member of either club, a supporter, or whoever – even a passer-by out walking his dog (this happened at a game I saw).

You might stand in for the referee yourself – many club secretaries have before and many will in future. If it happens that someone who turns up on the day is also a qualified referee (some players are), all the better. But a stand-in does not have to have any qualifications. So long as both sides agree to it, anyone can be a referee for a match at the level we are talking about. He'll need a watch and a whistle, and different colour clothing from both teams. He should also have a pencil and paper to write down the score and any bookings or sendings-off.

And here's the rub: once both sides have agreed to it, and the game has kicked-off, you can't change your mind about this stand-in referee. And though some stand-in referees do a great job, some don't know the Laws of the Game properly. But you made your decision before the match, and you're stuck with it – you should grit your teeth and get on with the game. The result should normally stand.

A stand-in referee may send a report of any bookings or sendings-off to your County F.A. – employing all the same powers over the match as does a qualified referee. And he or she can be paid the same fee as an appointed referee by the home club.

Some leagues are happy for you to play games with stand-in referees, especially if they know that there are some very good stand-ins available. Other leagues see it as a minefield to be avoided. If you do agree to play the match for points with a stand-in referee, it is a good idea to note on the official team-sheet that this was agreed, for the league secretary to read later.

2. BOTH SIDES AGREE TO PLAY A FRIENDLY MATCH WITH A STAND-IN REFEREE

A friendly officiated by a stand-in referee allows a game to go ahead with those who have turned up, but without much at stake. This means less pressure, any refereeing mistakes mattering much less.

The friendly can be played only if both teams agree to it. You may also need the permission of the groundsman for a friendly, since the ground's insurance may not cover unofficial matches in case of accidents on the premises.

The stand-in referee may, if you choose, be paid the regular fee for officiating the match, as a courtesy.

Important: this would also mean of course that the official fixture must be re-arranged. So after the game, the club secretary of the home club must contact the league secretary as soon as possible to explain what happened. He won't know that the official match needs to be rearranged with a new referee – unless you tell him.

3. BOTH SIDES AGREE NOT TO PLAY AT ALL, BECAUSE THERE IS NO OFFICIAL REFEREE

Some leagues prefer this option, usually because they have had chaos breaking out in games covered by stand-in referees. But other leagues don't like it because it adds another game to the fixture pile-up later in the season.

Important: again, this would mean that the official fixture must be re-arranged. So after the game, the club secretary of the home club must contact the league secretary as soon as possible to explain what happened.

If the two clubs cannot agree about what option to take, the game will just have to be called off, and all go home.

Club officials have refereed many a game in place of qualified referees. And some on occasion have done as well as many a qualified referee. If you feel happy about it, and your league is in favour, consider if you or anyone else at your club could step into the breach when needed.

ABANDONED GAMES

When a match is abandoned, before or after kick-off, it is almost always a bone of contention with one side or the other. There may be suspicion that one side is trying to get a game called off because they will lose the game. This is a difficult situation for the referee to sort out.

Only the referee has the power to abandon the game. The F.A. doles out its heaviest fines to any players who force a game to be abandoned through their behaviour. No matter how strong your feelings about something that has happened in a game, it is the referee's decision alone that counts.

REASONS FOR ABANDONING A GAME

This is up to the referee. If you feel you have a reason for a game being abandoned, your team captain should tell the referee. But, again, you will have to abide by the referee's decision. If he decides the game is to continue, it continues – you've done all you can within the Laws of the Game.

true stories

Flashpoint

There was a fixture we knew could get explosive – between two top teams in an amateur league. They were short of a referee for a league game. As it happened, one of their players was also a decent trainee-referee. Both sides agreed to him giving up his place in his team to referee the match. The complaint after the match was not about him. It was about an incident.

Two players, one from each team, had a fight during the match. One had a terrible temper. His club had given him a chance time and time again. This time he really let them down. He sank his teeth into an opponent's back.

The stand-in referee sent both players off for fighting. After the match, photos were taken of the teeth marks on the second player's back.

The League Management Committee would have been happy if the injured player had called in the police – it was a serious criminal assault – but we did not put pressure on those involved. It had to be their decision whether to call in the police or not.

The injured player and his club decided not to go to the police. They decided to ask us, the Management Committee, to take whatever action we thought right. We never felt more responsibility than at this moment.

We rang the County F.A. for their advice. They said they would not report it to the police themselves – that was up to those involved. They advised that if a complaint was made to our league, we could make our own decision. The County F.A. would get involved only if they received the referee's report.

Our stand-in referee did not want to make a report to the County F.A. So the County F.A. made it clear they had no further advice for us on how to deal with this. This brought home to us the risk associated with unofficial referees covering matches.

The onus was now on us, the League Management Committee. After a few meetings, giving the offending player and the clubs a chance to speak, we banned the player for one year. We made it clear to his own club that they had a responsibility after a year to decide if they could trust him.

Without him – and he was a talented player – the team got stronger, to their credit, and a year later went on to win our League Cup. They took steps to ensure their discipline record improved. They did not bring their player back into the team for several years. When they did they saw much-improved character in him.

For example, a serious leg-break could be upsetting for players of either side, as occurred in two games I recall. One time a referee and both teams agreed to abandon a game because no-one felt like playing on after seeing such a serious injury.

In a different game, a similar accident happened, but the injured player's team were on their own in not wanting to play on. They forced the game to be abandoned by refusing to play on. Because of this, the league awarded the three points to the other team.

true stories

'Unplayable, ref.'

If you find yourself on a pitch that turns into a swamp, remember that the decision on what is playable is up to the groundsman and the match referee, not the teams.

It was a horrible winter's day. My team was playing the league secretary's team, while I was vice-chairman of the league. We wanted to get the game over with, and, as I'd refereed games for both of these teams before, I was given the job. The rain got worse, cold and wind-blown. My team had the weather blowing their way first half, and took a three–nil lead. My friend the league secretary didn't like some of my decisions which made things more difficult.

When we saw the referee abandon the game on the next pitch on account of the rain, I was amazed. The pitches were muddy and greasy, but I've played in worse. But the losing team saw the other game abandoned, and at half-time they demanded their game be abandoned too. I refused.

I made my point that here is what the change in ends at half-time is for – their team would see the conditions (especially the wind) turn in their favour. They didn't want to know. They refused to take the field for the second half. I abandoned the game and made a report to the league, who awarded the game to my own team. They ruled that no team can call off a game unilaterally, however strongly the team felt about the circumstances.

A couple of years later, my friend the league secretary finally admitted his team were in the wrong, and that they had to lose the three points. He still thinks my refereeing was terrible, though.

RECRUITING MORE REFEREES FOR YOUR LEAGUE

Everyone would be pleased to see more qualified referees in grassroots football. One way is to encourage players to qualify as referees. At a club meeting, ask your team if anyone is interested on going on a referee's course. Your County F.A. will run such a course. It may cost just a few pounds.

This may appeal to players who do not get a regular place in the team, or who have to stop playing through injury. It's a chance to stay involved in the game and keep fit. In some regions, many referees are students making an extra few pounds a week to support their studies.

After gaining his badge, your new referee may be allowed to cover games in your own league for at least his first couple of seasons. This is a good way of boosting the number of referees in your league. As referees get more experienced, they may be called upon to cover more games in other leagues.

For details of courses in your area, contact your County F.A. Contact details are in Appendix II at the back of this book.

THE LAWS OF THE GAME

Everyone in football needs to understand 'The Laws of the Game', or the 'Laws of Association Football'. This means the rules for how matches are played, and the rules that the referee polices. This is different from your league's Code of Rules – those being the rules for how your league is administered – or indeed your Club Rulebook, which means the rules for how your club is run.

The F.A. publishes the 'Laws of Association Football' every year as a little book, usually in time for the start of the season. You can also download the Laws direct from the FIFA web-site. The site is at: www.fifa.com.

HOW ARE THE 'LAWS' PASSED ON TO CLUBS LIKE OURS?

When FIFA changes any of the Laws, it tells the confederations, such as UEFA, which then tells the national F.A.s, such as the English F.A. Then the F.A. tells the County F.A.s and your County F.A. tells your club. They normally tell you in writing, so carefully read any bumf they send you.

CAN NO LEAGUE CHANGE THE 'LAWS' IN ANY WAY?

No-one but FIFA has the right to change the Laws of the Game. Your County

F.A. referees know this. Whatever anyone else says, they apply FIFA's Laws of the Game. However, FIFA does allow national F.A.s in different countries some leeway about certain aspects of the game, such as how many substitutes are allowed in a match.

In addition, certain leagues may apply through the County F.A. for permission to change rules about the size of goals, ball, pitch and the length of the match. It is children's, veterans' and women's leagues that do so.

CAN WE PLAY THE GAME WITH LOCAL RULES?

If anyone tells you they play under different Laws in their league, do question it. The Laws are set by FIFA. If in doubt about whether the Laws are being applied correctly, consult your County F.A. or get a copy of the 'Laws of Association Football'.

The only edition of 'The Laws of the Game' to trust is an up-to-date one. This has been especially true in recent years – there have never been so many changes to the Laws in such quick succession. For the same reason, the Laws are not reproduced in this book. One Law, however, deserves some comment – Law 12.

Law 12 gives the referee the right to show a yellow or a red card for bad behaviour, including bad sportsmanship. What players often fail to grasp is that not only is foul language punishable, but abusive language is too. In fact, even making an offensive gesture without saying anything is enough to get a player into hot water. Questions of sportsmanship and disciplining players are covered in the next chapter.

CHECKLIST

■ read a copy of the 'Laws of Association Football'
■ find out who in your club could be assistant referees.

chapter 18

THE MATCH – DISCIPLINE AND SPORTSMANSHIP

One of the remarkable things about football is how it brings the best and the worst out of people. To get the best out of people, discipline and sportsmanship are important.

It's up to your club how to conduct discipline of its own members. This chapter maps out disciplinary measures commonly adopted by amateur clubs. It also covers what you can expect from officialdom, such as the County F.A.'s disciplinary measures used for dealing with misbehaviour at matches.

The subject of discipline can touch on almost all of your club's relationships, between your own club's members, with other clubs, with match officials and with league and F.A. officials. The sensible approach is to treat everyone on the basis that you need their goodwill and co-operation.

For more on dealings with match officials, see Chapter 17. For dealings with your league and the County F.A., see Chapter 3. For information on the systems of fines used by leagues to make sure clubs are properly run, see Chapter 14.

SPORTSMANSHIP

When discussing sporting behaviour, the question comes up of whether football has conventions in addition to the Laws of The Game. An example came up when a home team was being well-beaten in a match. They went 6–0 down when their offside trap was beaten. They argued that the goal should have been disallowed. Their arguments were, first, that the off-side decision was borderline, and, second, they believed there was a convention that a team being heavily beaten should get the benefit of any doubt.

They were sure of this convention, repeating it at later League Council meetings. No-one else had ever heard of such a thing. That's why it's important that clubs should know the rules. And in such a case the normal rule is that the benefit of any doubt in case of offside should be given to the attacking team, not the defending team.

It was a goal and that was that. Just supposing the referee had disallowed the goal, and the home team went on to score five goals themselves to claw the game back to 5–5: having disallowed the opposition's goal number six the referee might have been lynched.

But there do exist certain conventions to do with sportsmanship. Here are some main ones.

true stories

Out of the blue

Even the best run club has to be ever vigilant for discipline problems. Things go wrong at the most unexpected times.

There is the famous anecdote of a team being ten–nil up and then suffering a breakdown of discipline and getting into fights with each other – because they had no credible opposition on the pitch. A player psyched-up for a tough game may be poorly adjusted to an easy one. I would not have believed it – but when I saw this very thing happen with my own eyes, I had to.

There was a league match that my club won 14–2. A good day, until we were about 9–1 up in the second half, when one of our players suddenly lost his temper over a debatable offside decision – given by one of his own squad who was doing the assistant referee's job.

As we were already leading 9–1, you would expect him to take this decision on the chin. But no, he erupted. He ranted, he raved – a tantrum for all time. He heaped a torrent of verbals on the assistant's head, till one of his team-mates managed to calm him down.

SPORTSMANSHIP AND SERIOUS INJURY

In the case of an injury to a player who cannot get back to his feet – especially where the referee has not noticed the injury – there are two conventions. First, it is the done thing for the ball to be kicked out of play so that the injured player can be treated sooner. Second, it is the convention that, if play restarts with a throw-in after such a break, the thrower should return the football to the team that had possession when the ball was kicked out of play. You can do this – without putting your own team in danger of conceding a goal – by sending the ball towards the other team's defenders.

This convention is much-treasured in the U.K., as illustrated by the infamy that surrounded the incident when Kanu of Arsenal scored a goal, not realising that the throw-in he scored from had been intended by his team-mates to go back to his opponents.

SPORTSMANSHIP AND CHEATS

Cheats are a different matter. They may be less common in the U.K. than in some places, but they will always be with us. The thing to remember is that only the referee can judge a player guilty of cheating. The players must simply walk away from an incident, and not get mixed up in controversy.

If you are concerned that an opposing player is persistently cheating, you should ask your team captain to speak to the referee. He may ask the referee to keep an eye on the opponent concerned to see that it doesn't happen again. The final decision is still the referee's.

SPORTSMANSHIP AND THE NASTY STUFF

Most players know what behaviour is unacceptable. A few have to be told. No matter what the provocation, no-one can ever defend offences such as spitting at players, racial abuse, violent misconduct or abuse of officials. A wise club disciplines its own players for such things. Powers to deal with these problems also exist in the Laws of the Game, and are in the hands of referees and your County F.A.

SUPPORTERS' BEHAVIOUR

The F.A. believe that clubs have a responsibility for the behaviour of their supporters – that goes for both professional and non-professional clubs, even the smallest clubs. Pity a referee who tries to persuade a supporter to leave the field of play. This situation needs a confident and competent referee.

Your supporters' behaviour influences other people's opinion of you and your club – how well behaved they are, or not. In a league with a small number of teams, whose officials are in regular touch with the other clubs, a bad reputation can have knock-on effects. Where a club has picked up a reputation for bad behaviour, it has made their club secretary's relationships with the other club secretaries strained and stressful. The important subject of supporters' conduct at youth team games is covered in Appendix I at the back of this book.

true stories

'Get off the pitch!'

If you think that opposing supporters only need to be kept apart at professional matches, you might be in for a surprise.

I was watching a match on a park, when a man and a woman supporting opposing teams got into a bad case of the verbals. The problem started when the man, a substitute of the away team, yelled his disgust at the referee and the other team. He went on and on – no swearing, just strongly held opinions, pretty abusive in tone. The referee stopped the game and tried to take the substitute's name, but he seemed to refuse to give it – but he did leave the pitch after some persuasion.

The game restarted. The sub then walked right into the field of play to vent more of his disgust. But the referee seemed weak, and now just ignored the man – who then stayed on the field shouting his opinion.

The referee should have stopped the game again, with a view to the man being persuaded to leave the pitch, perhaps by his own side, but he didn't. Nor did he abandon the game. Instead, he tried to let the game continue as if nothing unusual were happening.

A woman supporting the other team was standing close by and yelled, 'Get off the pitch! Get off the pitch!' The sub turned and told her what he thought of her intervention. She was livid. Tension set in – later on, fights broke out between players.

Moral: this could have been avoided if the visiting team had made sure that their supporter behaved. The least they could have done to help the referee was to make their substitute leave the pitch.

The referee had been placed in a very difficult position, which he failed to resolve. He had no official linesmen to back him up. He was on his own.

Ultimately, the referee has the power to abandon the game if someone stops play from continuing normally like this, and the County F.A. hands out its heaviest fines in such cases. But the referee ignored the sub's presence on the pitch, not to mention his shouting. And it all went downhill from there.

DISCIPLINE

DISCIPLINE IMPOSED BY YOUR CLUB

When there are discipline problems, by far the best thing is to deal with them within your club. That could mean that the decisions are taken by your club's General Committee or a disciplinary sub-committee (if your club decides to set one up). Discuss whether to draw up a table of punishments for offences by members of your club, such as fines for abusing team-mates or officials. Generally, members of a well-disciplined club behave better in matches.

Ideally, any disciplinary decision taken by your club should be recorded in the club's Minute Book. If you do punish anyone at your own club, you need to think about whether it is a private matter between the General Committee and the player – or whether the whole team should know about it.

Keeping a punishment inside the club means that you do not have to notify either your League or the County F.A. if you don't want to. Depending on the disciplinary matter, you may want to let your league secretary know to reassure him that you are dealing with problems at your club yourselves.

The kind of offences that might merit discipline by a club against its own players or members include misconduct in training or in matches such as:

- persistent bad language
- persistent dangerous tackling
- fighting
- arguing with officials
- disobedience of club instructions
- excessive or unwarranted criticism of team-mates.

Other situations that might require club discipline are off-the-field offences such as players being persistently late, or regularly failing to pay subscriptions.

You may need the judgement of Solomon in all these things. Players may think an over-officious club official is not on his side. There are few alternative punishments available, however. Obvious punishments available to your General Committee are:

- fines (not too much, not too little to fit the offence)
- suspending players from matches (not for too long or too short to fit the offence)
- dropping a player for just one match
- expelling a player from the club.

Less earnest punishments used include:

- putting ten pence in a swear-box
- for players found guilty of less serious offences, insisting that they wear a horrible item of clothing throughout training (a woolly jumper with frilly patterns is embarrassing enough) for a week or two. This can be effective – no-one likes to be laughed at.

An unfortunate punishment, seen for not training properly, is to make the guilty party run extra laps of a field. Before imposing anything like that, consider how it may affect the development of his fitness. Excessive runs at the wrong time can do more harm than good to his physique, and, in the case of some children, may be especially inappropriate.

DISCIPLINE IMPOSED BY YOUR LEAGUE MANAGEMENT

If players are guilty of persistent bad behaviour in matches, it will probably attract the attention of your league's management. They get to hear of these things from County F.A. referees and from other clubs. The truth is that your League will normally be happy to leave this sort of problem to match referees and to your County F.A. The referee books a player, the County F.A. fines or suspends that player, and informs your league secretary. Your league secretary may of course monitor your team-sheets after matches to make sure you have not been fielding any suspended players.

A League Management Committee will rarely take things further unless club members' behaviour is so bad or so persistently bad that it is bringing the name of your league into disrepute and may damage your league's relationships with the County F.A. and with referees. In a severe case, the league may consider using its own power to impose suspensions and fines to punish a player or his club.

DISCIPLINE IMPOSED BY YOUR COUNTY F.A.

For some players it seems almost impossible to avoid being cautioned by referees and then fined by your County F.A. Let's look at the F.A. system for punishment.

As mentioned in Chapter 3, the most likely occasion during the season that you'll hear from the County F.A. is if a referee cautions one of your players in a match. You may be wondering how this system works. It is quite straightforward. The same system applies the same to big professional clubs as to small amateur clubs. This is only a rough guide. Your County F.A. can give you full details.

A BOOKING (YELLOW CARD)

- the referee sees an offence at a match and books the offending player
- the referee writes a report after the match and sends it to the County F.A.
- the County F.A decides to take no further action or to punish the player.

THE SECOND STAGE: if the County F.A. decides to punish the player:

- the County F.A. sends your club secretary a copy of what the referee reported, together with notice that the club or the player must pay an 'administration fee' within the next 14 days, or else get into more trouble. (This is £6 at the time of writing. If it is any comfort, you may like to know that a Sunday League player and a professional superstar, or their clubs, pay the same administration fee for a caution.)

- your club secretary tells the County F.A. that their letter has arrived
- your club secretary passes the County F.A.'s notice to the offending player
- the club or the player pays the 'administration fee' (the club secretary sending the money to the County F.A.),

or

THE THIRD STAGE: if the player wants to appeal against the booking
(the player can normally appeal only if it is a case of mistaken identity):

- within seven days of the match, the player writes a letter to request a personal hearing against the booking and gives the letter to his club secretary, who sends the player's letter to the County F.A.
- the County F.A. decides whether the appeal is worth a hearing – if they decide it is not, you have to accept the booking

or

THE FOURTH STAGE: if the County F.A. grants a personal hearing to the player:

- a County F.A. Disciplinary Committee meets for the player to prove it was a case of mistaken identity
- the player can normally win only by having the booking pinned on the player who really committed the offence
- if the player proves he is innocent, the guilty player gets the booking instead.

ANOTHER STAGE: for a player booked too often (usually the fifth time) in a season:

- the County F.A. charges the player with what they call 'continuing misconduct'
- the player, through his club, can write asking for leniency or else request a hearing to argue for leniency
- after these stages have been completed, the County F.A. may apply a punishment according to their current rules –– this usually means a fine and a suspension

A FURTHER STAGE: if the player picks up another three bookings in the same season, the County F.A. will go through similar stages to impose another punishment – usually bigger fines or longer suspensions.

A SENDING OFF (RED CARD)

- the referee sees an offence at a match and sends the offending player off
- the referee writes a report after the match and sends it to the County F.A.
- the County F.A. decides either to take no further action or to punish the player.

THE SECOND STAGE: if the County F.A. decides to punish the player:

- the County F.A. sends your club secretary a copy of what the referee reported, together with notice that the club or the player must pay an 'administration fee' (£6 at the time of writing) within the next 14 days (or else get into more trouble)
- the notice may include a fine to fit the offence and notice of any suspension
- your club secretary returns a message to the County F.A. to say he has got their letter, and tells them the offending player's full name, and a list of every affiliated club he has played for (the F.A. might fine you if you refuse to tell them)
- your club secretary also passes the County F.A.'s notice to the offending player
- the club or the player pays the 'administration fee' and the club secretary sends the money to the County F.A.

THE THIRD STAGE: if the player or the club wants to argue that the punishment is too heavy:

- the player or the club writes a letter to argue mitigation against the punishment and the club secretary sends the letter to the County F.A.
- the County F.A. decides whether they agree to give a lesser punishment – if they don't, you have to accept the punishment.

AN ALTERNATIVE STAGE: if the player wants to appeal against the sending off:

- the player and his club make sure the second stage has been properly followed
- the player writes a letter to request a personal hearing against the booking, and the club secretary sends the player's letter to the County F.A.
- the County F.A. decides whether the appeal is worth a hearing – if they don't, you have to accept the sending off.

or

THE NEXT STAGE: if the County F.A. grants a personal hearing to the player:

- the County F.A. tells the club secretary where and when the hearing will be
- the club secretary tells the player where and when the hearing will be
- the player can call others to be witnesses for his defence
- the County F.A. can call witnesses, too, such as match officials
- a cameraman can even bring video evidence
- a County F.A. Disciplinary Committee meets for the hearing

- at the hearing each side can ask the other questions
- if the player wins the hearing, that is the end of the matter

A FURTHER STAGE: if the player loses his hearing:

- the hearing will decide when the punishment starts
- the player may have to pay the County F.A.'s costs as well as accepting any punishment which the hearing decides fit, and...
- the player pays any fines and costs – if his club pays, the player must repay his club in full (if he is an adult).

ANOTHER STAGE: if the player or club wants to appeal after losing that hearing, different rules may apply in different counties; check with your own County F.A. for the rules that apply to you.

FINES

Your County F.A. should normally send you a booklet before the start of the season telling you of the different fines they impose for different offences. These fines will range from the smallest for, say, getting booked five times in one season, to the bigger fines for, say, causing a match to be abandoned, or (the heaviest) for assaults on match officials.

If there are any schoolchildren in your team, they cannot be fined by the County F.A., and, what's more, their 'administration fee' for a caution must normally be paid by their club for them.

SUSPENSIONS

If a player is suspended, this actually means that, believe it or not, he is not permitted to take part in, or even to attend, any association football match at any ground, be it professional or non-professional. Of course it is virtually impossible for the County F.A. to check whether a player is paying to watch a professional game when he is supposed to be suspended! But that's what suspension really means. A player charged with an offence of assault by the County F.A. will normally be suspended for 28 days as soon as he has notice of the charge.

BEING 'BLACKBALLED'

You may have heard this slang phrase. This punishment is reserved for the worst cases of persistent misconduct. A County F.A. has the power to suspend a player, or even a whole club, from association football for years. They have even been known to ban a player for life, otherwise known as being 'blackballed'.

CHILDREN
Normally, any child under the statutory school-leaving age who is called to a County F.A. hearing must be accompanied by a parent or, say, someone with experience of being a school-teacher.

MATCH OFFENCES AND THE LAW

An assault in a football match may be deemed a criminal assault. Although your County F.A. will be especially concerned about assaults on match officials, any assault on a player of either team could also be regarded as a criminal assault.

Let's hope you never need any of the following information, but with the number of sports-related assaults going to court being on the increase, some awareness of what the law holds is no bad thing. You need to know where the club and its officials and members stand in law if a match incident is brought to the attention of the police and the courts.

What follows on these pages is by no means legal advice and is not intended as any kind of definitive guide. If you are ever involved in any manner of legal dispute you are strongly recommended to seek professional legal advice.

HOW DO OFFENCES COME TO THE ATTENTION OF THE LAW?
Say a player has been assaulted in a match and someone wants it to go to court. Anyone at all who is concerned about it goes to a police station to make a complaint of an assault. If the police think the matter should be taken further, they will investigate the allegation. It should be said that, due to pressure on police time, they may prefer to stick to the more serious cases, and leave the rest for the F.A. to sort out.

If the police think that a court should look at the incident, they may arrest the person accused of assault. They will then hand the case over to the Crown Prosecution Service (CPS).

The accused may choose to get a solicitor to defend him. To pay for this, either Legal Aid (taxpayers' money) may help, or the accused will have to finance his case himself. Some details of legal aid are on this web-site: www.legalservices.gov.uk

If the CPS believe the police have put a decent case together, they can prosecute the accused person at the taxpayers' expense. This should start off in the Magistrates Court nearest to wherever the offence took place.

If the accused pleads not guilty, the magistrate may hear a trial, and decide on the fate of the accused. A magistrate can send someone to prison for six months.

For some offences, mainly the more serious assaults, it may be decided the case should go before a higher court, such as a Crown Court, probably somewhere near the Magistrates' Court. There, a jury will decide who is telling the truth, and a judge may pass sentence. This court can pass heavier sentences.

A person found guilty in any of these courts may appeal against his sentence or his conviction in a higher court. A solicitor can advise on all of these things.

WHAT KIND OF OFFENCES ARE WE TALKING ABOUT?

The Law for England and Wales describes different kinds of assault, all of which could potentially happen on a football pitch. Here is a brief introduction: again, what follows does not constitute any legal advice and is not any kind of definitive statement.

Remember that on the football field, some physical contact is legal. So, for example, you should not expect a court to see a legitimate tackle or shoulder charge as an assault. But spitting could be.

Common assault is the lowest level of assault. *Assault occasioning actual bodily harm* is more serious in that the victim must have received some harm on the body somehow. The latter offence could go to the Crown Court.

For both of these offences, if a blow is deemed to have been intended, whether it hits the person or not, that may still constitute an assault, so long as the accused was reckless about causing violence or intended violence.

If you are acting in self-defence because someone has attacked you first, it may not be assault to throw a punch back. Self-defence may be seen in court as a legal defence.

Unlawful or malicious wounding is more serious. *Causing grievous bodily harm with intent* is similar to unlawful or malicious wounding, except more serious again, in that it means that the accused really intended harm.

Whether from reckless or from intentional action, and whether or not the attacker made contact with the victim, wounding can range from the skin being broken, causing bleeding, to more serious injuries. The injury doesn't have to be permanent, but it should be something people would consider serious. Small cuts and bruises are more likely to be deemed a less serious offence, unless the victim is a child.

Another point about such assaults is that provocation may not be regarded as being a defence. Self-defence may be. It may largely depend on how much harm is caused.

SOME OTHER OFFENCES

Apart from offences of assault, there are other offences concerning behaviour in public. For example, police may charge someone with violent disorder in a case where three or more people have been using or threatening violence against someone. This charge would be successful only if it could be shown that the accused was at least aware that his behaviour could be seen in this way.

WHO WANTS THE POLICE INVOLVED?

Surely no-one goes to a football match expecting or hoping to end up in court as an accuser or the accused. But there is no doubt that more cases are going to court. If you want to make a complaint to the police, that is your right. Your league or your opponents or even your own club may not like the idea.

My own feeling is that too many men think the football field is a safe place for them to act criminally and inflict real harm on other people – but it is no good for them to hide behind remarks like, 'It's a man's game,' when we are talking about criminal assault. Real men can control their temper, or at least can face the music 'like a man' if they fly off the handle. If taking them to court helps to stop these assaults, then it may be argued that that is exactly what the law is for. Of course, proving a case in court is another matter altogether, and it can be an expensive business.

A GOOD TEAM SPIRIT

At the heart of any team's efforts to keep good discipline and sportsmanship is good 'team spirit'. It's not always easy to keep up team spirit in the club through the season – especially if players who have been dropped from the first eleven show their envy of those who are selected, perhaps with harsh words or sly digs.

Of course, when players are left out, you want them to have that desire to win their place back. The last thing the manager needs is players who are happy to be left out. If bad feeling develops, though, it is a situation to be dealt with quickly, not one to be allowed to fester between players. This raises the area of man-management.

Encourage substitutes and squad players to cheer the first eleven on. The reason is simple: if the team is winning, it takes pressure off everyone. And then it's easier too for squad players to play well if they come back into a winning team. Make sure that players understand that, especially when they are not selected to play.

Here is a simple guide to good sportsmanship; copy it for your players if you like.

- Never try to sway officials' decisions with protests and mass appeals.
- Never attempt violence to 'get your own back'.
- Never act as if injured when you are not.
- Never try to get an opponent booked or sent off – let the referee make up his own mind about showing a card.
- Never argue with referees or their assistants – referees can be new and inexperienced, too, and if you do not tolerate their mistakes, the game will run out of referees to cover matches.
- Never use foul language or abusive language at the football ground – it is an offence under Law 12 even if you are talking to yourself; it can mean a red card.
- Aim to play the ball – not your opponent under the pretext of 'going for the ball'.
- Keep in mind that winning fairly gives true satisfaction.

CODE OF CONDUCT

The above is the bare minimum for your players to follow. For the conscientious club, there is more to understanding good conduct. That brings us to the idea of a code of conduct.

The F.A. has a written Code of Conduct which they say applies to all football played by clubs affiliated to it. Many clubs have never heard of this, which may not be entirely their fault, since no-one may have told them about it. Nevertheless the Code is there. You can get a copy of it by contacting the F.A. directly. They have also put it on their web-site: www.thefa.com

Their Code is several pages long. It has advice for players and for coaches, for team officials and for match officials. It boils down to each person striving to give their best, while at the same time showing respect for the Laws of the Game and for all the players of both sides, match officials, club officials and supporters.

If you get a copy of this, it may be a good idea to talk it through at a team meeting, and give your players the chance to ask questions about it.

CHECKLIST

- decide whether your club should have a discipline sub-committee
- discuss whether to draw up a table of punishments for offences by members of your club
- discuss good conduct at a club meeting with the players.

chapter 19

THEY THINK IT'S ALL OVER... IT ISN'T

There is less to do after the game than before it – good news indeed. The bad news is that there's always something to be done in those moments after the match when your natural instinct is to relax. You may wonder what there could possibly be to do after the match worth any fuss, so here's a list of post-match duties to be attended to.

HOME TEAMS' JOBS

- take your own nets and goalposts back home if you have to
- make sure the referee and any assistant referees have been paid
- telephone the result.

BOTH TEAMS' JOBS

- leave the changing rooms as you found them
- collect subscriptions from players who took part in the match
- meet your league's deadline for sending in your team-sheet
- wash the kit.

In some competitions, you must also send a card to the County F.A. giving your marks for the referee's performance.

TAKING DOWN THE NETS AND POSTS

At some grounds you can be grateful that you never have to this. There are few moments in amateur football more grim than trying to undo ties from your wringing wet nets with frozen fingers in freezing February rain. This is especially true straight after the match when the away team and the referee are already back in the changing rooms getting warm and dry. A job that 'sorts the men from the boys'. It won't take long to notice which members of your team run straight indoors as soon as they hear the referee's final whistle. It's always the same ones – you'll know them because you will hear the same old excuses, usually about players being 'already late to meet someone'.

If some people really hate this task, here's one way to put it right. In Chapter 16 I suggested employing groups formed by members of your squad to put the nets up in turns. Well, the same groups can take them down again. The good thing about small groups is that players are more likely to stick together to do their bit. Just in case they forget, you should be at the changing rooms with a copy of the rota, and remind them whose turn it is. If you don't do that, the same few hardy souls will end up doing the work every time. If you have to take the goalposts down too, then the same applies.

If the pitch you hire has goalposts and nets put up and taken down for you by the ground-staff, you avoid all that grief. Such provision depends a lot on what region of the country your football ground is in, and how much you pay for it.

SEEING THE REFEREE AFTER THE MATCH

There are three reasons for the home team to see the referee after the match:

1. Straight after the match, the referee should have collected the match-ball. As the home team, you have to make sure your club gets its ball back from him.
2. If the referee did not collect his match fee before the match, he will want to receive his money now. If you are in a competition that provides any official assistant referees, that goes for them too. Don't forget to ask the referee to sign a receipt to say he's received his money.
3. For the home team especially, it is good to thank him for coming – no matter how the game went. It's only courtesy, of course, and after all, he could be your referee again pretty soon and you don't want to upset him.

PHONING IN THE RESULT

This is normally the last job exclusive to the home team: the home team's club secretary makes that important phone-call to report the result of the match (or sends an e-mail). The call is to your league secretary (or to whoever is running the competition in which you are playing). He needs all the results for up-dating your league tables with all the latest scores. Ask your league secretary what the deadline is in your league for sending in results.

One of the reasons your league secretary wants to avoid delay is so that he knows about any postponements. He needs to know the fixture is completed, or if bad weather, for example, forced it to be postponed. It's common sense, but it is amazing how clubs overlook this. They must think he is a mind-reader. If your game did not go ahead or was abandoned for any reason, the fixture needs re-arranging and he needs to know so he can book a referee, and so on.

Another reason is that most leagues put their results and league tables in a local newspaper. To get the scores into the paper, your league secretary will be working to a very strict deadline; if he misses it and the newspaper leaves your information out of its football news he could get the blame for the scores not being published – but he may still be waiting to find out the scores, too.

true stories

The league official's incredible shrinking afternoon

In one league, we agreed I would take the phone calls to collect the weekend's match results, instead of the league secretary, whose time was under pressure already.

Our games were on Saturday mornings. I wanted the results by Saturday tea-time. This was because I knew many club secretaries would be going out later in the evening, and, more than that, I had to fax the results and the latest league tables to the local newspaper by Sunday lunchtime to see them in the paper that week.

After a few weeks, there was a regular problem – I was only hearing half the results on the Saturday, either on my answer-phone or taking the calls myself. To get round this, I often had to telephone some of the clubs at about 4 o'clock on Saturday afternoon to find out their results.

This meant I could be making more than half-a-dozen calls, whereas each of those clubs needed only to make one call to me. But straight after a match the natural thing is to relax, and small jobs are easiest forgotten. So I was regularly chasing results.

And when I tried to phone some clubs, often no-one was home. It seemed obvious that people were out on a Saturday afternoon, at another match or shopping with their families, and having a normal life. One person not having a normal day was myself, sitting by the phone, devoted to putting those league tables together. Sad story, sadly true.

This is what running a league to deadlines can do to poor league officials. Have pity on them. Find out the deadline for phoning in the results and make that one call as soon as you can. Then you, and league officials, can enjoy the rest of the day.

CHANGING ROOMS

It is simply courtesy to leave the changing rooms in a fairly tidy state when you leave. First, players should have taken off their boots before they entered, so as not to leave a trail of mud and grass for someone else to clean up later. And empty water bottles and plastic bags left behind are only going to make your club unpopular with the ground-staff.

If you are last out, have a look round the room. It is surprising how often people rushing to leave forget to take shin-pads or footballs or items of clothing. The common cry a week later is, 'Has anyone seen my shin-pads?' Worse from the club's point of view is if parts of your expensive club kit are left behind, muddy socks left in a corner and so on. Last one to leave – often with a bag full of forgotten belongings and left-over garbage – should turn out the light.

COLLECTING SUBSCRIPTIONS FROM PLAYERS

This is a job for home and away teams, as detailed in Chapter 6. A reminder: many clubs collect a pound or two from each player straight after the match to make up club funds. This is a good reason for either the club treasurer or the club secretary to head straight to the changing rooms after the match, to collect the money before players get in their cars and go home. Remember to keep a proper record when handling cash.

TEAM-SHEETS

For home and away teams there is the important matter of completing team-sheets, normally for every competitive match. The only game that may not need a team-sheet is a friendly. After a match, complete two copies of the team-sheet in detail. A copy for your league secretary will normally be compulsory; the second copy makes your own handy record of your matches, which you are required to keep. (Check whether the referee and your opposing team need a team-sheet before the match.)

There is a deadline for sending one copy to your league secretary, and fines are common for clubs who don't do so straight away. I suggest you take to the match an envelope addressed to the league secretary with a first-class stamp already on it. Post it on the way home, and beat any deadline. If you leave it to the next day, it is more easily forgotten.

Expect your league to have its own unique design of team-sheet. You can see how it also fulfils the function of a match report. Here are some pointers to help you complete team-sheets:

- If you forget to note the time of kick-off, ask the referee.
- if you don't know the referee's name, ask him – before he goes home.
- Some leagues record 'sportsmanship' and 'man of the match', some don't.
- Details of the players' 'registration numbers', if required, should have been sent to you by your league secretary after your players signed for your club.

MARKS FOR THE REFEREE ON THE TEAM-SHEET

In most leagues you need to give the referee marks out of ten for his performance. Your league secretary will collect all these marks together to send them to the County F.A. or the local Referees' Association at the end of the season. Each referee's average mark is used as part of his assessment by the Referees' Association, and low marks may affect his prospects in the game.

There is often confusion about the marks a referee deserves, but you should let common sense guide you. For example, if a referee has a perfect game, until he makes a single costly mistake, should he get 9 out of 10, or 3 out of 10? Of course, 9 out of 10 is probably more fair, but it is surprising how many teams see it the other way – especially if they have lost the game.

To assess your referee, you could bear in mind his confidence and common sense. Judge how well he co-operates with his assistant referees. Then there is his

---

Drumton Football League Official Team-Sheet

Suggestion: take 3 copies of this form for each game:
1. give one to the referee before the game with players' names against their numbers;
2. immediately after the game post a completed one to the league secretary;
3. complete the other one and keep it for your club's own records.

Name of your team	....	Division or Cup	....
Ground played at	....	Corner flags at ground	Yes/No
Date of match	....	Time of kick-off	....
Home team	....	Home team score	(goals)
Away team	....	Away team score	(goals)
Referee's name	....	Mark for referee: /10	

(If referee scores less than 5, provide written explanation on back of form)
Marks awarded by your club for opponents' sportsmanship: /10
Man of the match in your team (given by opponents):

TICK THESE BOXES AS APPROPRIATE

	FIRST NAME	SURNAME	REGISTRATION NO. OF PLAYER	SUBSTITUTE (SUB) PLAYED	BOOKED	SENT OFF	NO. OF GOALS
GK							
2							
3							
4							
5							
6							
7							
8							
9							
10							
11							
Sub 1							
Sub 2							
Sub 3							
Sub 4							

Marks awarded by referee to assistant referees:

Assistant referees' names 1)   X... /10

2)   X... /10

Signature of referee after the match   X...............................

Signature of one of your club's officials   X...............................

Completed team-sheets should be posted immediately to:

The league secretary at **league secretary's address**

Failure to do so promptly may result in your club being fined.

fitness and how good his positioning is to follow the game. There is his general control of the game and how clear his signals are; his application of the Laws of the Game; how correct his decisions are; whether he plays good advantages; and how well he handles any major incidents. Bearing all of that in mind, it is obvious how unfair it is to give a referee very low marks for just one or two mistakes.

If you do give a low mark to a referee, say less than five out of ten, you may be required to give your league secretary an explanation in writing. It is normal to send this in with the team-sheet, perhaps written on the back of the sheet.

Some leagues do not require the referee's signature on the team-sheet, while others do. There is also a space on this team-sheet for the referee to mark his assistant referees, and these marks may be used by some leagues to present an award to the best assistant referee of the season.

The rest of it is straightforward to work out. As you can see on the sample team-sheet, some things can be filled in before the match, such as names of players; other things must be filled in during or after the game, such as details of bookings and goals.

WASHING THE KIT

At last we come to what is probably the final job after the match, apart from talking about the match itself. Here are just a few handy hints:

1. Make sure that all the players hand in all of the club's kit after the match – shirts, shorts, socks. Always keep all the kit together in one bag, or else things easily go missing, and before you know it you will be spending money on replacements.
2. Some launderettes offer a not-too-expensive kit-washing service.
3. On the other hand, you may prefer to write down a rota for everybody in your club to take a turn washing the kit – unless you want the same few to do the work every time – and take the rota to every match, so that you can tell a player when it's his turn.
4. Make a note of the name of the person who takes the kit home – you may need to call him to make sure he remembers to bring the kit to the next game. It is probably not a good idea to give the kit to anyone who is going to be away for a few weeks, if it is going to make it difficult to get hold of the kit before the next match.
5. To avoid clogging up a washing machine with mud, dump the kit in a few buckets of soapy water as soon as you get home. Leave it in the water for hours – mud should come off more easily – before putting kit in the washing machine.
6. Always check the washing machine is set for the right temperature before you turn it on. There should be instructions inside the shirts telling you the maximum temperature for a safe wash.
7. Consider whether you can afford to insure your kit against damage. Check any insurance deal to see what it covers. Insurance may be worthwhile if a

launderette accidentally ruins the kit; it's cheaper to have bought insurance than another kit.

Mind you, if you think someone in your club really lacks the common sense to do this job properly, think twice before asking them. Here are three examples of players without common sense:

- one player I know didn't wash the kit until the night before the next match. All the players had to put on a wet kit.
- another player just 'didn't have time' to wash the kit, and instead of giving it to someone else to do, he brought it back dirty to the next match. All the players had to put on a smelly kit. (The away strip had been left at home.)
- another player did not observe the maximum temperature for washing the expensive brand-new kit. He left the washing machine set for a high temperature. Afterwards the kit didn't fit the players – it shrank that much. Worse still, his club had given their old kit away to another team. Now they had to buy new kit – and probably thought how much cheaper an insurance premium would have been.

THE POST-MORTEM

Time should be taken for a common-sense approach to having a chat after the match about how the game went. People often call this the post-mortem.

But the only difficult issues I would discuss with my players straight after a match are discipline and behaviour, because if a player's behaviour was out of order you need to tell them so at the time – not days later when maybe it's time to let sleeping dogs lie.

One thing we are apt to do after a match is pick over the bones of our team's performance, the team selection, tactics and formation. But here's a different idea: don't let your team have any big discussion of the match straight after the game. Leave any discussion for a few days. Maybe a few minutes at a training session during the week would be enough to talk about the team's last performance. Here's why:

- when players come off the pitch, they are pumped up and likely to say things they will regret once everyone has calmed down – not good for team spirit
- players can go away thinking about their performance – not spend days fretting about how any changing room comments have upset them
- everyone has time to think calmly about what they want to say
- a discussion a few days later will be shorter, especially if players want to get on with their training session.

AFTER A DEFEAT

If your team has been beaten, avoiding a big discussion is sensible. Let the players make their way home instead – you could tell them you'll discuss the match with them later in the week.

The hour or two after a defeat is the worst time to start making decisions about how the team should play. Anxiety about the result takes over from common sense, and players start asking about changing the team-selection and tactics and the formation for the next game. But here's the rub – the changes being suggested have got nothing to do with the strengths and weaknesses of your next opponents, because everyone is thinking about the strengths and weaknesses of the opponents they have only just played. What works against one team one week may not work against the next team – because each team has different strengths and weaknesses.

Before you know it, the team and the formation are being chopped and changed every week, and it gets to the point where no-one is quite sure of their job on the pitch any more. It goes from bad to worse.

In any case, you may be too busy after a match collecting players' subscription money to have time to give the attention people deserve when they express their view.

Of course, many professionals do have a post-mortem after the game. These are famous for managers throwing cups of tea at the wall (and at players). It doesn't mean it would help a smaller club. The truth is that different managers have different styles – some get what they want out of players with a quiet word; others rant and rave. If players are not getting paid, ranting and raving is usually inappropriate.

HELPFUL THINGS TO SAY AFTER A MATCH

PRAISE: I've always tried to make a point of giving praise where it is due – without going overboard. Praise can make a player feel ten feet tall, and go into the next game with more confidence. And that (not over-confidence) is everything when you are looking for a good performance.

CONSOLATION: In the same way, if players have tried their best and been unlucky, it's important to console them. Tell them they have what it takes to turn things around, with a bit of luck, a bit more hard work, and most of all by sticking together. Don't leave them feeling like they are going to fail next time too. Make sure they realise it's in their hands to turn things around.

REMINDER: Finally, you could also give the players a reminder that they can discuss the team's performance later in the week, what might have gone right or wrong, and what resources the team has to avoid the same happening again.

Many clubs send the players home, and then have a private discussion involving just the manager and club officials. The same problem is still there, though – after the match people can say things that are rash. There is no absolute right or wrong here, and if you find it helpful to have a chat after the game and let off a bit of steam, it's your call.

CHECKLIST

- make sure you have enough photocopies of a blank team-sheet
- discuss with the manager whether your Club will have after-match 'post-mortems'.

chapter 20

GAME ON, GAME OFF

Postponed games and rearranged games can be a minefield of misunderstanding between clubs. I've already written about how league officials spend hours on the phone at weekends when fixtures hit crisis point due to misunderstandings. Demands for games to be called off rank high among regular crises. Full rules about postponed games should be in your own league's Code of Rules. In one league, two years running we asked the AGM to amend our league rules to tighten up the procedures for having games called off. In the first place we brought trouble upon our own heads by setting out with a regime too lenient, if not downright easy-going.

Check the rules in your league to find your deadlines for requesting postponements. I should stress that the normal rule is this: even after you apply for a game to be called off, the game is still on – until your league declares otherwise. The league should let you know when they have made a decision on an application to call your game off. You may know that some teams do try to call games off without consulting anyone – illegally.

Difficulties can be safely avoided by staying on top of simple administration in two ways (see 'Top Tip' on p236).

true stories

Stricter but fairer rules for all

In our league's first season – on account of the league being new – we allowed teams to ask for games to be called off as late as a Thursday night, before the games on Saturday morning. We soon regretted this, since clubs often said they could not raise a team for the coming Saturday, and used our rules to get their game called off. Games got called off week after week. A fixture pile-up grew quickly.

One or two teams were even said to have had games called off because they couldn't put their best team out, when eleven players were available. That would be against the spirit of the game – teams can't pick and choose the date to play to give themselves a better chance over their opponents.

So we agreed to change the rules. We knew of another league in our region, where clubs couldn't call off games unless they gave a month's notice – of course even then the final decision was the league's, not the club's. But our clubs were not used to such advance planning, not yet anyway. So our new rule was that clubs couldn't make a request for a game to be called off unless they gave at least one week's notice. We agreed that any club who called off a game with less than a week's notice could lose the three points for that game – at the discretion of the Management Committee.

A pleasant development was that the same teams began to put out eleven players regularly. We got fewer calls for games to be cancelled, but still too many for the league to be happy. There was another fixture pile-up in the spring.

This prompted our next change. We felt that if we went further, things would be smoother, and teams would be better organised. We asked the next AGM to rule that in future clubs couldn't make a request for a game to be called off unless they gave at least two weeks' notice (or risk losing the points). The clubs voted for this too.

It worked. Teams got better at planning. We received still fewer calls to cancel games. No-one likes to forfeit three points. And this is better than a world where games get cancelled so late as to force teams to telephone all their players to pass on the message about the cancellation at short notice.

HAVING GAMES CALLED OFF: QUESTIONS AND ANSWERS

Following are typical answers to questions that are likely to be aired when injuries and fixture pile-ups upset your plans. Sooner or later every club faces these problems – where they may be forced to play with a depleted squad, or face fixture congestion that can disrupt normal human daily life. I'd emphasise that the answers given below are based on typical league rules. You should always check if there are any variations in your own league's rules.

Q. If we object to anyone cancelling our game, can we force it to be played?

A. No, it's not up to either club. But what you can do is put your point of view to the league secretary – and, if your objections are justified, the League Management Committee may be more likely to take your side because they want to see fixtures completed on time if possible. The final decision will be for the League Management Committee normally.

Q. What reason do you need to get a game called off?

A. Submit your own reasons for the request. There could be a variety of reasons, such as a snowfall preventing the away team from travelling to the home ground, or out of respect for a bereavement, for example.

Q. So what reasons are not good enough to cancel a game?

A. It's not enough for a club to say that they can't put out their best team. It's not enough even to say that you don't have eleven fit players – because normal rules say that so long as you have seven players that's enough to start the game.

Q. Isn't it unrealistic to ask a team to play with just seven players?

A. It's harsh, but those are normal rules found in the Laws of the Game. I've known teams play with just ten players on a few occasions, because that was the best they could get. In any case, you could always sign more players; you will have advance notice of when these fixtures are; and somehow all the fixtures have to be completed before the season ends.

Q. Who should we contact if we want a game called off?

A. Call the league secretary, unless you're told any differently (some leagues have a fixtures secretary for this purpose). It's courteous to contact the secretary of the other club about the fixture too, to let him know what you are trying to do and why.

Q. Can a team cancel a fixture on their own say-so?

A. No, they cannot. Normal rules are that a fixture can be cancelled only when the League Management Committee says so. Regardless of what any other team may ever tell you about a game being called off, a fixture stands until the league says otherwise. Contact the league secretary if you are not sure where you stand.

Q. If we are the away team for the next match, and we don't get a courtesy call in advance from the home team – does that mean the game is now off?

A. It shouldn't – normal rules are that the game is still on. So you'd still have to turn up – any team that doesn't turn up risks losing the three points to the other team. Phone the league secretary to tell him if you have not had a courtesy call from the home team; he may punish them with a fine.

true stories

'I want my fee'

Try as we might as league officials to keep fixtures under control' there was one occasion when we found ourselves seemingly up the creek paddle-less. We thought all was taken care of for the coming Saturday's games to go smoothly. Referees were booked. We'd had no requests for the weekend's games to be called off. All seemed well.

On the Friday night the league secretary got a telephone call from referee asking to be paid his fee for his Saturday match that had been called off. We didn't know anything about games being called off. No-one had consulted the league, and clubs can't call off games by themselves as if no-one else counted. Only the league can order games to be re-arranged, and only the groundsman and referee can say a pitch is unplayable. One club can't do this to another club.

We understood that the groundsman had not made any announcement. We wanted to get to the bottom of this mystery at once. The referee said he had come home to find a message had been left for him saying the pitch was waterlogged. He rightly pointed out to us that so long as the owners of the pitch or the groundsman didn't close the ground, then it was his decision as to whether the pitch was playable – only up to him, not up to clubs. That's how we saw it too. All the same, he had this message that the game was off, and he'd said his piece, so now he just wanted paying. The league secretary promised the referee his money straight away, of course.

Next we had to find out what was going on between these clubs. We would have liked to tell the home team to turn up for the fixture or else risk losing the three points without playing. But we had no luck with our attempts to contact the home team who had made this decision to cancel their game. No-one was home.

So, with his personal Friday evening once more in tatters, the league secretary next phoned the away team to put the questions to them instead. They said they'd had a phone message just the same as the referee, informing them that the game was off. They'd had to ring all their players to tell them not to turn up for the game.

Now it seemed clear that the home team was acting alone in calling this game off. This is against the league's rules – the same rules that all the teams signed up to before the season. Someone at the home club hadn't read the rules, or was making them up as he went along.

The league would have been within its rights to award the three points to the away team. We would have preferred the away team to turn up with the referee,

The league would have been within its rights to award the three points to the away team. We would have preferred the away team to turn up with the referee, silly though it seems, to make it plain that the home team had failed to fulfil its fixture. But now there would be no referee there. In the event, the away team made the whole thing easier by offering to play the game on a new date. This showed a great spirit towards the game, so the league's Management Committee agreed, and the game was rearranged. We fined the home team though.

Q. What if a team effectively cancels a game without permission?

A. As I said above, such a club may be deemed in breach of their fixture requirements under normal rules. They may stand to lose the three points. And what's more, there's usually a rule giving the league management the right to inflict other punishments on a club at its own discretion.

Q. What happens if one of the teams doesn't turn up for the match anyway?

A. In many leagues, the missing team will forfeit the three points. Check your own league's rules.

Q. Is it ever worthwhile to ask for a game to be called off at short notice?

A. This depends on your league's policy, but there are bound to be serious circumstances which could lead to a game being called off, more than could be listed. One footballing reason why games may be re-arranged is to accommodate County F.A. tournament fixtures. However, even in this case you would hope to have decent notice of cup dates to make it easier to change league fixture dates.

Q. What if we're still in doubt over whether a game is on, right up to match day?

A. If, after discussing the fixture with the league secretary and the other club, you're still in some doubt about the fixture, then it's simple: the normal thing is your team turns up. That's it. If your club finds it has wasted time and money, take it up with your league secretary.

top tip

1. Keep your list of fixtures up to date

Amend your list of fixtures whenever a game is called off or rearranged. Write down any new match-date clearly. Whenever you find out the date of a rearranged fixture for your team, put it in your diary. If your players keep copies of the fixtures, give them a revised fixture list too, so that they aren't caught by surprise making other plans when a game is due.

2. The courtesy call matters more than ever

Making the courtesy call from the home team to the away team matters more than ever for rearranged games (see Chapter 12). One team or the other can often get confused about the date of a rearranged game. The courtesy call will bring any such problem to light before it's too late to save the day.

COMMUNICATIONS BREAKDOWN

Most misunderstandings about fixture dates boil down to a simple failure of communication. You can see why most leagues insist on the home team's courtesy call to the away team. It is also why it's best to contact the league secretary to let him know if any club is forgetting to make the courtesy call to your club – that is, when you are the away team.

CHECKLIST

■ find out your league's rules about postponing games.

chapter 21
CRISIS AT THE TOP

One thing I've tried to do in this book is to lift the lid off what it's like to run an amateur football club. Well, there may be times when running a club seems too much trouble. What follows are very personal thoughts about surviving a season at the helm in amateur football.

POOR PERFORMANCES IN MATCHES

Playing matters are not the main point of this chapter. But bad results and pressure on those running the club usually go hand-in-hand – for amateur clubs as for professional clubs. When a team has lost a few games in quick succession it can become like a runaway train. It may be a cliché, but winning and losing are habits. When losing becomes a habit, everything seems to go against a club.

For example, when a club is on a losing streak it takes every effort of the whole team to get out of the rut. It must work hard to make its own luck. If it plays a little below par, its mistakes on the pitch will be punished by the other teams.

On the other hand, it often seems that a team on a winning run can make mistakes and survive. It's a hard one for anyone to explain. Teams on a winning run seem to get an extra bit of luck in the way a loose ball comes to them, or a deflected shot gets them a goal, or a referee's mistake works out in their favour. When you are losing, few of these things seem to go your way. Many footballers get very superstitious about this, which is no good thing at all, because it is up to the team alone to turn these fortunes around. That's why to break a losing streak, a team – all eleven players – must give maximum effort. Usually eight or nine hard-working performances will not do. You want eleven players working together.

For that, team spirit must be good. The points to remember are:

■ all your players need to feel that they have a fair chance of making it into the team at some point

- players need to be kept informed of what is going on at their club
- players need to look after each other, whether they make the team or not
- when match results are good, everyone feels a lot better than when they lose.

In sport you need room for the highs and the lows, for the joy of victory, for learning to cope with defeat. Without highs and lows the game would be bland. And the lows can hurt. It has often been said that football breaks your heart.

There are always plusses. You are always building bridges and friendships in the game. But during a tough, competitive season, the person running the club can get pushed to the limit. The club secretary has a lot to sort out. Things will go wrong: on the field in performances, results or behaviour; and off the field over organisation or money or the spirit in the club.

POINTING FINGERS

And here's a thing – when things go wrong, someone always points a finger at the person running the club, rightly or wrongly. People are apt to see it like this – you run the club because you think you can sort out the problems. The club secretary is seen as a top dog because he organises the club, and top dog is expected to get things right.

You'll be under some pressure at times. Especially if things do go wrong, no matter whose fault, people will look at you for answers, maybe even as someone to blame. But taking the top job means you need to be able to handle that bit of pressure.

When 20 people are standing around you at a football ground with minutes running out to kick-off, all expecting you to have answers to problems, that is a spot of pressure. Honesty counts for a lot, of course. If you are honest about any slip-ups, most people will respect you for it. And if people are mistaken about blaming you for anything, then you could be honest with them about that too.

Being gracious under pressure is a big part of running a club so that its members are kept happy, because the job you took was to run things and sort things out. People will probably expect nothing less.

We all make mistakes. When I've been very lucky, I've managed to put things right before anyone else has even noticed anything was wrong. But you always have to be open and ask people to help you or let you get on with putting things right. And that's why people expect you to deal with a bit of pressure calmly.

On match-day, adrenaline is pumping, tempers can get frayed. You find out the character of the people around you when things go wrong. (And you find out more about your own character too.) If things don't go smoothly, someone one day is going to blow his top, and people want someone to take it out on. It's not just the referee who gets this. Most of us who have run clubs have been on the receiving end of a tantrum.

Usually, we can put these things down to a bad day. But over a long season a harassed club secretary wakes up some mornings thinking something like this: 'I do all this work. Unpaid. And I get more hassle than help. And I've had enough. It's time to give it up.'

Usually that's all forgotten as soon as you get to the ground for the match. But what do you do if the day comes when organising the club isn't fun anymore? Those who feel the pressure most tend to really care about their club – it's in caring so much that they bring so much pressure on themselves. That's strange but true.

OPTIONS WHEN THE PRESSURE IS TOO MUCH

There are different ways to approach the situation when you are not getting enough help. Here are a few:

1. struggle on for now as you are
2. improve the structure of your club to simplify the work
3. stay on as secretary but delegate more work
4. stay on as secretary but train a deputy
5. resign as secretary, but stand for election to another post on the General Committee to pass on your knowledge when elections come around
6. give the club notice that you will resign from your post at the end of the season
7. just resign immediately
8. call a vote on whether to disband the club – and how soon to disband.

The next few pages go into these very different options in more detail.

1. STRUGGLE ON FOR NOW AS YOU ARE

There are good reasons why you might feel it's not time to quit as club secretary. The obvious one is that no-one else wants the job. Here's another: you're still learning the job. One of the most important things in life is learning from mistakes, in all walks of life. You are growing into a new role. Most of us, when we start something completely new, don't start all that well. But we get stronger in our new role if we learn. It takes time to learn the ropes.

I've known clubs where a new club secretary seems to come along every six months; no-one is ever in the job long enough to learn enough to do it well. In any walk of life, bringing in a new face brings new energy but it also brings inexperience. You have to do a job to know what it's really like. So deciding when to quit and move on is a big decision all in all. That's why you may well ask: is handing over the job to someone else the best idea? There is always the chance that someone else can fill the job, but what will it mean? There are other alternatives, if you feel now is not the time to resign, to relieve pressure.

2. IMPROVE THE STRUCTURE OF YOUR CLUB TO SIMPLIFY THE WORK

Take time to think for a while whether there is room to improve the structure of your club. Remember the three most common crises at amateur clubs are: a communications breakdown; not enough people off-the-park to help in the running of the club; not enough money to pay a club's bills.

Have these been any source of aggravation to you? If you don't have enough support from the people in your club, it's time to call a club meeting to ask your members these questions: Are things going to change for the better? How are they going to change?

3. STAY ON AS SECRETARY BUT DELEGATE MORE WORK

Have another look in Chapter 4: 'Building the structure of your club', at some ideas for sharing the work of running your club. Start delegating work sooner rather than later. Think of any things you don't have time to do. Have ideas ready for what other people could do for you, to reduce your workload.

4. STAY ON AS SECRETARY BUT TRAIN A DEPUTY

It's also a good idea to let someone else watch the work you are doing, so that they are like an understudy. They will learn enough to give you help when you need it. With support, you may be able to ride through the troubled waters.

5. RESIGN AS SECRETARY, BUT STAND FOR ELECTION TO ANOTHER POST ON THE GENERAL COMMITTEE TO PASS ON YOUR KNOWLEDGE WHEN ELECTIONS COME AROUND

If you just change the face at the top, is your club any better off? If you decide to step down as club secretary, you may want to stand for election to a different job on the General Committee. If your club votes you in, this would be a chance to share the lessons you've learnt with the new management and carry on helping in some way with the running of your club. There is more than one job to be done, after all.

You, as an experienced club secretary, will know things a new secretary hasn't learned yet. So does it profit anyone if the new man stumbles over the same problems that you might have faced? While you now understand how to avoid these problems, it doesn't follow that he has any clue about them. So your continued presence on the Management Committee could have value.

If you feel things are getting too much to carry on regardless, then talk to someone, anyone, and make plans to share the work out, even if it's just a temporary help. You do no-one any favours if things are left to drift.

6. GIVE THE CLUB NOTICE THAT YOU WILL RESIGN FROM YOUR POST AT THE END OF THE SEASON

People usually call it 'burn-out'. If you're at the end of your tether, what then? Sometimes you think of how you've handled this bit of pressure before. But what if you feel the responsibility becomes a millstone? If it is more than you can bear, then be aware: it's not time to pass the blame, but it may be time to ask this question: 'Is it time to pass on the job to someone else?' You will probably know when it's time to go.

true stories

Where's the manager?

A friend ran his club as secretary and manager and resources officer all rolled into one. Near the end of a tough season he was under extra personal strain as relatives of his were in ill-health. Not knowing this myself at first, it was a surprise when he was not returning phone calls. Under the strain, there was a lack of communication between him and his players and the league. It's easy with hindsight, but it might have helped if he'd asked his players to take on more of his job of running the club till the end of the season. They hadn't done it before, but it looked a good time to learn.

On a Saturday morning the team assembled at their home ground. The manager didn't. The away team did. And everyone was waiting. The manager had the nets for the goals, not to mention the corner flags. After a while, it seemed clear he wasn't going to turn up. A few days before that, the manager had told his treasurer there was a chance he might not turn up, but, with no word since, no-one knew for sure what was going on.

To be fair, they acted quickly. The visiting team said they could drive back home to pick up their own nets. Eventually, they got the game started.

The gaffer left his club a few weeks later, pretty fed up with the whole thing. It was a shame that things couldn't have been resolved a better way sooner.

When your time to resign comes, speak to the other officers at your club, such as your chairman and treasurer. At clubs where one person still runs everything it may be that you could talk to your senior players to let them know what's happening. The things to talk about are the best time for you to quit, and maybe to talk about who could take your place. To make your intentions clear, you could write a short letter and copy it to each of the people on the General Committee so that they know what's going on. The best time for a replacement to be appointed is usually at the club's Annual General Meeting when all the members can vote.

7. JUST RESIGN IMMEDIATELY

If you cannot wait till the club's AGM to get a replacement, ask the General Committee to appoint someone to take your place sooner. Remember that the General Committee normally has the power to appoint a replacement at any time (that's if you have Club Rules like the ones suggested in Chapter 4).

8. CALL A VOTE ON WHETHER TO DISBAND THE CLUB – AND HOW SOON TO DISBAND

Unfortunately, even when you close a club down, this means paperwork. For most unincorporated clubs (those that are not Limited Companies, which is most of them) this is not too much trouble.

First, a decision to disband should be made formally by your General Committee or – better – by an Extraordinary General Meeting of your club. If possible, complete your fixtures for the season, the fairest thing for the other clubs. If you can't, don't forget to tell your groundsman. In any case, as soon as possible tell your club's members and players and your league secretary of your club's decision to disband.

You need to tell your County F.A. too. They would ask that you let them know in writing that you are disbanding as soon as possible – before December 31 during the season, in fact. Of course, in a state of crisis such decisions are often not made until the end of season, but try to oblige the County F.A.

An issue bound to arise is what to do with the club's assets (property) and liabilities (unpaid bills). In a typical park football club all the members jointly own the property, and may be jointly responsible for unpaid bills – depending on what you agree to in your Club Rules. After all, the General Committee's Officers are normally, in effect, the club's caretakers, not its owners.

Your club should of course try to pay any debts it has. Following that, if the club has any assets (such as cash) left over, ensure everything is above board. Often, such assets may be transferred to another club, to a competition (such as your league) or to an affiliated association (such as your County F.A.). For some clubs winding up, the assets amount to a few pennies, if that. For advice, speak to your County F.A.

If your club is a Limited Company, as many senior clubs are, then there are more rules to follow when winding up. You should find these rules in the F.A. Handbook, or ask a solicitor or your County F.A. for advice.

HOPE

Of course, a time to call it a day will come to all of us – but it needn't be the end of all you have achieved. It may still be possible for a club to be organised better so that those who take over your job get the help they need.

true stories

A club standing on its own two feet

The first time I was a club secretary, I lasted a year. I had failed to build around myself a properly organised network of helpers to lighten my load. After a year, with its share of highs and lows, great victories, players' tantrums and organisational hiccups, things came to a head. Short of back-up on the organisation side, short of emotional support from the club, I was exhausted and decided to quit. I'd built the club from scratch – it meant a lot to me, so deciding to quit led to a few private tears. But exhausted, I had to let go of the reins. I resigned after the last game of the season.

I played a few more games for the club too, but friends persuaded me to make a fresh start at a new club. I left with regrets about not being there to help the club further. But what happened to that club since has given me heart. After a few changes, they settled on a new management team and the club learnt to stand on its own feet. It went from strength to strength. But, for other people to come through, it first needed me to step out of the way and make room for them.

There were moments when the club almost folded, but they pulled through. That club had to learn to run itself – if it was going to survive – and with the work of a small group they did well. I just hope their future club secretaries keep a small group together on the General Committee to share the load.

CHECKLIST

■ consider what jobs your club could offer to others.

chapter 22

ONE SEASON ENDS...

So the games are over and the close season, as they call it, arrives. And if you have been the club secretary for a season, you'll know how much you deserve a pat on the back, a bit of a break. Reflect on what you as club secretary have achieved. You've done so much work – probably more than you expected, perhaps at times unnoticed by others. But think what that effort did for the club.

I've seen a rag-tag bunch of lads turn into a more mature group of men, ready to own up to their mistakes, ready to support each other. The quiet ones have come to know the others better. The louder ones have learned when to hold their tongue a little more. Lads have grown up in front of me for their own good and the good of the team. Football has had a part to play, exposing their weaknesses, challenging them to give their best for the sake of the team. Some of them now have greater self-esteem and greater respect for each other.

Of course football brings times of trouble: injuries, lack of discipline, bad language, rows. But football also provides an arena where problems can be faced.

All of this is why governments and welfare groups are turning back to team sports like football for the good they can do. You are playing a part in this, even if you didn't mean to.

It's not easy to acknowledge all the good things that happen, but awarding special club trophies is a popular way of doing so.

TIME FOR PRIZES AND PRESENTATIONS

On a shelf in my home are two trophies – but not for my very average footballing abilities. One is from a club and one from a league, in thanks for hours that I spent on the footballing cause. Long after individual matches are gone – when no-one else remembers that world-class tackle I made, or the laser-guided crossing – trophies and medals still stand for something.

Many clubs make a point of having a special occasion to mark the end of the season. Lots present shields to players who have excelled themselves. Here are some popular ideas for what to give awards for:

- Team's choice for player of the year
- Supporters' choice for player of the year
- Club's leading goalscorer of the season
- Most improved player of the season
- Club man of the year (for someone who has contributed a lot of effort to the club)

Some clubs just present a 'Player of the Year' award.

ORDERING MEDALS AND TROPHIES

As club secretary you have a busy job, so why not ask someone else to organise the presentation night, the medals, the venue, the food, the tickets, and so on. Ask around your team and there may be someone who knows how to organise a good party. There is a knack to organising an event like this.

We kept things simple. In most towns there is a shop that sells trophies and medals and will engrave the name of the prize and the name of the winning player on the trophy. Prices for this differ greatly. Shop around.

At the end of every season these shops get a rush of orders from many clubs. That means you shouldn't leave it to the last minute. As soon as you can, place an order for your trophies and engravings. Once you have bought a shield or trophy, you can use it again and again, getting new names engraved each year.

THE VENUE

It's probably best to ask your players where they would feel comfortable having a presentation night. Here are a couple of ideas.

I know one young team who, after their last game of the season, simply go to their local pub for a buffet meal, and present the trophies there, with a few quiet speeches in their corner. If you want to do this, ask the landlord for permission. Some landlords are even so generous that they offer a free buffet to help your party along (perhaps with lots of salt to build your thirst).

Another team I know makes a bigger occasion of it. They book a function room, a bigger buffet, a disco, and sell tickets. They book a special guest from the footballing world to present the trophies. They make it a night out for their spouses and children and friends.

One important question is how much money you can spare. Remember that, in a few weeks, your club will need to start paying its bills for the next season. It is very important at this time of year that you watch how the pennies are spent. If you hire a venue you might be able to sell tickets to make the event pay for itself.

YOUR LEAGUE AWARDS CEREMONY

Even if your club decides not to have a party, there will almost certainly be an evening to go to – one organised by your league. Try your best to support events like this. The league's end-of-season party is probably the last time you will see the other teams until the next season.

After a hard season I think it's great to see all the teams turn up, and to show respect to the teams who have won something. Sadly, some teams don't feel the same about it. I've heard various excuses for some clubs not joining in league celebrations, all quite sad. The fact is that when your turn comes to pick up some silverware you will want to hear the applause to go with it. So each of us should do the same for others.

The end of the season is miserably drab without a good party, whether you did well or not. It's so soon before the work in preparation for next season starts, so you want to give your club at least one good night a year. So if your league wants you to sell tickets to your players, why not use your influence to get them and their partners and friends to go and enjoy themselves together.

TIME TO REFLECT

After the pat on the back and celebrations, it is time for thinking. Get your club's General Committee to meet for an hour or two – there are things to talk about. The end of the season is a chance to assess what went well this year – and what didn't.

Why not have a glance over the first half of this book again to prepare yourself for planning for next season? Ask yourselves if there was any danger in the season from the three most common crises at amateur clubs: a communication break-down; not enough help; not enough money. And here are some more questions your General Committee might discuss at the end of a season:

1. Has the club paid all its debts and completed all its paperwork for this last season? Or is there still work to finish?
2. When should you hold your club's Annual General Meeting? You should give your players and other members plenty of notice of the AGM.
3. Do your club's officers want to be officers for another year? Or will there be resignations?
4. Will the manager or coach carry on for another year?
5. Did you have enough players for each game? Or do you need to sign new players to make your squad a little bigger?
6. Your home ground: what condition was your pitch in during bad weather? Will you stay at the same pitch next season – or will you look for a new ground?
7. Do you need to buy any new kit or equipment for next season?
8. Has the club got enough money to start next season? And how can you raise more funds?

All of these things are for your General Committee to discuss. Remember to keep the minutes of the meeting. A club secretary's work goes on...

TIME TO PLAN

What happens next? It all starts again. As club secretary you will be the busiest member of the club at this time of year. The good news is that obviously you don't have to go back and buy all that expensive club equipment again, or find a whole squad from scratch. But for the club secretary the paperwork is starting again. Those forms you filled in before last season will need to be filled in again. Of course, if there is no sign of the forms arriving, telephone the appropriate authorities – now you know from experience who they are (the pitch owner, league secretary, County F.A.). Now that you've done it before, why not draw up your own timetable of your deadlines?

Of course, different forms have different deadlines. What's more, some of these forms will mean bills to be paid – you are going to need a chat with your club treasurer to make sure your club is able to start paying.

Late May/early June is a good time to chase up any forms you have not received. Don't wait till mid-summer to fill them in and send them back. Remember that it is quite common for your club to get fined if your forms are returned late. Remember, too, which pieces of paperwork need attention sooner than others – those are the jobs to concentrate on next.

PITCH RENTAL APPLICATION FORM

In many parts of the country, pitches are booked on a first-come first-served basis, so just because you had your pitch last season may mean nothing. Don't take your pitch for granted.

Around the end of the football season, telephone your pitch agency and ask them whether you should have received an application form yet, to book your pitch for next season. Get the ball rolling.

BOOKING YOUR PITCH AGAIN; QUESTIONS AND ANSWERS
Q. What if no-one sends me an application form for the pitch by May or June?
A. You chase them up. Phone, and make sure they have your correct address for them to send an application form to you.
Q. What if we can't pay the bill?
A. See Chapter 6 for money-raising ideas. Before you know it, a bill for hundreds of pounds will land on your desk for next season's pitch. Be warned – your club needs to have money left in the coffers at the end of the season.
Q. What if we want to move to a different ground?
A. You have every right to apply to hire a different pitch, but once you sign a

contract for a pitch, you may be expected to pay for it.

Q. Do I need to tell the pitch agency if we are leaving their ground?
A. It is common courtesy to tell them. They may have a waiting list for teams wanting to use that pitch, so do tell them if you don't want it any more.

Q. How do we find a new home ground?
A. See Chapter 7 for ideas.

Here is a reminder of other forms you will need to see before next season:

FORM	WHERE TO GET IT FROM	ANY COST?	ANY DEADLINE?
County F.A. Affiliation (you cannot play without this)	County F.A. unless your league secretary sends it to you.	YES	YES
County F.A. public liability insurance deal	DITTO	YES	YES
County F.A. Competition Registration (joining will be optional)	County F.A.	YES	YES
League Registration	League secretary	YES	YES
League Cup Registration (may be optional)	League secretary	YES	YES
League Rules	League secretary	NO	YES
Player insurance	High Street insurance companies or County F.A.	YES	Check with your league

Having done all that last season, at least you know what is involved. Before you know it, you will be getting the fixture list for next season from the league secretary, and starting your pre-season training.

MEETINGS

But before that there are two important events coming round: Your club's annual general meeting and your league's annual general meeting. This is different from the end of season parties. You will find an explanation of how to hold your club's

AGM in Chapter 4. It's your chance to ensure you have officers appointed to run the club next season.

As for the league's AGM, don't forget that attendance is usually compulsory. Your League Council Meetings will probably continue. These are valuable in the summer. With the pressure of matches some time away, you have more time to chat to other club secretaries and the league secretary to find ways of improving the running of your club, or to pass on to them lessons you have learnt.

The time may come when so much paper and so many meetings are a thing of the past. The Internet, e-mail and mobile phone text messaging are helping many clubs' communications already. The advantages of the Internet are that it can speed up the business of sending forms to league secretaries, and save money on paper and postage. The downside, for now at any rate, is that what usually makes a piece of official paperwork valid is someone's signature, hand-written in ink. E-mail has not entirely replaced that tradition yet. And those weekly courtesy telephone calls before matches may still be the norm for many club secretaries, but in the future e-mails or text messages will probably become more common.

But, with or without technology, it will be club secretaries who keep their clubs ticking over. So, be it the present or the future, welcome to running your own club.

CHECKLIST

- ask if anyone is prepared to organise an end-of-season event for your club
- set a date for the next AGM.

appendix ▌
YOUTHS IN FOOTBALL AND THE CHILDREN ACT 1989

Whether your team is an open-age team, girls' team, boys' team, girls' and boys' mixed team, if any children are in your team, you'll need to pay extra attention to ensure that they are properly protected. That's the least anyone would expect, even if you only intend to take a few children out for a kick-around. In these days of greater awareness of how children have been ill-treated by some in positions of trust, the need is clearer for care and for the right things to be seen to be done. Howard Wilkinson's 'Charter for Quality' put forward a recommendation that any adults who give children the chance to play football should themselves be trained in child protection. Contact your County F.A. to find out if they run such a scheme.

This Appendix is not intended as a full statement of a child protection policy or as legal advice, but only as basic introductory information.

Let's consider the Children Act first, and then ideas for what you can do to protect children at your club.

THE CHILDREN ACT 1989

For most football clubs, the Children Act can be thought of as lots of helpful ideas – recommendations on child protection. For certain groups, there are regulations to follow too. So the first thing you need to know is if you can just make use of the recommendations, or if your club is in the smaller group covered by regulations. Your club is in that smaller group if you can answer 'Yes' to each of these three questions:

1. Among the children in your club, are any aged five or six or seven?
2. Are any of those five- to seven-year-olds with you, on more than six occasions in the year, for more than two hours?
3. Is someone else other than you the usual carer of those children?

If you answer 'Yes' to all three questions, then child protection regulations are something you need to know about. And for all clubs with children of any age, there are also recommendations to consider.

REGULATIONS: GETTING A 'CERTIFICATE OF REGISTRATION'

The first thing to know is how to register your club to comply with the Children Act 1989. This is a legal requirement. Don't delay with this, because it could take months spent on paperwork, meetings and police checks before you get your Certificate.

Ofsted are the people to speak to. Their helpline is 0845 601 4771; or see www.ofsted.gov.uk.

SOME CRITERIA

Here's the sort of criteria you should expect to meet:

1. Making sure the space the children play in is not too small for the number of children.
2. Making sure enough facilities are available. (For instance, one toilet may be enough for 20 children at the most, and one hand-basin for 25 children at the most.) Ideally, children and adults should have separate facilities.
3. Making sure enough adult helpers are available. For each adult in charge, there should not be more than 12 to 15 children, but how many exactly may vary. Ideally, there should be a few leaders anyway, because a solo leader is more at risk of being under suspicion of wrong-doing. Think of two adults as the minimum. If the activity is out of doors, and most football is, you may be asked to double the number of adults to keep an eye on the children.
4. Making clear to everyone that one particular adult is in overall charge. Ofsted may prefer that adult to have some kind of certificate for working with children.
5. Paying a fee to cover the costs of registering your club, and another fee for an annual inspection by the authorities.

The authorities are likely to ask you for documents to take this forward such as:

1. Two references for each adult. References from friends or relatives are not enough. They should be of a more professional nature, but at least one should have something to say about the adult's previous work with children.
2. Police check forms completed for each adult helping out with your club. You should ask the adults for their consent before you do a police check on them. If any of your adult helpers do not want a police check done on them, it may be wiser not to let them help with the children at all.
3. Health-wise, a document showing that you personally have a suitably clean bill of health for coming into contact with other people's children.
4. A written plan for how you will run your club. Details might include how you are recruiting helpers and how you will organise a complaints procedure.

You may also be required to attend an interview to establish that you are a fit person to run this kind of activity.

It's a lot to do, but it is required – if you are looking after children of such a young age for such lengths of time – and you should get some help with the procedure from the authorities as part of the process of registering your club. Such regulations may cover a smaller group of children, but recommendations are for everyone. So let's look at how much you can do for sensible child protection.

RECOMMENDATIONS: GROUPS FOR YOUNGER CHILDREN

First, if a few of your children are aged from five to seven, you may think about letting them play in a smaller group on their own, away from the larger children, and most smaller children will be glad to have their own game. This of course means you need extra adults to keep an eye on them.

I am assuming that you are not taking any children less than five years old. If you do, ask Social Services or Ofsted for advice. One of the safest things to do is to ask the child's parents to accompany such a young child.

Avoiding behaviour that might arouse suspicion may not be as obvious as you think – think about how any of your business with the players might look to other people, if you're not sure. Social Services or Ofsted may again have more detailed guidelines on how to run out door activities and how you should conduct yourself so as never to come under suspicion of any wrongdoing.

Here are other recommendations.

If the children play outdoors – have one adult for every seven children. If all the children are over 12 years old, then one adult for every 10 children may be fine. But there should still be at least two adults in charge.

Where there are both girls and boys – have at least one male and one female adult in charge.

Insurance – the kinds of insurance appropriate here would include personal accident insurance to cover the adults and children of the club and public liability insurance, for example. Make sure the parents know whether you have bought insurance or not and know the limits of any insurance cover you have bought. It is best to hand out an information sheet to get such information across.

Let everyone know who is in charge – this avoids confusion and messages being given to the wrong person.

Have a qualified first-aider and a first-aid kit – and if there are any accidents tell the child's parent or guardian yourself. In the event of any serious injury, say a broken bone, keep a written record of the injury to the child, including how the injury happened and what treatment the child was given by your club. When children play, it may reassure parents if the job of first-aider is given to a woman rather than to a man, as this job involves physical contact, and a woman rather than a man may be less likely to be regarded with suspicion. It is sad that anyone may be viewed with suspicion, but clubs must deal with the world as it is: in this day and age, such are public perceptions of who might pose a danger to children. A sensitive approach to parents' concerns is advisable.

USEFUL STEPS FOR AWAY GAMES

Recommendations given above are suitable for home and away matches. Next let's cover things specific to away games. For travelling with children to away games, or other outings, there are sensible steps to take. They begin before the day of the outing. The order in which things should happen may go like this:

Consent forms – you may wish to get a consent form for every child to go on the outing, each form being signed by a parent or guardian. Ask your Social Services office for copies of this kind of form, as they may prefer you to use their own form. Keep these consent forms for at least a few months, just in case someone wants to complain about something.

Where and when – make sure that children and their parents always know the correct times and places for being dropped off and picked up. Especially make sure that the children know exactly where and when to meet beforehand, so that no-one is left behind, confused, and probably in tears. It's good sense to take care when choosing your picking-up and dropping-off points. The best way to inform the parents is in a letter, telling them the times and places for dropping off and picking up their child; what type of transport you are using; the name of any travel company you are using; the address of the football pitch where the children will play, and a contact telephone number of a third person in case they are worried. (A third person is someone else, not travelling with the group. Every time you travel, before you go, give this person the names of all the children on the trip. Make sure the third person has the phone number of all the children's parents/guardians (to call them in case of an injured child, for instance) and make sure that all the parents have the phone number of this third person, so that they have someone to call if they are worried. As for phone numbers, land-lines are more reliable and therefore usually preferable over mobile phone numbers. When you have returned safely from the trip let this third person know you're back, to save them from worry too!)

The register – just as in school, keep a register with the children's names in. Take it for every trip, making sure that all the children who travel are marked in the register. Then you can check on the way home that none of them is missing.

Transport – it may be unwise to carry other people's children in your own car. This may attract suspicion towards you. Normally, only an emergency is a suitable time to carry children in your own car. If this is the case, remember to check that your motor insurance carries passenger liability (and is current!).

In any case, children should sit in the rear seats only – not too many of them – and there should be no adults with them at all in the back. (This also protects the adults from any unexpected suspicions or allegations.) The children should wear seat-belts.

You should be satisfied that the person driving is capable of supervising children on a journey. If possible use a minibus or a coach and make sure you have a driver who is competent for handling this kind of vehicle before you entrust the children's safety to him or her! And whether you use your own vehicle, or hire one, make sure it is road-worthy.

There should be at least two adults in a minibus with the children, not just the one driving. The other adult should sit nearest to the door in the back. As for the children, they should be one to a seat, in forward-facing seats, belted-up, and never moving around the minibus while it is in motion. Luggage should not block the aisle.

Journey breaks – if the journey is quite long, do plan for where the children can go for a toilet break, and where the driver can take a rest break.

Preventing children from getting lost – a popular idea to save children from getting lost from their group is to give each of them something identical and brightly coloured to wear, to be spotted easily. This might be a rucksack, hat or T-shirt, or even the football kit. You should not encourage them to journey home in a mud-soaked football kit, of course.

Lost children – tell all the children exactly what to do if any of them gets lost. You could tell them to meet in a particular place, for instance, and when you arrive show them the place – they will remember better if they see the place for themselves. If it is possible to leave someone at this meeting place to watch out for waifs and strays, that would be ideal – but if you are short of staff it is better to keep the staff with the group of children. Of course, the adults should know any plan beforehand too!

If there are any very young children, you may wish to put sticky labels on them. The label should NOT give the name of the child, but could give the address and phone number of an emergency contact, the name of your club, the registration number of the minibus or the name of the coach company, or, in some cases, the registration of the car. The label might also mention: the name of the person in charge of the trip, and the time and place where the children will leave from.

The club's cheque book – one of the handiest things to take with you for some emergencies.

First-aid kit – you still need to take this for away games, remember.

Injuries – in case of a serious injury, you should get in touch with your contact person ('third person') as soon as possible and ask them to phone the parents or guardians. It should be added – but hopefully unnecessarily so – that in the case of the death of a child you should also call the police immediately and don't alter any of the equipment at the scene until the police have said so.

Then there are things you don't have to do. It's as well to know these pretty normal don'ts.

WHAT YOU SHOULD NOT HAVE TO DO

Medicines – don't give any medication to children. Some children can self-medicate. Otherwise this is normally the job of the parents or guardian or a specially trained person – if medication is necessary you could insist that a parent or guardian comes on the trip too.

Dressing/undressing – don't help the children to get dressed or undressed – the children should be independent. They may have a friend (another child) who helps them anyway – it is a good idea to encourage the children to find help from other children they are comfortable with. If it is really unavoidable for an adult to help a child with problems in dressing, the adult should take care so as not to act suspiciously – ensuring other adults are present is a good start.

Toilets and washing – don't give help to the children to go the toilet or to wash their hands or any other part of themselves. Children should be independent. If you know a child will need assistance, ask a parent or guardian to come on the trip to help the child. If there is no such help, such a child probably should not be on the trip until the child or the parents/guardians can solve the problem themselves.

It may be necessary to escort a child as far as the toilet or washing facilities, but an adult should never enter a cubicle with a child. Ideally adults and children should have separate facilities.

If it is necessary for the adults to supervise the business of changing, washing and toilet visits, the adults should still never act in an over-protective way, or be very demonstrative, and the adults should always be in pairs.

Good practice to teach your colleagues is: 'never get into a situation where you are the only adult alone with children in some place – especially for long periods of time;' and: 'Avoid rough games with a child and generally avoid any inappropriate physical contact.' Similarly, never let an adult make any sexually suggestive remarks to a child – it won't do to say, 'It was a joke.' In the same way, if a child makes an inappropriate remark to an adult, the remark should always be challenged straight away.

Sleeping arrangements – I am assuming you won't have to stay overnight anywhere. If there is an overnight stop, seek guidance from Social Services.

WHAT TO DO IF YOU ARE SUSPICIOUS OF OTHER ADULTS' BEHAVIOUR

Any child protection course should train you to be aware in particular of the danger of physical or sexual abuse of children. It is perfectly all right for you to warn someone if they are acting suspiciously.

You should not keep your worries to yourself. You may wish to tell the other adults in the club of your concerns, and to remind all the children not to be alone with any adult when they are with the club. As soon as possible, you should notify the Social Services, who can consider with you how best to notify parents and the police of any concerns. You should write down exactly what you have seen or heard as soon as possible.

If someone wants to speak to you about a matter of concern – say the parent of a child wants to see you – ask someone else to be there as an independent witness. If anyone asks you to discuss or admit legal liability for something, you have the right to take your time, think about it, maybe speak to your club's insurers or see a solicitor, and later come back to whoever has made the request or complaint with your answer. Ask them for contact details. The truth of a situation is the thing to establish first. Remember, if anyone is pushing for a confrontation, you have the right to call the police to come and calm things down.

If a child chooses to confide in you that they have been abused in some way, stay calm, don't interrupt, listen, tell them it's not their fault. Tell them you will write down what they have told you, so that you can pass it on to someone in authority. Do just that. Don't pry and don't promise to keep it secret. Don't make negative remarks about the alleged abuser, and don't promise that you will make everything all right.

If anyone, child or adult, makes an allegation, the allegation should be questioned, but it should also be followed up properly. It must be written down, as should contact details of witnesses, so that you have a proper record. You need not assume anyone is guilty, and you don't have to be the one to investigate it. If concerns seem well-founded, Social Services can advise you. You could also turn to your local Police Child Protection Team, or to the NSPCC, whose Helpline is 0808 800 5000.

CRIMINAL CHARGES
It should be noted that if allegations involving a member of your club in any way are brought to the attention of the police, you may be asked to co-operate with a police investigation. For more information on the criminal law, see the section on the courts and the police near the end of Chapter 18. An important thing to remember, if you have to answer an allegation against yourself, is that you may seek advice from a solicitor.

WHAT IS CHILD ABUSE?
It is understood that child abuse takes many forms. Most people are aware of the threat of sexual abuse to children, but, at the other extreme, neglect of children is also seen as a form of abuse. This would not be the place to discuss kinds of abuse. Instead, here are some pointers – with a football situation in mind – of how to help to prevent different kinds of abuse of children at your club.

BULLYING
In any group of children, even children you think you know well, bullying can be a problem. Let the children know that they can always approach the adults if they are being bullied. Act quickly to root out any bullying. If you make the atmosphere of your club encouraging and supportive, that atmosphere should spread among the children too. Stay vigilant for an outbreak of bullying, be it physical or verbal, such as name-calling.

SEXUAL ABUSE
Getting police checks carried out for all the adults in your group is a sensible step to help prevent abuse. You can get information about this from Social Services or your local police station. Following the sensible steps elsewhere in this Appendix should help too.

PHYSICAL ABUSE
An F.A. coaching course is a good idea for learning how to avoid exercises which

may be harmful to children, and common sense on the coach's part will help. It is not good to force children into exercises simply physically too difficult for them. Give the children footballs of an appropriate size. For under 11s, size 3 or size 4 footballs are appropriate, not size 5. Other points: don't make anyone play with an injury; and avoid punishing naughty children with hard physical exercises.

NEGLECT

To prevent neglect of children's safety, one thing you can do before any game is to make sure the equipment is safe. Especially ensure that goalposts and crossbars are secure – portable goals should be anchored. And never let children swing on the goalposts: this results in serious accidents if the posts give way. The number of tragic deaths of children involving goalposts speaks for itself.

If the weather is bad, let the children wear extra clothing if they want, and if they get thirsty let them drink. It is a good idea to take bottles of water to training and to matches. Children, like adults, often forget to bring water.

You should make sure that children are not left without supervision, or left out of activities. Perhaps other children will ignore a child they think is somehow below themselves, but it is up to your coaching to make sure children don't get excluded. You could choose exercises with the ball that all the children can join in with – and making sure that all the children warm-up properly together and warm down afterwards is helpful.

Another idea is for adults to play in the children's teams in training and pass the ball to any children who seem ignored by the other children. Some unkind children will protest when you deliver the ball to less skilful children if they do not 'rate' them: pay little heed to such protests – it's up to your club to create an atmosphere where all the children are encouraged. However, the adults must not make any kind of physical challenges which present a risk to the children – it's not enough to say a play for the ball was 'a fair challenge' when the bodyweight of an adult is pitched against that of a child.

EMOTIONAL ABUSE

Let the children enjoy their game, regardless of the result. Avoid the negative kinds of criticism. Especially avoid blaming children or making any sarcastic remarks ridiculing their efforts. Children can take this sort of thing to heart. It is not right to expect a child being verbally abused simply to 'toughen up'. Stop the verbal abuse. Don't let anyone get carried away if the children do badly.

In fact, going over the top about their success when they do well isn't very clever either. Praise should just be honest. Anything more may look like favouritism, and this can have the effect of isolating a child from other children, who may want to knock the 'golden boy' off the pedestal you put him on.

Parents who are supportive of their children in the team are a welcome sight. But don't let adults pressurise the children – the children are not there to live out the dreams of their elders. Over-enthusiastic parents at matches don't think of their screaming and shouting as abuse – but then they do not realise the pressure the children feel.

SUPPORTERS AT CHILDREN'S MATCHES

In fact, some of the worst behaviour in football in recent years is the behaviour of some parents at children's matches. You will probably understand the urgent need to put things right if you have seen adults screaming at children to win at all costs, yelling abuse at other parents, at officials, and, in the worst cases, fighting.

Some parents get over-involved emotionally. There is no perfect solution in an imperfect world, but here is a simple suggestion to counter this behaviour, if you are running a youth team and encounter this sort of problem. The idea is to make the child's chances of playing in the team conditional on the good behaviour of that child's own supporters. It's not a new idea – in the past people have tried to solve such a problem by expelling a whole family from a team.

One thing to avoid is giving the impression that a club is making up rules as they go along. One suggestion is to give the parents or guardian of every child a simple letter to sign, setting out the rules – the rules being that the child will be left out if the parents misbehave.

Once they have signed that letter or form, you can hold them to it. They have given you a promise, and you have the proof in writing. People who use letters like this say that it has helped to improve the behaviour of supporters at children's games, although it's pretty rough on the children – they might be blameless.

If you do this, make sure that you do have a form for every child. Take blank forms to the matches – so that you can get the form signed in front of you if that's the only way to get it done. And if someone refuses to sign, explain simply that you have to have the same rule for everyone. You can't have one rule for one, and a different rule for the others.

If someone does refuse to sign, do not let their child play for your club. It's a tough policy, but fair. Children need to be protected from the excessive behaviour of some adults. What you are doing is for the good of the whole team.

The letter could go something like this.

PROMISE OF SUPPORTER'S CONDUCT

Write the child's name here: ....

To the club secretary of ....
Football Club

As a parent/guardian of this child, I want him/her to enjoy being part of this club.

I believe that for this child to improve his/her own performance is more important than to win. I say so because this child is as valuable to me whether he/she wins or loses. I know that every time the team plays, the children risk losing – I will only ask him/her to try his/her best because I am aware of the pressure the children already feel. At matches I will not damage the atmosphere of encouragement by criticising the children or others openly.

I understand that if the conduct of myself or fellow supporters of my child is ever deemed negative and destructive by the club's General Committee that my child will automatically lose his/her place in the team for any period of time to be set by the General Committee. I accept these rules as binding on all involved in the club.

Name of parent or guardian: ....

Phone number of parent or guardian: ....

Address of parent or guardian: ....

Signature of parent or guardian: ....

Date: ....

And the most important thing of all? Don't let any of your club officials be hypocrites. Club officials have to show the supporters a good example of how to be supportive of the children. No-one will respect club officials who don't practise what they preach.

F.A. GUIDANCE

The F.A. has published a document on child protection in football. It is called: 'The Football Association Child Protection Policy'. For a copy of this, contact: The Education and Welfare Advisor, The Football Association, Lilleshall Hall, National Sports Centre, Nr Newport, Shropshire, TF10 9AT.
Telephone: 01952 603136

MINI-SOCCER AND THE CHARTER STANDARD

In matches recognised by the English F.A., children are not to play 11-a-side football until 10 years old. That's been the rule since September 1999. Children under the age of 10 play mini-soccer instead.

Millions of pounds are being spent to make the right size pitches with the right size goals available. Mini-soccer means having fewer players on smaller pitches so that all players get more touches of the ball, to produce more skilful young footballers.

You may also wish to apply to go on the F.A.'s 'Charter Standard for Children' courses. The Charter has criteria to encourage the sort of things discussed in this chapter, and some rewards for clubs that meet the standard. Contact the F.A. for details.

CHILD PROTECTION COURSES

There are many child protection courses available, such as those run by the F.A. They are usually not too expensive. Courses should include: how to understand what is and isn't abuse; the best way to run sport for the children's good; how to be eagle-eyed to spot any abuse that is going on; and steps you can take if something is amiss.

A CODE OF CONDUCT

An important part of coaching children is showing them the right spirit to play the game in, and teaching them to respect other players and officials. See Chapter 18 for more on this. You may want to look at the F.A.'s Code of Conduct, since this has advice for coaches and players. You can get a copy of it by contacting the F.A. directly. They have also put the Code of Conduct on their web-site. www.thefa.com.

top tip

Keep the extra load of arrangements for child protection from falling on the already burdened shoulders of the club secretary. Why not create a new post in your club of Child Protection Officer, whose job it could be to make arrangements such as described in this Appendix. Your child protection officer could also be made the person in charge on outings such as away games. Remember, though, that the child protection officer can only do so much: child protection is everyone's responsibility.

It may be a good idea to mention to the children from time to time things from the Code of Conduct. Especially for younger children, a lengthy discussion at a team meeting is not the way to get ideas across, because they have a shorter attention span. Just keep reminding them of how they should behave, and you may wish to give them the chance to ask questions about it.

As mentioned, this Appendix is not a full statement of how to protect children. It is only basic introductory information. So do give thought to attending a child protection course, seeking advice from your local Social Services or from others experienced in child protection, and reading further on the subject.

appendix II

USEFUL CONTACTS IN THE UK AND AROUND THE WORLD

CONTACT DETAILS IN ENGLAND

The English Football Association
25 Soho Square, London, W1D 4FA
Telephone: 020 7745 4545
Web-site: www.thefa.com

The Women's Football Association
shares the same address above.

The Women's Football Co-ordinator
The F.A., 9 Wyllyots Place, Potters Bar,
Herts., EN6 2JD
Tel: 01707 651840

English Schools F.A.
1-2 Eastgate Street, Stafford, ST16 2NQ
Tel: 01785 251142
Web-site: www.esfa.co.uk

COUNTY F.A. ADDRESSES IN ENGLAND

The County F.A.s have begun to run courses on Effective Football Club Administration. If you find that your County F.A. details have changed from those published here, you should be able to get up-to-date details from the English F.A. headquarters – and you will find their contact details above. For ease of use, the list splits England into its northern, southern and midlands portions, the mid-portion including east and west England.

I have not published telephone numbers as these have changed the most frequently in recent years. To obtain up-to-date County F.A. telephone numbers, phone the national F.A. or see the F.A. web-site at www.thefa.com.

NORTHERN ENGLAND

Cheshire County Football Association
The Cottage, Hartford Moss Recreation Centre, Winnington, Northwich,
CW8 4BG

Cumberland County Football Association
17 Oxford Street, Workington,
CA14 2AL

Durham County Football Association
Codeslaw, Ferens Park, Durham,
DH1 1JZ

East Riding County Football Association
50 Boulevard, Hull, HU3 2TB

Lancashire County Football Association
The County Ground, Thurston Road,
Leyland, Preston, PR5 1LF

Lincolnshire County Football Association
P.O. Box 26, 12 Dean Road, Lincoln,
LN2 4DP

Liverpool County Football Association
Liverpool Soccer Centre, Walton Hall
Park, Walton Hall Avenue, Liverpool,
L4 9XP

**Manchester County Football
Association**
Sports Complex, Brantingham Road,
Chorlton, Manchester, M21 0TT

**North Riding County Football
Association**
Broughton Road, Stokesley,
Middlesborough, TS9 5NY

**Northumberland County Football
Association**
Whitley Park, Whitley Road
Newcastle upon Tyne, NE12 9FA

**Sheffield and Hallamshire County
Football Association**
Clegg House, 69 Cornish Place, Cornish
Street, Shalesmoor, S6 3AF

**Westmorland County Football
Association**
Unit 1, Angel Court, 21 Highgate,
Kendal, LA9 6AG

**West Riding County Football
Association**
Fleet Lane, Woodlesford, Leeds,
LS26 8NX

MIDLANDS AND EAST AND WEST
**Birmingham County Football
Association**
County F.A. Offices, Ray Hall Lane,
Great Barr, Birmingham, B43 6JF

**Cambridgeshire County Football
Association**
City Ground, Milton Road,
Cambridge, CB4 1FA

Derbyshire County Football Association
Units 8–9, Stadium Business Court,
Millenium Way, Pride Park, Derby,
DE24 8HZ

**Herefordshire County Football
Association**
County Ground Offices, Widemarsh
Common, Hereford, HR4 9NA

**Leicestershire and Rutland County
Football Association**
Holmes Park, Dog and Gun Lane,
Whetstone, Leicester, LE8 6FA

Norfolk County Football Association
Plantation Park, Blofield, Norwich,
NR13 4PL

**Northamptonshire County Football
Association**
2 Duncan Close, Moulton Park,
Northampton, NN3 6WL

**Nottinghamshire County Football
Association**
7 Clarendon Street, Nottingham,
NG1 5HS

**Oxfordshire County Football
Association**
P.O. Box 62, Witney, Oxon,
OX28 1HA

Shropshire County Football Association
Gay Meadow, Abbey Foregate,
Shrewsbury, SY2 6AB

**Staffordshire County Football
Association**
County Showground, Weston Road,
Stafford, ST18 0BD

Suffolk County Football Association
The Buntings, Cedars Park,
Stowmarket, IP14 5GZ

Worcestershire County Football Association
Craftsman House, De Salis Drive, Hampton Lovett Industrial Estate, Droitwich, Worcestershire, WR9 0QE

SOUTHERN ENGLAND
Bedfordshire County Football Association
Century House, Skimpot Road, Dunstable, LU5 4JU

Berkshire and Buckinghamshire County Football Association
15a London Street, Faringdon, Oxon, SN7 7HD

Cornwall County Football Association
1 High Cross Street, St Austell, PL25 4AB

Devon County Football Association
County H.Q., Coach Road, Newton Abbott, TQ12 1EJ

Dorset County Football Association
County Ground, Blandford Close, Hamworthy, Poole, BH15 4BF

Essex County Football Association
31 Mildmay Road, Chelmsford, CM2 0DN

Gloucestershire County Football Association
Oaklands Park, Almondsbury, Bristol, BS32 4AG

Hampshire County Football Association
8 Ashwood Gardens, off Winchester Road, Southampton, SO16 7PW

Hertfordshire County Football Association
County Ground, Baldock Road, Letchworth, SG6 2EN

Huntingdonshire County Football Association
Cromwell Chambers, 8 St John's Street, Huntingdon, PE29 3DD

Kent County Football Association
69 Maidstone Road, Chatham, ME4 6DT

London Football Association
6 Aldworth Grove, Lewisham, London, SE13 6HY

Middlesex County Football Association
39–41 Roxborough Road, Harrow, HA1 1NS

Somerset and Avon (South) County Football Association
30 North Road, Midsomer Norton, Bath, BA3 2QD

Surrey County Football Association
321 Kingston Road, Leatherhead, KT22 7TU

Sussex County Football Association
Culver Road, Lancing, BN15 9AX

Wiltshire County Football Association
Covingham Square, Covingham, Swindon, SN3 5AA

CONTACT DETAILS IN THE CHANNEL ISLANDS AND THE ISLE OF MAN
Guernsey County Football Association
Corbet Field, Grand Fort Road, St Sampson's, Guernsey, GY2 4FG

Isle of Man Football Association
P.O. Box 53, The Bowl, Douglas, Isle of Man, IM99 1GY

Jersey Football Association
Springfield Stadium, St Helier, Jersey, JE2 4LF

CONTACT DETAILS IN WALES
Football Association of Wales
Plymouth Chambers, 3 Westgate Street,
Cardiff, CF10 1DP
Tel: 029 2037 2325
E-mail: info@faw.org.uk
Web-site: www.faw.org.uk

CONTACT DETAILS IN SCOTLAND
Scottish F.A.
Hampton Park, Letherby Drive,
Glasgow G42 9BA
Tel: 0141 616 6000
E-mail: info@scottishfa.co.uk
Web-site: www.scottishfa.co.uk

That same address is shared by:
Scottish Amateur Football Association
Scottish Junior Football Association
Scottish Schools' Football Association
Scottish Women's Football Association

CONTACT DETAILS IN NORTHERN IRELAND
Northern Ireland F.A.
20 Windsor Avenue, Belfast, BT9 6EE
Tel: 02890 669458
Web-site: www.irishfa.com

CONTACT DETAILS IN THE REPUBLIC OF IRELAND
Football Association of Ireland
80 Merrion Square, Dublin 2
Tel: (00353) 01 703 7500
E-mail: info@fai.ie
Web-site: www.fai.ie

SOME OTHER CONTACTS IN THE UK
The National Coaching Foundation, funded mostly by Sport England, provides training for team coaches, including for coaches of children and disabled players. It has regional offices in Wales, Scotland and Northern Ireland. For details contact their headquarters:

Sports Coach UK (The National Coaching Foundation)
114 Cardigan Road, Headingley, Leeds, LS6 3BJ
Tel: 0113 274 4802
Web-site: www.sportscoachuk.org

The English Federation of Disability Sport helps to organise some opportunities for footballers with disabilities to play. It has no funding to give away. Contact:

English Federation of Disability Sport
Manchester Metropolitan University, Alsager Campus, Hassall Road, Alsager, Stoke on Trent, ST7 2HL
Tel: 0161 247 5294
Web-site: www.efds.net

The armed forces organise football for servicemen. The Army Football Association, for instance, has over 600 affiliated clubs, one part of building camaraderie within the armed forces. Contact details are:

Army Football Association
Clayton Barrack, Thornhill Road, Aldershot, GU11 2BG

Royal Air Force Football Association
502 Allces Pol (RAF), Room 625, St Giles Court, 1–13 St Giles High Street, WC2H 8LD

Royal Navy Football Association
H.M.S. Temeraire, Burnaby Road, Portsmouth, PO1 2HB

FOOTBALL ADDRESSES IN THE REST OF THE WORLD

Next are details of the many headquarters of organised football around the world. At the top of the world-wide structure is:

FIFA (Fédération Internationale de Football Association

or International Federation of Association Football)

FIFA
P.O. Box 85, 8030 Zurich, Switzerland
Telephone: 0041 1 222 7777
Fax: 0041 1 222 7878
Cable address: FIFA Zurich
Web-site: www.fifa.com

Under FIFA are six Confederations. You should be able to tell which Confederation looks after football in your part of the world.

THE SIX FIFA CONFEDERATIONS

AFC (Asian Football Confederation)
Asian Football Confederation
AFC House, Jalan 1/155B, Bukit Jalil,
Kuala Lumpur 57000 Malaysia
Telephone: 0060 3 8994 3388
Web-site: www.footballasia.com

CONMEBOL (Confederación Sudamericana de Fútbol)
(or South American Football Confederation)
Autopista Aeropuerto Internacional y Leonismo Luqueño, Luque, Gran Asunción, Paraguay
Telephone: 00595 21 645 781
Web-site: www.conmebol.com

CAF (Confédération Africaine de Football or African Football Confederation)
CAF, PO BOX 23 Abdel Khalek Sarwat Street, El Hay, El Motamayez, 6th October City, Egypt
Telephone: 0020 2837 1000
Web-site: www.cafonline.com

FOOTBALL CONFEDERATION – Formerly known as CONCACAF (Confederacion Norte-Centroamericano y del Caribe de Futbal OR Confederation of North, Central American and Caribbean Association Football)

Football Confederation
725 Fifth Avenue, 17th Floor, New York, New York 10022, USA
Telephone: 001 212 308 0044
Web-site: www.concacaf.net

OFC (Oceania Football Confederation)
OFC Ericcson Stadium, 12 Maurice Road, PO Box 62 586, Penrose, Auckland, New Zealand
Telephone: 0064 9 525 8161
Web-site: www.oceaniafootball.com

UEFA (Union des Associations Européennes de Football or European Union of Association Football)

UEFA
Route de Genève 46, Nyon 1260, Switzerland
Telephone: 0041 22 994 4444
Web-site: www.uefa.com

appendix III
FURTHER READING AND BIBLIOGRAPHY

FIFA PUBLICATIONS
Laws of Association Football
(A new edition of this book is published each year)

F.A. PUBLICATIONS
Some bookshops say the F.A. will not let them sell publications such as the F.A. Handbook. Instead the F.A.'s publications may be obtained directly from the F.A. or through a company called Coachwise by mail order – which may mean paying before you have seen the goods. Contact details are:

Coachwise, P.O. Box HP86, Leeds, LS6 3XW
Tel: 0113 279 1395

The F.A. does not have its own bookshop. For more details of F.A. publications contact this F.A. office:

The Football Association Limited, 9 Wyllyots Place, Potters Bar, Herts., EN6 2JD
Tel: 01707 651840

Titles include:

The Football Association Handbook Rules of The Association And Laws of the Game.
(A new edition of the Handbook is published each year)

County Football Association Club Administration Manual (available free from your English County F.A. – a thin

publication introducing the issues involved in running a club)

Charter for Quality (Howard Wilkinson's national blueprint for coaching)

National Facilities Plan for Football

OTHER PUBLICATIONS
Investing in the Community – A Report by the Football Task Force submitted to the Minister for Sport on January 11, 1999.

Guidance on Football Related Legislation – Home Office Circular 3/4/2000

Health and safety of pupils on educational visits – published by DfES Publications (Department for Education and Skills), 2001

Denton Wilde Sapte TransMiT newsletter - Sport Issue 4, 2003 (April)

Charity Choice – Tenth Edition published by Waterlow Information Services Ltd., London, 1998

Flat Back Four: The Tactical Game written by Andy Gray with Jim Drewett, published by Boxtree, London, 1999

Football Fitness and Skills written by Pete Edwards published by Hamlyn, London, 1997

The Guinness Record of World Soccer
written by Guy Oliver
published by Guinness Publishing Ltd.,
1997

Soccer for Girls
written by Graham Ramsay
published by Benford Books, New Jersey
USA, 1998

Soccer Skills: Tactics and Teamwork
written by Charles Hughes
published by HarperCollins Publishers,
London, 1996

The Soccer Referee's Manual
Written by David Ager
published by A & C Black, London,
2002

**Handbook of Football Club
Management**
Written by David and Andrew Ager
Published by the Crowood Press Ltd,
2003

The Hon. Treasurer
written by Roderick Boucher
published by Elliot Right Way Books,
Tadworth, 1994

**London Football Association Coaching
Course programme 2000**

**Brent Children's Play Service Off-site
Activities Guidelines**

PERIODICALS
On the Ball
(the F.A. magazine for women's football
in England)
published by Moondance Publications
Ltd, Gateshead, monthly.

Team-Talk
(the F.A. magazine for the men's football
Pyramid in England)
published by Tony Williams Publications
Ltd, Taunton, monthly

The Non-League Paper
(the newspaper for Conference and
Pyramid Leagues football)
London, weekly

appendix IV
CHARITABLE SOURCES OF MONEY

Ask a public library for a book listing charities that donate money to good causes and you may be handed a volume as thick as the phone directory. There are far more agencies willing to support deserving causes than most people realise, with many different reasons for giving money. While it may be confusing having so many different sources of funding, if one funding agency turns you down, another may support you.

Here are some charities and some general sources of funding that are especially interested in supporting sport at non-professional level.

THE FOOTBALL FOUNDATION

The Football Foundation was launched on July 25, 2000, to put money into pitch and ground improvements at the grassroots of the game. With money coming from a share of the broadcasting rights enjoyed by the Premier League, plus more from the Football Association, the Government, and Lottery money from Sport England, it should have funds worth around £50 million a year. But then, to get football pitches across the country up to scratch there is a lot to do. From making school pitches into decent surfaces to play on, right up to making safety improvements to the stadiums of Pyramid clubs, the work will go on for years.

As the Foundation develops, they intend to have a wide range of programmes to support the development of grassroots football, including better coaching for children. Contact details are:

Football Foundation, 25 Soho Square, London, W1D 4FF
Tel: 020 7534 4210
Web-site: www.footballfoundation.org.uk

The Football Foundation's Safety and Improvement Panel will take on the safety improvements to football grounds for which the Football Trust was responsible.

THE NATIONAL LOTTERY AND THE SPORTS COUNCILS

Sport is one of the good causes for money raised by the National Lottery. The Sports Councils have to be careful to follow guidelines for sharing out such public funds, and that means you have to answer lots of questions to get money from them.

If your club has or needs its own building and facilities, note that the Sports Councils will consider applications for capital projects, but you should find out their criteria first. For example, if you want to up-grade a school playing field, success in obtaining Lottery funding may depend in some cases on it also being of use to the local community.

Another point is that the Lottery will not provide all the money for a project. They may give the majority, while expecting you to raise money from other sources. The Lottery has published some helpful booklets to explain their many projects, with titles such as 'Access for Disabled People', 'Car Parking', 'Financial Projects', 'Floodlighting', 'Planning Permission and Statutory Consents', 'Sports Pavilions and Team Changing Accommodation', 'Turf pitches – Synthetic', and various booklets on educational facilities for community use.

Sport England
The English Sports Council (called Sport England) has these aims:
- get more people involved in sport
- get more places to play sport
- get more medals through higher standards of performance in sport.

It pays special attention to the part to be played in sport by women, disabled persons, ethnic minorities, through National Lottery Funds, local authorities and governing body investment. A lot to think about.

Sport England answers to Parliament. Its work is jointly funded by the Exchequer and the National Lottery. Money from the Exchequer is for maintaining sports infrastructure. National Lottery funds are for the development of sport. To find out if they have any schemes in your area that could help your club, and for details of funding or booklets, contact the national office or the regional offices, which deliver Sport England's schemes at regional level. Here they are:

National office
Sport England, 3rd floor Victoria House, Bloomsbury Square,
London, WC1B 4SE
Tel: 08458 508508
web-site: www.sportengland.org

Sport England regional offices
Sport England, Aykley Heads, Durham, DH1 5UU
Sport England, 4th floor, Minerva House, East Parade, Leeds, LS1 5PS
Sport England, Astley House, 23 Quay Street, Manchester, M3 4AE

Sport England, 1 Hagley Road, Five Ways, Birmingham, B16 8TT
Sport England, Grove House, Bridgford Road, West Bridgford,
Nottingham, NG2 6AP
Sport England, Crescent House, 19 The Crescent, Bedford, MK40 2QP
Sport England, Ashlands House, North St, Crewkerne, Somerset, TA18 7LQ
Sport England, 51a Church Street, Caversham, Reading, RG4 8AX

Sport England and the Lottery Fund
As mentioned, this is mainly of interest if your club has its own building and facilities. For details of the Sport England Lottery Fund or to get an application pack, call Sport England. Their funding schemes include:

Community capital programme
For capital funds, apply using the Community Capital Projects Fund application pack. To get this, call 0345 649649. Be prepared to answer a lot of questions on the form.

This programme funds community capital facilities projects such as sports halls, football pitches, and upgrading existing facilities for more people to use. You will still have to find at least 35 per cent of the money yourselves. This scheme includes:

The Priority Areas Initiative (PAI)
This is money set aside for deprived areas in cities and the countryside. If you have a project that fits the scheme, you will still have to find at least 10 per cent of your funding from somewhere else.

The School Community Sport Initiative (SCSI)
The idea is for schools to get upgraded sports facilities and make them available to the community. You still have to find at least 20 per cent of the funding from somewhere else. Rules include that:

- the project must cost more than £5,000
- it must be run by a bona fide organisation that can't raise enough funds from other sources
- the project has to lead to a significant increase in the number of people taking part or a measurable improvement in sporting standards.

That means explaining how the project will benefit the wider community. Priority is given to those projects emphasising involvement from disadvantaged groups.

The other Sports Councils in the UK
Sports Council for Wales
Sophia Gardens, Cardiff, CF1 9SW
Tel: 029 2030 0500

SportScotland
Caledonia House, South Gyle,
Edinburgh, EH12 9DQ
Tel: 0131 317 7200

Sports Council for Northern Ireland,
House of Sport, Upper Malone Road, Belfast, BT9 5LA
Tel: 028 9038 1222

As a side note, the UK Sports Council (now called UK Sport) takes responsibility for issues that need to be handled at UK level, such as controlling drug use in sport.

OTHER FUNDING SCHEMES

Sportsmatch

Sportsmatch is about how the sponsorship of grassroots sport is a way that businesses can reach new customers, support their employees or get involved in the local community. They encourage businesses to sponsor sport by matching the business's donation with government money. If you have a sponsor for your team, this may interest you.

How it works is this: Sport England can match every pound of business sponsors' money with a pound from government funds. It can put in around £3 million every year. It has made more than 2,500 awards to various sports, and says that together with sponsors' money this has generated some £40 million for grassroots sport – especially for youths, and those with disabilities and other disadvantaged groups.

The point is that sponsoring grassroots sports can be effective for businesses, and much cheaper than sponsoring professional sport. Sponsors' logos should go on kit or on other places for advertising. There are criteria you have to meet, and you still have the job of finding that business sponsor whose donations may be matched by Sportsmatch. The organisation may sponsor clubs, but not individuals or competitions. Details of criteria are available from:

Sportsmatch Scheme Manager, Institute of Sports Sponsorship, 3rd Floor, Victoria House, Bloomsbury Square, London WC1B4SE.
Tel: 020 7273 1942
E-mail: info@sportsmatch.co.uk
Website: www.sportsmatch.co.uk

Your local authority
Your local authority, be it a city, county, borough or parish council, probably puts more money into sport in your area than anyone else. To find out if they have money to give out you'll have to ask them. See my section on hiring local authority pitches in Chapter 7 to find out how to contact a relevant department at your local council. Ask them if they have a Local Authority Advisory Sports Council, the usual name for the office that arranges the donations.

The Football Association Torch Trophy Trust
You can only apply for this one if affiliated to your County F.A. (See Chapter 3 for information on affiliating.) If you are only after a small rather than a large grant, this may be the one for you. There is money here for using sport to help with education and to support individuals who want to help with the organisational side. Grants are available for improvements to grounds and changing rooms too. Write for details to:

Torch Trophy Trust, 25 Soho Square, London, W1D 4FF

The Foundation for Sport and the Arts
This organisation provides a great deal of funding for grassroots sport. Write to:
The Foundation for Sport and the Arts, P.O. Box 20, Liverpool, L13 1HB
Tel: 0151 259 5505

The Prince's Trust
A very good one for disadvantaged groups to apply to, and aimed at 14–25-year-olds. It is keen on how sport helps individuals to become more self-confident. Details are available from:

The Secretary, The Prince's Trust, 18 Park Square East, London, NW1 4LH
Tel: 020 7543 1234
Web-site: www.princes-trust.org.uk

The Football Association Youth Trust
The organisations in mind for this money are schools and universities. Write to:

The F.A. Youth Trust, 9 Wyllyotts Place, Potters Bar, Herts., EN6 2JD
Tel: 01707 651840

SportsAid
For SportsAid, you must be a member of a national squad and in genuine financial need. SportsAid gives priority to athletes pursuing careers in particular sports.

They include women's association football. The idea is to encourage sport of a high standard among young people, especially those disadvantaged by disability, poverty and social factors. They hope to see this help with education and integration into society too.

A regional grant is usually £150–£250 per year. For details write to:

SportsAid
3rd floor, Victoria House, London, WC1B 4SE
Tel: 020 7273 1975
Web-site: www.sportsaid.org.uk

Army Sports Control Board Trust
No surprises here. Sport in the army is the intended target for the money. Contact:

Director, Army Sports Control Board, Clayton Banks, Aldershot, Hants, GU11 2BG.
Tel: 01252 348568

Police Property Act Fund
The police believe in young people taking part in sport instead of hanging around with nothing to do. So your football club, or the person keeping it going, could apply for a grant to help run the club. Write to the Police H.Q. in your county. If you can't find the H.Q. address, ask for it at a police station. Address your letter to: The Secretary, The Police Property Act Fund

top tip

This list is only the tip of the iceberg. If you cannot find support here, it's not the end. Check one of those directories of charities at your local library. You will never have enough time to write to every one, because there are so many. And don't forget other ways of raising money – some are suggested in Chapter 6.

Other funding for ground improvements
When contacting any of these funding agencies, give a brief outline of why you need money and ask for an application form. Ground improvement funds may be available from The Football Foundation, The Football Trust, The Football Association Torch Trophy Trust, The National Lottery and the Sports Councils.

Details of those organisations are given earlier in this Appendix. Then there is...

The National Playing Fields Association
This may only be worth consideration if the facilities you use are owned by the NPFA in the first place. Their facilities are normally managed locally. If the local management turns out to be the local council, that may rule out grants. Contact

The National Playing Fields Association, Stanley House, St Chad's Place, London, WC1X 9HH
Tel: 020 7833 5360
www.npfa.co.uk

The National Sports Centre Trust
Bearing in mind their funds are to help public use of facilities, they run various schemes to improve facilities. Details are available from:

The National Sports Centre Trust, 9 Wyllyotts Place, Potters Bar, Herts., EN6 2JD
Tel: 01707 651840

Your local authority
To find out if your local authority has money to give out you'll have to ask them. See my section on hiring local authority pitches in Chapter 7 to find out how to contact a relevant department at your local council. Ask them if they have a Local Authority Advisory Sports Council, the usual name for the office that arranges donations.

Your council rates may be costing your club a lot of money, so telephone your local authority about rate relief on your sports ground. A typical requirement to qualify is that you should be a non-profit organisation, but you should ask your local authority for guidelines since it is their decision who gets rate relief in their district. The contact details you need should be on your rates bill.

OTHER SOURCES OF FUNDING
From time to time other sources of funding become available under one scheme or another, so it is a good idea to keep in touch with the County F.A. or Sport England who often hear about such things early on. Good football magazines often have up-to-date news on funding schemes. There is no foolproof way to know about them all. It's up to your club to keep your ears to the ground, and ask around.

Often others in your own league will know about funding sources you have not discovered – another reason to meet up with them at your League Council Meeting. And if you find a new source of money, why not let the other officials in your league know the next time you go to your Council Meeting?

THE CHARITIES COMMISSION

You can find out more about charities that could make a donation to your club from the Charities Commission. A public library near you may have a copy of the book, 'Charity Choice', that the Commission publishes every year, listing every registered charity in the UK. This one really is as thick as a telephone directory. For further information about the work of charities, contact your nearest office:

Charity Commission, Harmsworth House, 13-15 Bouverie Street, London, EC4Y 8DP
Tel: 0870 333 0123
web-site: www.charity-commission.gov.uk

Charity Commission – Liverpool
2nd Floor, 20 King's Parade, Queen's Dock, Liverpool, L3 4DQ

Charity Commission – Taunton
Woodfield House, Tangier, Taunton, Somerset, TA1 4BL

index